Journeys
After
Adoption

Journeys
After
Adoption

Understanding Lifelong Issues

Jayne E. Schooler and Betsie L. Norris

BERGIN & GARVEY
Westport, Connecticut • London

Library of Congress Cataloging-in-Publication Data

Schooler, Jayne E.
  Journeys after adoption : understanding lifelong issues / Jayne E. Schooler and Betsie L. Norris.
    p. cm.
  Includes bibliographical references and index.
  ISBN 0–89789–816–8 (alk. paper)
  1. Adoptees—Psychology. 2. Adoption. 3. Birthparents—Identification. 4. Life cycle, Human. I. Norris, Betsie. II. Title.
HV875.S3645 2002
155.44'5—dc21   2002016485

British Library Cataloguing in Publication Data is available.

Library of Congress Catalog Card Number: 2002016485
ISBN: 0–89789–816–8

First published in 2002

Bergin & Garvey, 88 Post Road West, Westport, CT 06881
An imprint of Greenwood Publishing Group, Inc.
www.greenwood.com

Printed in the United States of America

The paper used in this book complies with the Permanent Paper Standard issued by the National Information Standards Organization (Z39.48–1984).

10 9 8 7 6 5 4 3 2 1

From Jayne Schooler:

To Matthew Andrew Goetz, my nephew, a remarkable young man to
whom much has been given
and
To Dr. Gregory Goffe, used by God as an instrument of healing
in my life.
Thank you both for being a source of encouragement and support.

From Betsie Norris:

To my families: adoptive, birth, and step, for loving me and
supporting me,
especially my dad, Brad Norris, for being an extraordinary role model
and inspiration.
And to all the members of Adoption Network Cleveland for allowing
me to share in their lives.

Contents

Acknowledgments

No project like this could have been completed without the willingness of so many to share their lives, their stories, and, in many cases, their pain. It is truly impossible to thank each one who touched this project in some way; however, we would like to express our appreciation to the following:

To our editor, Lynn Taylor, who captured the vision for this project and has been an incredible support and encouragement.

To Pat Johnston, publisher, Perspectives Press, who saw the worth and value of using Searching for a Past as the springboard for this more in-depth treatment of the lifelong issues in adoption. She told us it needed to be done.

To Dr. LaVonne Stiffler, who not only contributed her own excellent work for this project, but gave many insightful editing hours to us.

To Dr. Deborah Fravel, who sacrificed personal time to add a dimension to this book that will have lasting impact.

To Holly Pressley, whose help in the early reediting stages of the original work was extremely valuable.

To many who have shared their stories and perspectives, including Lisa Kimes, Jonelle Blair, Howard Dulmage, Nancy Kukla, Sylvia Mauser, Jeanne Hood and Donni Linden, Tammy Pasela, Patti Jo Burtnett, Tom Nelson, Denice Bertino, Reneka Howard, Ai Loan Nguyen, Monica M. Byrne, and so many others too numerous to mention. Without you this book would not have been possible!

To the following professionals who took time out of their extremely busy lives for interviews and chapter critiques of the original publication *Searching for a Past*: Dirck Brown, Kate Burke, Bonnie Carroll, Susan Cox, Ronny Diamond, Susan Frivalds, Marian Parker, Joyce Maguire Pavao, Sharon Kaplan Roszia, Randolph Severson, Anu Sharma, Nancy Ward, Curry Wolfe, Linda Yellin, and Kay Donley Ziegler.

From Jayne: Thank you to my husband, David, for his every continued support and to God for continuing to open doors to new and broader experiences.

From Betsie: Thank you to Kay Ariel, Linda Bellini, and Kirtsen McNamara for helping me through the important and difficult year in my life that happened to coincide with the writing of this book. Thank you to my son, Elliot, for making my life joyous.

Introduction

What would it be like if you were Richard? Richard's memories of growing up adopted are happy and filled with feelings of love and security. However, in spite of all that, he has a missing piece. He wants desperately to meet his birthparents and even at forty-four years old struggles with how to bring up the subject with his adoptive mother. He loves her and doesn't want to hurt her, but he must know.

What would it be like if you were Linda? Linda, now forty-six, relinquished a child for adoption twenty-six years ago. She has not told anyone about her secret. Her son comes to her mind and into her heart quite often, but Linda does what she always has done—attempts to stuff away those thoughts and feelings. It has been a secret for so long, yet she longs to see him, or, at least to know if he is okay.

What would it be like if you were Fred and Margaret? The Duttons adopted their three children in the early '70s. At that time, the agency assured them that if they were good parents, their children would never need to search. Recently, their daughter came to them and said she wanted to search. Feelings of failure and fear of loss gripped them.

All of these individuals have been on their own journey after adoption. Each perspective is different. Each individual thinks about and feels the issues of his or her life in varying degrees of wonder, curiosity, fear, and pain.

From the vantage point of history in this country, adoption has loomed under a cloak of secrecy for decades. Professionals in the world of adoption over the last seventy years believed it would be best to create a new world for all those involved in the adoption circumstance. What they believed this new world should be was:

- a place in which adoptees would forget the past as though it didn't exist
- a place in which birthparents would sublimate the relinquishment experience and move forward as though it never happened
- a place where adoptive parents would exist in total anonymity

The springboard for *Journeys After Adoption* is an earlier published work titled *Searching for a Past: An Adopted Adult's Unique Process of Finding Identity*. From that publication this newest work has grown and greatly expanded in focus and content.

The goals for *Journeys After Adoption* are threefold. One goal is to present a historical look at the past practices of adoption as it touched the adoption triad: adoptees, birthparents, adoptive parents and siblings, and to offer lessons from those on the journey. A second goal is to provide a resource for all members of the triad as they grapple with the decisions and processes of search and reunion. A third goal of this project is to provide support to those generations living with the effects of these past practices.

For simplicity, coauthor, Betsie Norris is quoted frequently throughout the book when she reflects on her personal experiences as an adoptee or as founder and executive director of one of the nation's largest regional organizations serving the adoption triad.

A special note, much of *Journeys After Adoption* addresses adopted persons and birthparents. Only one chapter addresses the needs of adoptive parents, and that focuses on issues found in search and reunion. This was done intentionally, due to the extraordinary amount of literature available to adoptive parents today.

An important note also is that the issues of growing up in openness and in transracial/transcultural adoptive families have not been addressed in great detail. A growing amount of literature is available around transracial/transcultural issues. Those who grew up in a level of openness are just now reaching adulthood and this holds the possibility of another project. However, we have included in the appendix two essays written by young women, one that experienced growing up in openness and one that was adopted internationally.

Journeys After Adoption is designed to meet the informational and practical needs of the following groups:

1. Adult adoptees, birthparents, and adoptive parents
2. Foster parents
3. Adoption and foster care support groups

4. National organizations that focus on the needs of adoptees and birthparents
5. National organizations that focus on the needs of adoptive parents
6. Adoption professionals who work with and educate adoptive and foster parents
7. Mental health professionals who work with children or adults who are touched by adoption in some way

Fate's Echo

D. Thomas Nelson

Mom and Dad:
You adopted me
You plucked my tiny soul
From a living limbo
And showed me the way
You took me in warm arms
And truly made me
A part of your life

And when I cried—
You were there
When I laughed—
You smiled
When I was wrong—
You righted me
When I succeeded—
You rejoiced

I need to find the answers
To the questions of my past
Of my history
Of these fundamental elements
That have mingled with
your nurturing and
Have created the man that
I am

And when I told you this
You understood

I love you, Mom and Dad
I will not leave you
For you are forever—
Mom and Dad

Mother and Father:
You created me
A moment in time
Fate had called your names
And I am the echo

A decision was made
Were you courageous?
Were you in fear?
We were separated
But by distance and shadowed secrets

Yet, Mother and Father
You have always been near
For inside me you exist
Never touching
But always touched

For your gifts, my eternal gratitude
For to you whom I cannot remember
I have never forgotten

PART I

A Look at Issues and Their Impact

CHAPTER ONE

Secrecy in Adoption and the High Cost It Required

Lying and secrecy make a problem part of the future; openness and honesty make a problem part of the past.[1]

Kristen, a tall, beautiful woman with an expressive personality, black hair, and an engaging smile, always enjoyed family Christmases. It was both the holiday time and her birthday. This holiday brought an extra joy, because Kristen was awaiting the birth of her first child. Since she was a small child, the family always celebrated her birthday right along with the holiday. This year, even at thirty-seven, it would be no different. The entire clan was there. However, after the usual rite of Christmas and birthday songs and the opening of presents, a causal conversation with a cousin forever changed Kristen's perception of her family and who she was.

Kristen and her cousin Laurie were setting the holiday table together when Laurie asked, "How does it feel to be having a baby and someone that will look just like you? Knowing your own birthmother and Russian Jewish heritage now must make it even more special. I'm so glad she found your family when she did!" Kristen, who had known she was adopted since she was young but always, thought she was Italian, sat stunned and shocked, just mumbled a reply and quickly finished her task.

Later that afternoon when the celebration had quieted down, Kristen asked her mother to come into a back bedroom. Kristen hesitantly relayed the earlier comment from her cousin. Her mother sat quietly and then said simply, "Yes, your birthmother found and contacted us about a year ago asking to be put in touch with you. We weren't sure what to do, and didn't know if you'd want to know, so we didn't tell you."

Kristen's mother continued to share with her what she now knew about her birthparents. Including the fact that she was Russian and Jewish, even though they'd always told her she was Italian so she'd feel like she fit in with her adoptive family. Questions flooded Kristen's mind like, Why didn't you tell me? Who else knows my story was changed? Why didn't you just ask me if I'd want to know instead of keeping this door closed to me, after all I'm an adult now! Like many adoptees, Kristen had not talked much to her adoptive parents about how she felt about being adopted. Like many adoptive parents, her parents had not asked.

What causes this lack of communication about adoption? Why is adoption so often the undiscussed family secret? A glance back at the societal attitudes present at the time of adoption of today's generations of adult adoptees will help us recognize how past viewpoints shaped adoptive parents' thinking and actions.

THE ORIGIN OF SECRETS IN ADOPTION

Kristen's experience mirrors the experience of many adopted adults whose adoption was not openly discussed, only discussed to a point, or whose birth history was altered, omitted, or falsified. Not only did the reconstructing of an adopted person's background profoundly affect them, but it also greatly impacted their adoptive parents and birthparents, as well.

Adoption within a Societal Context

"Years ago," according to Sharon Kaplan-Roszia, "myths were perpetuated through the adoption community. One myth taught those whose lives were touched by adoption that the most healthy attitude for all members of the triad was to make a clean break."[2] That break meant no looking back—no information passed on, a story left untold. Many adoptive parents of decades past were taught and therefore believed this myth and others that fueled secrecy, forced denial and lies, and created unexpected heartbreaks.

"Adoptive families were told to act just like biological families," Roszia commented. Birth certificates were amended to represent the adoptive parents as biological parents, a procedure some adopted persons now call "legal fiction." To compound the legal fiction, the original certificate of birth was most often sealed away. Although social attitudes about adoption have changed dramatically over the last decade or two, this "legal fiction" is still supported by the majority of state laws and agency policies. While adoption placement practices are gradually changing for the better, there are today generations of adoption triad members (adoptees, birthparents, and adoptive parents) whose adoption originated in the past, who are stuck today to deal with the mores and norms of those past times.

From history's earliest days until the present, the practice of adoption has served a variety of functions, according to Ken Watson, author and retired adoption professional. It has spanned a continuum of needs from "providing a royal family with an heir, to adding 'indentured' hands, to making a family financially self-sufficient, to emptying orphanages to save community dollars."[3]

In recent decades, adoption has served two additional functions—to meet the needs of couples whose dreams of a family were shattered by infertility and to provide a solution for birthparents who found themselves facing an unintended and untimely pregnancy.

What emerged from the latter two functions of adoption during the middle decades of this century was an idealistic picture, one that characterized a perfect solution to a societal problem. As Dr. Miriam Reitz, a family therapist, and Watson state: "Adoptive families and adoption agencies collaborated to present adoption as what it can never really be—a chance for birth parents to go on happily with their lives, for children to grow up in trouble-free families, and for adoptive parents to fulfill themselves and find immortality through children to whom they have sole claim by virtue of adoption."

Ken Watson remarked that "the implications of the adoption on the subsequent development of the child or family was either viewed as inconsequential or denied altogether." These perceptions—"we are just like a biological family: adoption has no reference to the future, and things are best kept a secret"—further established a precedent on how children were told about their adoption and what they were told, if they were told at all.[4] In addition, it was not unusual for agencies themselves to edit or even fabricate information that was told to the adoptive parents at the time of the adoption.

Little thought was given to the impact the lack of information would have on an adopted child, his or her relationship with the adoptive family and eventually the birthparents, if a reunion occurred. The lack of information also made the adoptive parents' job more difficult, and caused tremendous wrenching pain to birthparents.

Adoption practitioners of the day followed a prescribed course—create a new world. It would be a world in which adoptees were told to forget the past, as though it did not exist. Adoptive parents were told to create a new reality and given freedom to exist in total anonymity with no pressure for disclosure. Birthparents were insensitively shoved aside and told to erase the present events from their memories.

Whenever a secret exists, a question must be asked: "Who is being protected by whom and from what?"[5] Secrecy in adoption practice was well intended. It was assumed that if anonymity of all individuals involved was protected it would be in the best interest of all involved.

However, a major problem existed. No one really gave anyone any choice. No one asked, "Do you want this protection?" Secrecy infiltrated adoption practice with many goals for everyone involved.

Goals of Secrecy for Birthmothers

• The birthmother could more easily resolve her feelings about the placement.
• The birthmother would be protected from the label of "fallen woman."
• The birthmother could forget about the child and move forward, living her life as though the experience never happened.

However, as birthmothers have come forward and spoken of their needs, it is clear that these goals failed miserably. (This will be discussed in further detail in chapters five and six.) In fact, one state's intervention in unsealing records is just a sampling of what would be discovered throughout the country. "Since 1980, Michigan has given birthmothers the opportunity to choose whether or not identifying information about them could be made available to their relinquished children when they reach 18. Over 98 percent of the mothers have chosen to make this information available."[6]

Goals of Secrecy for Birthfathers

• The birthfather could just move right ahead with life—no concern
• The birthfather would never have to assume parental recognition—no responsibility

These goals failed miserably for birthfathers. For many, many birthfathers, now one, two, three, or four decades away from any involvement in their child's life, it is common knowledge that (if they knew) they have not forgotten. Although not much is known about birthfathers because of their silence (fully chosen on their part or dictated by societal norms), small studies and support groups give insight to a much larger picture. One birthfather gave his voice to the pain: "There is no stopping the wondering. I hurt every day. I can't go any place without wondering if the young lady walking past me might be my birthdaughter. I would give anything to meet her, to know what type of life she had."

Goals of Secrecy for Adopted Persons

- The child would be protected from the label of "illegitimate."
- The child would be more easily integrated into the family.

These goals also failed for adopted persons, as well.

Most who were adopted were born to unmarried parents and, thus, the effort to protect the child from "shameful" facts of his or her birth. Often, false and more socially acceptable explanations were given (adoptee support groups share with considerable ironic humor stories of the large numbers of couples that seem to have perished in automobile accidents leaving no kin, or records that have been destroyed in a fire). The connection, however, between secrecy and stigma is intuitively known by children and, as an adoptee wrote, "an important aspect of secrecy is the easily made assumption that if one is not allowed to know something, especially about yourself, it must be bad. The recursive relationship between secrecy and stigma is clear. A stigmatized person is protected by secrecy but secrecy promotes stigmatization."[7]

What about goals for the adoptive parents? They didn't work, either.

Goals of Secrecy for Adoptive Parents

- The family could portray their structure as that of a biological family.
- They would never have to tell anyone
- The pain of childlessness could be hidden
- And . . . no one would have to look back.[8]

Robert Jay Lifton, psychiatrist and adoption advocate, in a court appearance on the sealed record issues testified, "I think that continued secrecy about the information concerning one's natural parents poisons the relationship between the adoptive parents and the adoptive person. What it does is build an aura of guilt and conflict over that very natural, healthy, and inevitable curiosity. Both of them get locked into that aura of guilt and conflict concerning the whole subject."[9]

WHAT DO FAMILIES KEEP FROM EACH OTHER?

Family secrets—haunting words that evoke unsettling memories, disturbing thoughts, and uncomfortable feelings. A family secret—something that hides in most every family cedar chest; information that is banished to a darkened attic, buried under dust and cobwebs, hoping to remain forever under lock and key. What types of things do family members keep from one another? Why do families keep secrets? What impact does secrecy have on family relationships? Why has secrecy shadowed adoptees, their adoptive families and birth families?

Families keep secrets from one another around potentially embarrassing, shameful, humiliating, or painful events. A teenage love relationship, an untimely pregnancy, an adoption plan, financial mismanagement, serious mental or emotional illness, a criminal history, drug use—all fill the compartments of that darkened cedar chest.

When Robert was twenty-three years old, his father died suddenly. He had a tremendous relationship with the man he called his hero. His world shattered one afternoon as he and his mother took a walk through a neighborhood park. On that bright, sunny day clouds overshadowed the memories Robert nurtured of his father. On that day, his mother told him of a relationship that she had had earlier in life. At nineteen she had fallen in love with a man who loved her and left her. After his departure, she discovered she was pregnant with Robert. When Robert was eight months old, she met David, the man Robert knew as Dad. David never formally adopted him.

"We intended to tell you all along, son," she related through a trembling voice. "I kept putting it off."

WHY DID WE KEEP SECRETS IN ADOPTION? SECRECY AS A TOOL FOR ...

When Jennifer was twenty years old, she experienced an unplanned pregnancy. Feeling overwhelmed and inadequate to parent, she made an adoption plan. That was twenty-one years ago. She has told no one of her secret, not even her husband and family. Why? Control. As long as she kept her secret, she alone would have absolute control over it.

In her book, *Family Secrets*, Harriet Webster comments, "secrecy is a tool we use to adapt what has happened to us [or our children]. Through the conscious, deliberate concealment or disclosure of information, we take some control of our life and exercise a degree of power over those with whom we interact."[10] *We used the tool of secrecy to keep control.* Why else did we keep secrets in the world of adoption?

Individuals and families keep secrets from one another to keep a blanket of secure protection over them. The less other family members know about a particular past circumstance or event, the less vulnerable that person is to hurt. The less others know the less chance that the family member will be placed under the microscope of unhealthy commiseration, unconscious criticism, judgment, or blame.

One rainy afternoon, when Carla was fifteen years old and her older adopted sister, Rachel, was seventeen, they were cleaning out the upstairs attic. They stumbled onto a shoe box full of old newspaper clippings. The articles told the grisly details of Rachel's birthmother's death at the hands of her father. The articles related the aspects of a very messy trial and his subsequent imprisonment. Rachel, now thirty-four, relates what happened:

I can remember sitting there stunned. I always knew I was adopted, but was always told that my mother died of cancer and that my birthfather couldn't handle his grief and me, too. I confronted my mother with the information and she said, "We just wanted you to be shielded from such a hurtful history." From that moment to this, I have had trouble reconciling that image with what I thought. If I had grown up knowing the truth, it would have been a lot easier for me now as an adult.

We used the tool of secrecy to feel protected or to protect. There are still more reasons adoptive families and birthparents kept secrets from each other and from those outside the family, who could provide love and support.

Candy and Joyce had been close friends for nearly nine years. They shared hurts, joys, hopes, and dreams. Yet, there was still something that Joyce had never shared. While they were finishing their usual Thursday afternoon lunch together, Joyce opened up.

"I need to tell you something that I have told no one since we moved here. I need to tell you that I when I was eighteen, I had a baby and placed him for adoption."

Candy responded, "Why didn't you ever tell me? There wasn't any reason to keep that from me."

"I just couldn't," Joyce said. "I have always been ashamed of the fact that I didn't keep my baby. At that point in time, you just couldn't. I have always thought of myself as not worth much because as someone said years ago to me I 'got rid' of my problem. I thought if you knew, you wouldn't want to be my friend anymore." We used the tool of secrecy because of our sense of shame. It is a shame that leaves us feeling defective and without power.

To keep control, to protect or be protected, to hide shame, all these are reasons why families kept secrets about their adoption experience. Another reason people kept secrets was to hide their public persona—their image. If people knew about their adoption plan or their adoptive status, would life be different for them?

Masking one's secret of childlessness through an adoption by never talking about it, either inside or outside the family, used to be a routine mode of family communication. Living as if an adoption plan never happened used to be a familiar route taken through life by birthparents years ago. Not telling a child about his adoptive status, or asking that child not to reveal it to others, was also a means of quietly handling a child's placement in the family as well as the image of the family itself. This type of denial is now seen to impair adoptive parents' ability to grieve their own loss. What did that type of family secrecy do to children?

Parents are forceful people in the lives of their children, Watson says. They occasionally, through the strength of their authority press a child into silence (if the secret is found out) in order to protect their public image. A child who feels that mentioning adoption in anyway outside the family is a threat to the family's image, begins to wonder what is really important—appearances or reality. "Are reputation and image so sacred that they must be preserved at any cost?"[11]

Questions begin to fill the mind of this silent child. "If my parents choose to protect the image of the family and if I am a sacrifice that has to be made in the process, "the child wonders," how can I be worth anything?"[12] *We used the tool of secrecy to guard our public image and reputation.* There is yet one more reason why families used the tool of secrecy.

Fourteen-year-old Michael joined his adoptive family at two years of age. Michael had been severely neglected, often left an entire day by himself. The condition in which he was eventually found by social workers was beyond deplorable. It was beyond disgusting. Both of Michael's adoptive parents feel that the least said about Michael's past the better. If it is not talked about, it will be forgotten. The entire family maintained the attitude that bad things belong buried in the past. *We used the tool of secrecy to forget about the past.*

THE HIGH COST OF KEEPING SECRETS

Secrets are powerful things. Secrets within any family distort reality, undermine trust, and destroy intimacy. Secrets create exclusion, destroy authenticity, produce fantasies, evoke fear, and kindle shame. For those touched by adoption, there is a high cost to pay.

Secrets in Adoption Distorted Reality

Lois Roberts, now in her early fifties, grew up as an only child, loved, almost worshipped by her parents. Occasionally, her mother would say to her, "We couldn't have any children and then you came along." The phrase had no real meaning to Lois.

Following the sudden death of her mother and the subsequent resident nursing home care needed by her father, a family secret emerged. As Lois visited with her father, each time she entered the room he would ask the same question, "Are you adopted?" Puzzled, Lois contacted family members who confirmed the truth. All the other relatives knew. Everyone knew but Lois.

"I have a lot of questions," Lois stated. "I feel a sense of abandonment. I feel like the whole world is on the inside of a glass and I am on the outside. My prevailing emotional feeling is that everybody marches along to a family rhythm and I don't know what mine is and now it is too late. I don't know what my reality is. I should have counted somewhere enough to be told the truth."[13]

"While some secrets can bring people together by giving them a sense of intimacy and sharing," says author Betty Jean Lifton, "secrets can be destructive if they cause shame and guilt, prevent change, render one powerless or hamper one's sense of reality."[14]

Secrets in Adoption Undermined Trust and Intimacy

When Holly found out that her older sister was adopted, it impacted her relationship with her mother. "My mother and I had always been close. I felt I could tell her everything. When I was seventeen she told me the family secret that Heather had yet to find out. She was adopted. What keeping this family secret did to our relationship was subtle and gradual. I found myself sharing less and less with her, guarding what I did tell and always wondering in the back of my mind, what else she hasn't told me."

Secrets in Adoption Created Exclusion and Division

Keeping a secret puts family members into exclusive clubs—those who know it and those who do not. Secrecy in adoption impacts many arenas in the secret-keeper's life. In order to keep the secret, the secret-keeper has to carefully guard all communication with others close to him. This defense mode often leads to distance, anxiety, and awkwardness in relationships with intimate others.[15] Where there is exclusion and division from one another based on secrecy, the probability of mutual caring, mutual understanding, and mutual honesty is seriously diminished.

Adoptive parents Charles and Marybelle Jenner were advised at the time of their adoption over forty-five years ago to keep it a secret. When Kathleen joined their family at four weeks of age, family members and close neighbors knew of course. The parents were advised not to tell Kathleen, because "it wasn't necessary. She is just like a biological child to you."

"Somewhere in my heart and mind," Marybelle related, "it didn't feel right not to tell her. But we followed our worker's instructions. We lived under a shadow of anxiety wondering if she would ever find out. We wondered which one of our relatives would be the one to tell her. I wish we had followed our own instincts. Kathleen discovered her adoption papers while helping us move. The repair work in our relationship still continues today."

Secrets in Adoption Destroyed Authenticity

In families where secrets are kept, another problem emerges. It is the creation of the family mask. What the family members seem to be on the outside to one another is not what is truly on the inside. In secret-keeping families, the sense of authenticity is lost, says author Michael Mask.[16] For some birthparents, this becomes a lifelong sentence.

Living with secrets, Mask offers, meant remaining entangled in a web of deception, even if the motive was pure and protective. Deception in adoption was so destructive it broke trust and caused confusion. When the truth was kept secret, then corresponding emotions were denied or repressed; defense mechanisms rose to take their place. When some young and impressionable birthmothers, driven by the societal expectation of secrecy were told, "don't think, don't ask, don't see, don't feel, don't tell," they lost their sense of what was real. They became inauthentic.

I relinquished a child for adoption when I was seventeen. My first taste of being inauthentic occurred at the maternity home in 1964. When I was checking in, the matron of the home handed me a short list of names to choose to go by while at the home. I could no longer go by my real name nor could I tell anyone there my real name. Once my son was born, I was told to forget the experience and not to tell anyone about it. For many years, I denied the depression I experienced was caused by the relinquishment, but finally I am no longer repressing that reality and allowing my self to deal with those issues of my past.—Caroline

Secrets in Adoption Produced Fantasies

Kathy, now forty-two, was quite imaginative as a little girl. She knew that she was adopted, but her parents only had sketchy information from the agency. They told her what they had, but they too also wondered what they were not told. Kathy, while growing up, often drew pictures of the house she imagined her birthmother lived in. It was a two-story house on a large farm with lots and lots of animals. Since Kathy was an only child, she dreamed of having brothers and sisters who loved to play with her.

It wasn't until Kathy was an adult that the truth of her birthfamily came to light. Her birthfather was unknown, and her birthmother died shortly after Kathy's birth. Her parents were never given that information from the agency, and the unstated reality for adoptive parents was that one didn't ask.[17] Because Kathy and her parents never knew the truth, Kathy created one for herself. It was a "truth" that would serve her only for a season until the "real" truth came crashing in.

Secrets in Adoption Evoked Fear

"I grew up never knowing anything about my past. No one would ever answer my questions so I stopped asking them," Kirsten related. "Because of that, I also was never able to share an overwhelming fear I had with my parents. I grew up with the fear that some day I was going to wake up and nobody would be there. They would have all left me alone. I just wonder . . . maybe I was adopted because I had been abandoned."

When secrets are kept, there is a vacuum that must be filled. That vacuum is filled with a pre-occupation with the secret. That preoccupation then leads to anxiety and fear. "Secrecy . . . creates a feeling of chronic vulnerability," says adoption author and open adoption proponent, James Gritter. ". . . Fear alters our ability to gather and interpret information, decisions are often based on fantasy-enhanced speculation rather then the fact. Secrecy can accentuate the distressing feeling of being different from others."[18] And when one feels different and doesn't know why, fear is a constant companion.

Secrets in Adoption Kindled Shame

Jim, age forty-five, knew he was adopted, but he didn't know why. He always felt it was about him, like there was something wrong with him that his birthmother couldn't handle. The truth was, his birthmother loved him very much, but as a young teenager forty-five years ago, it was impossible for her to raise him. She had no family support. Jim's adoptive parents knew the whole story, but they, as many parents of that generation, assumed that the less said, the better—for everyone. The only problem was that Jim was left with believing there was something "wrong" with him, that he had been unlovable from birth. A feeling of shame haunted his thoughts and impacted his relationships. He wasn't alone.

"I could never talk about adoption in our house. It was like the family's secret word. If I brought it up, you would have thought I'd said a dirty word," commented Jim. "I grew up thinking that because adoption was never talked about, it was a horrible secret. If there was something wrong with adoption, there must be something terribly wrong about me."

The power of secrecy to disrupt positive emotional development can be seen in the life stories of many adoptees, birth parents, and adoptive parents. Author and adult adoptee Robert Anderson says, "One does not build a house on a sandbar or a personality on a pile of problematic secrets. Feeling secure about oneself is difficult when basic aspects are unknown and frightening. It is all too easy to worry about what might be at the core of the secrets with the possibilities limited only by one's imagination."[19]

WHAT LESSONS HAVE WE LEARNED?

By walking back through adoption practices generally accepted in the decades of the '40s, '50s, '60s and '70s, we have learned that secrecy in adoption demanded a high cost. For all members of the adoption triad touched by the practice of secrecy, we have discovered that this secrecy:

- distorted reality
- undermined trust and intimacy
- created exclusion and division
- destroyed authenticity
- produced fantasies
- evoked fear
- kindled shame

The institution of adoption is now changing from within. Over the last twenty years, and with increasing velocity in the last several years, practices and policies are being influenced by adopted adults, birth parents, and adoptive parents speaking out openly about their experiences, feelings, and needs. However, change comes slowly and, in the meantime, we have generations of people in our country who, although existing in today's social reality in every other way, are stuck with adoption laws, policies, theories, and myths of the past.

In the chapters to come, we will look in greater depth at the members of the triad and at the lessons we have learned from their life experience. We will also add a voice of support to those who are on the frontier of change in adoption practice, so that those who are touched by the adoption experience will move through life in an emotionally, psychologically, and spiritually healthy way.

NOTES

1. Quote from Rick Pitino, "Lead to Success," *Reader's Digest*, May 2001, 73.
2. J. Schooler, *Searching for a Past*. (Colorado Springs, CO: Piñon Press, 1995), 40.
3. Ibid.
4. Ibid., 41
5. E. Imber-Black, *Secrets in Families and Family Therapy*. (New York: W. and W. Norton and Company, 1993), 89.
6. Ibid.
7. Ibid.

8. R.G. McRoy, H.D. Grotevant, & L.A. Zucher, *Openness in Adoption: New Practices, New Issues.* (New York: Praeger, 1998).

9. Imber-Black, 95.

10. Harriet Webster, *Family Secrets: How Telling and Not Telling Affects Our Children, Our Relationships and Our Lives,* (Reading, Mass.: Addison-Wesley, 1991), 11.

11. Ibid., 202.

12. Ibid.

13. Schooler, 105–106.

14. Betty Jean Lifton, *Journey of the Adopted Self: A Quest for Wholeness* (New York: Basic Books, 1993), 22.

15. M. Weinrob and B.C. Murphy, "The Birthmother; A Feminist Perspective for the Helping Professional," *Woman and Therapy.* (1988): 30.

16. Michael Mask, *et al., Family Secrets* (Nashville: Thomas Nelson, 1995.

17. Betsy Keefer and Jayne Schooler, *Telling the Truth to Your Adopted or Foster Child: Making Sense of the Past* (Westport, Conn.: Bergin and Garvey, 2000), 39.

18. James Gritter, *The Spirit of Open Adoption* (Washington, DC: CWLA Press, 1998), 73.

19. Schooler, 14.

CHAPTER TWO

Lifelong Psychological Presence: Can Family Members Really Be Invisible?

Deborah L. Fravel

Tiffany and Matt stood before the minister, Matt proudly holding Chad, their six-month-old son. Chad wiggled in his father's arms, slightly uncomfortable in his crinkly white new clothes, sensing that his parents were a little nervous. As the minister began the christening ceremony, Chad began to suck his pacifier with renewed intensity. A brief sensation overtook Tiffany and she turned, looking at the empty space to her left and behind her. At the reception following the ceremony, when Matt asked Tiffany what she was looking for, she explained, "I felt her there, Matt. I can't explain it, but for a minute there it felt like Chad's birthmother was standing right there beside me!"

Cassandra shifted nervously in the skimpy paper gown as she answered the nurse's questions, routine for an annual medical exam with a new physician. "How many children do you have?" This is one of the questions she always dreads, one she always struggles to answer. Not to mention Nikky, the name she calls her first child, seems somehow unfaithful. Cassandra dearly loves Nikky although she hasn't seen her since the day Nikky was born. There is never a week that passes without thoughts or questions about Nikky flitting through her mind. At the same time, mentioning Nikky has many other implications. She doesn't believe it is necessarily everyone's business that, when she was fifteen years old, she made an adoption plan for Nikky. Cassandra swallowed hard as she heard the nurse ask, "How old is your oldest child?"

Julianna was turning eleven today. She wanted to ask her adoptive mother a question, but was uncertain how to bring it up. She went out to the playhouse in the backyard and practiced how she would say it: "Do you think my birthmother thinks about me on my birthday? I think of her. I hope she thinks of me."

Experiences like those just described are fairly common when adoption is part of a person's life. These accounts capture a phenomenon, psychological presence, which has only recently begun to be understood and explored in the adoption world. Tiffany felt the psychological presence of Chad's birthmother. When Cassandra's nurse asked her certain questions, she felt Nikky's psychological presence. "Psychological presence," simply put, refers to some person being in a family member's heart, or on his or her mind. *It is the symbolic existence of an individual in the perception of other family members in a way that influences thoughts, emotions, behavior, identity, or unity of remaining family members.*[1]

Under ordinary circumstances, people do not separate psychological presence and physical presence. For example, imagine this comment at the breakfast table: "Wow, Uncle Manfred was really psychologically present last night at dinner, wasn't he?" This question might actually cause some alarm in the minds of people who overheard it. The truth is, it is only when the two types of presence do not match that people are even aware of psychological presence. In this chapter, we will first lay some groundwork for a better understanding of psychological presence, and then we will address it specifically as it relates to adoption.

BOUNDARY AMBIGUITY

Psychological presence was first identified by Pauline Boss, family therapist and professor of family science, toward the end of the U.S. war in Vietnam.[2] Boss was working with families of missing-in-action soldiers. She observed that some families were troubled when the missing, physically absent soldier/father was psychologically present in the family in a way that kept the family from going about its usual life. Dr. Boss determined that, when there is a mismatch like psychological presence with physical absence, a condition called *boundary ambiguity* occurs.

Boundaries

Why is this condition called boundary ambiguity? Although people do not ordinarily think of families as structures, it is helpful to realize that, like structures, families do have boundaries. Some of them are visible, tangible boundaries, like the walls of a house. Other boundaries are intangible and invisible, like the idea about just how much the family members will reveal to people outside the family about their finances. Even though this latter kind of boundary is invisible, it is still very evident to family members if the boundary gets violated. For example, when Julie says to her teenage sister, Nora, "I just hate it when Mom and Dad argue about the credit card bill that way," both sisters accept that as an appropriate comment. However, if Julie storms in the back-door and snorts indignantly, "That busybody neighbor asked if Mom and Dad argued about buying our new car!" the whole family knows immediately that the neighbor, an outsider, has overstepped their family's boundaries.

There are many other ways to think of boundaries, and those ways apply also to families. For example, boundaries can be permeable or impermeable. They can be fixed and rigid, or movable and flexible. Healthy boundaries in families compare to well-built components of buildings susceptible to earthquakes—properly constructed, they provide a stable base for the family, but still allow for movement and change within the family. And, just as a good architect designs a building to prevent it swaying too close to nearby buildings, healthy family boundaries also allow for movement and exchange between the family and the outside world, but with some breathing room.

For example, under ordinary circumstances, one parent in a household might be responsible for reading bedtime stories, carrying out the garbage, and locking up the house at night. People in the family are secure in this routine, because they generally know what is going to happen, when it will happen, who will be there, and who will do what. However, in a healthy family, that parent can go away on a trip, and other people will move to cover the bases usually covered by the traveling parent. An older child may help with the bedtime reading, a neighbor may carry out the garbage, and the other parent will lock up the house at night. Family members are not ruffled by the absence of one parent, because the boundaries are flexible and permeable enough to bend without breaking.

Understanding boundaries is important because it is around the boundaries that conflict and stress are likely to occur in all families. For example, when an adult child gets married, family boundaries need to expand to embrace the in-laws. Although marriage is usually a joyous occasion, it is nonetheless also a stressful time. Another example of boundary changes happens when a grandparent dies. The boundaries contract, causing a different kind of stress.

Boss called the mismatch between physical absence and psychological presence *boundary ambiguity*, because it can create uncertainty about the nature of family boundaries. The uncertainty is a perfect setup for family stress. If someone is psychologically present but physically absent, family members may even wonder whether that person is inside the family, or not.[3] The uncertainty doesn't require the family to go out and buy new furniture for someone to physically sleep in, but it does require a parallel accommodation in the person's heart and mind—moving the emotional

or mental furniture, if you will, to make room for the person's psychological presence. Family boundary issues involve such concerns as loyalty and inclusion or exclusion.

Roles

One of the ways families regulate their internal and external boundaries is through the use of *roles*. Roles in families compare to roles in theater productions: different actors have different roles. Roles help family members know who they are: "I am the oldest child." When Susan asked Cinda why an adult neighbor bought her some school clothes, Cinda replied, "Because she's my play aunt." With this answer, Cinda signaled her friend that there is someone in her life playing a family role.

Roles also help family members know how to behave toward one another, who is responsible for certain tasks, and the location of certain limits. When Nita says to her classmates, "We don't usually have Christmas stockings at our house, because my stepfather knows that is something my dad likes to do for us," she is demonstrating that people in their family have negotiated their roles. The man in the role of stepfather does certain things, and the man in the role of father does certain other things.

Roles also help families keep a sense of balance in their lives, because roles usually come in matched sets: parent-child, mother-father, sister-brother, grandparent-grandchild, and so on.[4] Family rules are often based on roles: Parents bathe in the upstairs bathroom; children bathe in the downstairs bathroom. Family rituals may also be associated with roles: "At our family reunion, the fathers always help their children light the fireworks."

Roles are an important consideration in boundary ambiguity. If a person would normally occupy a certain role, and that person is only psychologically present, it may lead to confusion for the rest of the family. It may feel disrespectful to assign that role to someone else, yet the *activity* or behavior required from the person in that role must be fulfilled in some way. This is not possible when the person is physically absent.

BOUNDARY AMBIGUITY IN ADOPTION: LOOKING AT THE PAST, LEARNING FOR THE PRESENT

For many years, birth and adoptive families alike were instructed to "get on with" their lives, to act as if the other party, the corresponding birth or adoptive family, did not exist.[5,6] More recently, based on feedback from adoptive parents, adopted persons, and birthparents, adoption professionals came to realize that it is healthy for everyone involved to acknowledge the existence of the other triad members. Now, new knowledge and understanding about psychological presence provides yet another consideration to add to that acknowledgment: For adoptive families and birthfamilies, touched by adoption many years ago, to examine, understand, and manage the unrecognized dynamics of psychological presence during the intervening years.

Recent research shows something many adoption professionals and triad members have always believed—that birthmothers are nearly always psychologically present in adoptive families.[7] Likewise adopted children are nearly always psychologically present to birthmothers.[8,9] With new adoption openness practices, physical presence has added even more complexity to this mix. Although the practice of closed adoptions has diminished, there remain a fair number of people whose adoption occurred when this style was standard practice. In closed adoptions the birthparents and adoptive parents are physically absent to one another. In more open arrangements, birthparents and adoptive parents are physically present to one another, although not all the time. Therefore, in all adoptions there is high potential for boundary ambiguity, at least some psychological presence, and at least some physical absence.[10] Exactly how does psychological presence occur for families, and what practical meaning does this have for members of the adoption triad?[11]

Boundaries and Roles in the Adoption Triad

Boundary issues have always been commonplace when adoption is part of a family's picture. Adoption occurred because a child moved from one family to another. Two things are immediately obvious about this situation: The first is that the adoption left some kind of space or void in the birthparents' family and, simultaneously, adoption created a need for expanded boundaries in the adoptive family. Let us consider these two situations separately.

Boundaries in the Birthfamily from the Past to the Present

When a child moved from his or her birthparents to adoptive parents, a void was created in the family of the birthparents. This is not to suggest that the birthparents lacked confidence that the adoption was the right decision, or to deny any relief the birthparents might feel at knowing the child had a good home. It simply meant the now-adopted child was once physically there with the birthfamily and now she or he is not there. Although a few birthmothers report never thinking about the adopted child, research shows this to be the exception. Most birthmothers think about and feel for the child fairly often.[12] Although research does not yet extend that far, some birthmothers and adoption professionals speculate that this remains true throughout a birthmother's lifetime.

To put it another way, the child remains psychologically present to the birthmothers, although physically absent. The birthparents report finding themselves in the curious situation of having to maintain a boundary flexible enough that as the adopted child grows toward and into adulthood, it will include him or her psychologically, but not physically. This task continues to affect their daily lives in various ways.

Most birthmothers reserve a very tender, special place in their hearts for the adopted child. For them, it is unthinkable not to cherish and nurture thoughts and feelings related to the adopted child. Problems have occurred when they attempt to do so. For many birthmothers, few family members and friends related to or understood the loss and the psychological presence of the now physically absent child. The child was never mentioned aloud, but remained sheltered only in the silence of a mother's heart. Problems emerged for birthmothers in determining *how* to accommodate the child's psychological presence into their lives. For example, they may want to somehow include the absent child in the celebration of holidays, but are uncertain of exactly how to accomplish this. This is an issue associated with national and religious holidays like Thanksgiving and Christmas, as well as with family holidays.[13] Marla's and Mariah's stories are examples.

This year, Marla bought Stephen a bandana. She chose it, in part, because it was something small and flat. Every one of the eight Christmases since Stephen went to his adoptive home, Marla had bought a gift of this type, something she can hide under the tree during the holiday season, then move to the scrapbook she is keeping to give him someday when they meet. Her husband, who is not Stephen's birthfather, smiles a sad smile, wishing there were something he could do to make it easier for Marla, but knowing this is an important ritual that she needs to observe.

Mariah, whose child is also eight, dreads the coming of Justin's birthday. It is the anniversary of one of the most important days of her life, and she wants so much to observe it in some way. However, her family refuses to talk about Justin and charges her to "forget about it" and move on.

Marla and Mariah are, in their own ways, dealing with the psychological presence of their birthchildren. They are struggling with how to keep these precious children in their hearts and minds, while still respecting the decision they know was necessary for everyone's well being.

Boundaries in the Adoptive Family from the Past to the Present

At the same time adoption left a void in the birthfamily, it created a need for expanded boundaries in the adoptive family. This need for expanded boundaries that included birthfamily members, at least minimally in discussion or more openly with a level of contact, was left virtually unattended and largely denied for decades. Although adoption is nearly always a highly sought-after circumstance in the adoptive family, it nonetheless continues to require some adaptation on their part. Total inclusion of the child throughout his or her life was a part of what the adoptive parents expected when the adoption occurred. Although adoptive parents were acutely aware that their child came into the world as the child of other parents, they were not prepared for the need to make space for the birthmother, as well, in their hearts and minds. She nearly always becomes psychologically present in the adoptive family, and families were not assisted in the healthy management of that presence.

As the years pass, the unspoken conversations continue. At first, it may be only the adoptive parents who are dealing with the psychological presence of the birthmother. As time passes, the boundaries stretch as her psychological presence within their family increases. When the child grows and begins to ask more specific questions, the birthmother's psychological presences may become more and more evident in the family. Molly and Larry's story demonstrates the progression.

At first, Molly and Larry thought of their child's birthmother with awe, grateful that she was able to entrust them with this most precious of all gifts, her child and their son, Devin. The day they brought Devin home, Larry made a silent pledge to the unknown birthmother, promising her that she would never, ever have reason to regret that they have the child she gave birth to. That was only the beginning of a long, silent relationship with her, but there were times when the thoughts and feelings about her caused them a little unease.

As Devin grew older, he began to understand better the answers his parents gave when he asked questions about his birthmother. He began to tell people there were four people in his family, and Molly and Larry knew the fourth person was his birthmother. The first time he said it, Molly and Larry felt very uncomfortable with it, and talked to each other about it into the wee hours of the next morning. Ultimately, they decided that Devin was obviously speaking about his perspective, and they would just follow his lead. Over time, they noticed that Devin became selective about when he said there were four people in his family. They noticed that he mostly said it to close relatives who would understand what he was talking about, without requiring an explanation.

For Molly and Larry, Devin's birthmother was always psychologically present, in a very positive way, but when their boundaries were stretched, it created some temporary discomfort for them. Knowing how important it was to acknowledge Devin's reality, they allowed their boundaries to flex according to Devin's needs, and eventually noticed some equilibrium occurring in the expanding and contracting boundaries.

When Psychological Presence Disturbs the Family's Boundaries

Often, when a family's boundaries are disturbed because of psychological presence, it is related to issues concerning roles. In general, difficulties are associated with family membership, problems determining whether someone has a role in the family, or issues concerning the way those roles are filled. For adoptions that are now decades old and birth-family reunions are now in the pictures, the questions still arise.

One challenging feature of roles in families involved in adoption is that duplicate roles are created. For in reality, a birthmother often has two sets of children, the one she made an adoption plan for, and the ones she is parenting. By the same token, adopted persons have two sets of parents, one set of birthparents, and one set of adoptive parents. Both of these situations impact roles and relationships for a lifetime.

People grow up being taught a certain set of behaviors that are associated with roles. However, the behaviors and expectations that are taught about being a parent are related to being the biological parent of children then raised in that parent's home.[14] When adoption becomes part of the picture, roles get blurred, and usual behaviors and ideals have to be individually redefined. Historically, a birthmother operated with the only choice she thought possible: completely dismissing the role of "child" from her domain. But that is not a viable alternative for many women. Society's requirement for a birthmother to carry a child in her body for nine months, to make a plan that ensures that child's whole future, and to then suddenly and simply, completely dismiss that child has proven extremely difficult to meet.

Another option available to a birthmother is to consider the child hers in name only, and privately. This has the unfortunate side effect of giving the birthmother no social support, giving her also nowhere to go with the psychological presence. What remains for the birthmother is an ambiguous role contained within an ambiguous boundary: This is really my firstborn child, but not the oldest child I am parenting. For the children I am parenting, I am mother. For this adopted child, I am *a* mother, but not *the* mother. Connie's story provides insight into this ambiguity.

Connie chatted nervously with her good friend and neighbor, Jessica. Connie was speculating about what it would be like if she got to meet her birthson, Andy. Jessica knew all about Connie's adoption experience, and she was accustomed to listening to Connie talk her way through issues that came up from time to time. "I just wish, I'm not sure how we, I just wouldn't know how to say what we are to each other. Because he already has parents, you know, and yet, what am I if I am not his parent, too? And what is he to me? He's my son, of course, but yet Billy [the oldest child she is parenting] is, well, Billy has always known he is my only son. But yet I know Andy is my son, too. How would I say it? I wouldn't want him to call me Mom. He could just call me Connie, but if he wanted to he could think of another name for me."

For Connie, the roles of mother and of son are blurred by the fact that the son is psychologically present to her, yet physically absent. She doesn't want to give that up, of course, but it presents a challenge to weave together the roles her two sons have in her heart and mind.

For adoptive families, roles present similar issues. Adoptive parents must parent fully. They want to love, nurture, protect, and otherwise parent the adopted child. Like birthmothers, adoptive parents are *a* parent, but not *the* parent, and the birthmother's role is one that they must weave into the fabric of their family life. For adopted persons and adoptive families of times past, there was no weaving of the birthmother into the fabric of family life. The issues were unidentified, therefore they were not addressed by professionals assigned the job of preparing families for adoption. Families, in turn, did not address them either. However, unlike the adoptions of yesterday, the weaving of the birthmother's psychological presence into the family is now happening. The weaving of roles requires careful negotiation, and many issues that might ordinarily be taken for granted must be reprocessed with acknowledgment of the birthmother. For example, do they consider her a family member? She is, after all, a blood relative to part of their family. Often, these role issues are associated with *how* to include and honor the birthmother while still keeping secure boundaries in the adoptive family. Stephanie's experience illustrates this idea.

Stephanie dragged her feet as she ambled home from school. The coming Sunday was going to be Mother's Day, and she always dreaded it, in a way. Of course, she wanted to do something nice for her mom, Ginger. She and her dad always plotted to have a big surprise for Mom on Mother's Day. This year, they were giving her the Siamese kittens she had fallen in love with at the pet store a few weeks ago. The thing was, though, that Stephanie really wanted to do something for her birthmother this year. She didn't even know her birthmother, but as she had gotten older and learned more about how she came into the world, she had gained a new respect for what her birthmother had done for her. At the same time, she didn't want to offend Mom. A few times, when Stephanie mentioned her birthmother, Mom had had just a quick look on her face that let Stephanie know it made Mom uncomfortable.

When she got home, Stephanie dumped her books on top of the washing machine and walked into the kitchen. Mom was sitting there. "Steph," she said with a smile, "look! Our church newsletter came today, and there's an article announcing that people can put a rose in the church Sunday, in honor of their mothers. Would you like to donate a special one in honor of your birthmother?"

Stephanie broke into a big grin. It was a perfect idea, made extra special by the knowledge that Mom was the one who thought of it!

In spite of her occasional discomfort with the subject, Stephanie's mother acknowledged the psychological presence of the birthmother. She was confident in her own role of mother, and this helped her devise a creative way to help her child embrace the psychologically present birth-mother in her life.

Other Facets of Psychological Presence

Psychological presence comes to the adoption triad through many avenues. One avenue is more cognitive, or head oriented, and may involve thinking or worrying about the physically absent person.

Adrienne, an adoptive mother, thinks a lot about the birthmother of her new infant son, Jeff. She wonders how Jeff's birthmother is doing, and whether she would be pleased if she could see the bright colors Adrienne chose for Jeff's bedroom. Sometimes she even imagines taking Jeff's birthmother on a tour of their house. She thinks a tour might help the birthmother be able to see that Jeff is okay and that his new parents love him very much.

Tim, a fourteen-year-old who was adopted as a toddler, sometimes thinks to himself in the middle of a soccer game, "When I meet my birthmom, I want to remember to tell her about that cool play we just made!"

These scenarios illustrate a triad member preoccupied with, worrying about, or thinking about the physically absent triad member.

Another avenue for psychological presence to occur is more emotional, or heart oriented.

Sometimes when Brenda is in church, she feels intense emotion as she thinks about Cliff, who has been in his adoptive home for eight years. She knows his adoptive parents, and tears slide down her face as she thinks for the thousandth time how she wishes she could have raised him. She squares her shoulders and reminds herself what a good home his parents have provided for him, how happy he is, and how well adjusted he seems. She knows in her heart that she could not have raised him, and she is grateful to his adoptive parents.

The same day, Cliff's adoptive father grins broadly as he watches his son constructing a model dinosaur. He remembers the last time Brenda visited, and is amused to see Cliff grip a piece of the model with the same quirky finger coordination he noticed Cliff's birthmother use when she was unwrapping their birthday present for her. He makes a mental note to share this observation when he sees Brenda next, because he knows it will please her to hear about it.

To What Degree, and of What Nature?

Even though psychological presence is a fairly common occurrence in adoption, its nature varies a great deal from person to person, triad to triad. It can range from a very low degree to a very high degree, and it can be a very positive experience, or a very negative one. Of course, there are many degrees between high and low, as well as shades of positiveness and negativeness between the extreme points.

Meghan looked down at her sandals as she walked across campus to her accounting class. She smiled to herself as she realized how nice it was to be able to see her toes. She remembered the autumn of her sophomore year, when she was very pregnant about this time of year, and her toes were only something she could feel at the end of her foot. The thought triggered a question in her mind. "I wonder if Toby will want to play in the leaves when they fall?" She made a mental note to look in the child development book she kept on her bookshelf, to see how two year olds play. She would also try to remember to ask Jan and Tim, his adoptive parents, when they met the next time. She really didn't know much about children, but she wanted to learn, so she could let Toby grow up in her mind, in the long time periods between those visits.

For Meghan, Toby is psychologically present nearly all the time, very close to the surface of her conscious awareness. She was very pleased when she met his adoptive parents, and she knows he is in a good home. She sees Toby once a year, and she wants to be a positive influence in his life. For this reason, she has chosen to keep a moving picture of him in her mind. The mental notes and the child development book are evidence that she not only feels Toby's psychological presence, she is also doing things to foster it. Toby is very highly psychologically present to Meghan. For her, psychological presence has positive qualities. She intentionally embraces it, nurtures it, and feels better for having experienced it. The psychological presence that Meghan perceives contrasts sharply with that of the birthfather, Jack.

Jack jogs out of his residence hall, away from campus, moving toward the city park. As he runs, he thinks about the daily quizzes in his physics class, and groans to himself as he remembers the C− at the top of his last quiz. As he jogs by a daycare center, Jack thinks briefly about that awful autumn two years ago when Meghan was giving birth, and a flash of the newborn boy moves before his eyes. He would give anything if he could go back and relive the spring semester when Meghan got pregnant. He shakes his head vigorously, as if shaking the image from his head, just as he has chosen not to participate in the visits with the boy's adoptive parents. Next time, he will jog another route, to avoid this daycare center. He forces himself to think again about the physics quiz.

Toby is also psychologically present in Jack's heart and mind, but differently than for Meghan. Jack does not particularly like to dwell on what happened. He loves Toby, but thinking about him leaves Jack feeling uncomfortable and unsettled. Thoughts and feelings about Toby occur fairly infrequently, and that is just fine with him. He tries to think about Toby as neutrally as possible, often not even thinking of him by name. When the thoughts do happen, he gets rid of them as fast as possible. For Jack, the frequency of psychological presence is much less, and it has a more negative quality to him than it does to Meghan. He has developed strategies to keep it at a comfortable distance.

Sarah rolls around on her blanket on the floor while her adoptive mother, Rachel, sits nearby. As she does most days, Sarah plays with her toys for a while then lets them drop one by one as she eases down to lie on her side. She begins to coo a rhythmic sound that signals she is starting to go to sleep. From time to time, her small smile accompanies the cooing. Rachel is still grateful that this seems to be Sarah's preferred way to go to sleep. At the same time, however, Rachel believes the little smiles mean Sarah is thinking about her birthmother. She wonders if Sarah's birthmother used to sing to her. Once she tried to sing to Sarah herself, and Sarah sat straight up and started fretting. So Rachel sits quietly beside Sarah as she falls asleep. Rachel thinks the bond is kind of neat, in a way, but at the same time she is not completely comfortable with the whole idea. Then she gets frustrated with herself for feeling the discomfort. Often she reasons, "Well, she had more time inside her birthmother than she has had with me so far." The truth is, though, that she hopes this does not continue. It just makes her feel uneasy, like someone else is taking part of something that is hers. She feels kind of silly for thinking this, because she knows the adoption is legal and permanent, but still . . .

Sarah's birthmother is psychologically present to Rachel. She believes there is some kind of bond between Sarah and her birthmother. Rachel is struggling with issues of the "mother" role. She highly respects Sarah's birthmother for the wonderful way she took care of her health during the pregnancy, and for loving Sarah enough to let her go. But Rachel grew up in a home where the parents and children were biologically related to each other, and she cannot figure out exactly where this other mother fits in their family. For her, the psychological presence has a mixed nature, causing her some pleasure and some discomfort. Rachel appears to still be "in process" about all this.

Jill moves restlessly at her desk, wishing the hours would past quickly so she could go home to her apartment and her new boyfriend. She is a little uncomfortable this morning, because this is the first day back on the job for one of Jill's coworkers, who has been out on maternity leave. Later, Jill will say a "Welcome back" to her coworker. But Jill cannot allow herself to join the crowd around her coworker's desk, oohing and aahing over baby pictures. She has learned over the past couple of years that there are certain things she has to avoid, in order not to think about Cassandra, the baby she bore. Cassandra was adopted through a closed adoption.

A Closing Word

This chapter addresses a phenomenon that scholars of family studies are only beginning to understand. Knowledge about boundary ambiguity and adoption is a process that is unfolding. In addition, the study of families never yields answers that are absolute. There are always at least a few families, or a few individuals, who vary from the majority or from a pattern. Are those few families, or few individuals, "wrong" or "bad"? Absolutely not! People are very different from one another; the combinations that occur when different people come together create a sort of family fingerprint or dynamics that are totally unique to that family. For this reason, an individual reader may find that parts of this chapter "work" for him or her, but other points just do not apply with regard to the adoption in his or her experience.

WHAT LESSONS HAVE WE LEARNED?

1. *When adoption is part of a family's experience, psychological presence of one or more people is very likely to occur.* Some people with adoption experience have told us that knowing about psychological presence has put a name to something that had nagged at them for years, thereby bringing them a deeper sense of personal peace. This is not too surprising, because naming a stressor is often the first step toward effectively managing that stressor. Some parties to adoption may have experienced feelings of guilt or shame associated with what they now know is psychological presence. Psychological presence in adoption makes adjustment more complex. So, although knowing that psychological presence is a common phenomenon may not be the *whole* battle of adjustment, it is a healthy step along the way.

2. *Once people identify the phenomenon as psychological presence, they then perceive more choices about how to deal with it.* Some people choose to embrace the psychological presence and savor it; others feel comfortable with a little more distance. It may be helpful to think specifically. "Is there some way that psychological presence is affecting my (or my family's) sense of boundaries?" or "How might my role as_____be different because of psychological presence?" Often, the answers to these questions will help a person know how to start dealing with it. For example, a person who has been trying to keep fairly firm boundaries, thinking it the healthy thing to do, may decide a little more flexibility is in order.

   Some people like being able to plan ahead of time for events and circumstances. These people often experience relief when they learn about psychological presence, simply because they can think ahead about ways to manage their feelings or change their thinking, before psychological presence becomes a bigger issue for them. A little self-analysis may help a person identify certain triggers that prompt psychological presence, or feelings associated with it. Once the triggers are identified, the person is better able to plan ahead about how certain situations could be handled. A man who gets anxious whenever his role as adoptive father feels violated may be able to proactively define what he wants his role to be, and how he will be comfortable having the birthfather psychologically present.

3. *Other people can help.* For some people, knowing about psychological presence may not bring complete peace. If a person feels "stuck" or unsettled in this regard, it may be helpful to locate a support group, or find a counselor who can help him or her talk through it. There are many resources available to people whose experience includes adoption, and some of the resources are available at no cost (see appendix three).

NOTES

1. D.L. Fravel, "Boundary Ambiguity Perceptions of Adoptive Parents Experiencing Various Levels Openness in Adoption" (Doctoral dissertation, University of Minnesota, 1995), *Dissertation Abstracts International* 56 (10): 4160.

2. P. Boss, "A Clarification of the Concept of Psychological Father Presence in Families Experiencing Ambiguity of Boundary," *Journal of Marriage and the Family*, 39 (1977): 141–151.

3. P. Boss, *Family Stress Management* (Newbury Park, Calif.: Sage, 1988).

4. R. LaRossa and D.C. Reitzes, "Symbolic Interactionism and Family Studies," In P.G. Boss, W.J. Doherty, R. LaRossa, W.R. Schumm, and S.K. Steinmetz (eds.), *Sourcebook of Family Theories and Methods* (New York: Plenum Press, 1993): 325–355.

5. A.B. Brodzinsky, "Surrendering an Infant for Adoption: The Birthmother Experience," in D. Brodzinsky and M. Schechter (eds.), *The Psychology of Adoption* (New York: Oxford University Press, 1990): 295–315.

6. M. Reitz, and K. Watson, *Adoption and the Family System* (New York: Guilford, 1992).

7. D.L. Fravel, H.D. Grotevant, P.G. Boss, and R.G. McRoy, "Adoption openness and the psychological Presence of Birthmothers in Adoptive Families," forthcoming.

8. D.L. Fravel, R.G. McRoy, and H.D. Grotevant, "Birthmother Perceptions of the Psychologically Present Adopted Child," *Family Relations*, 49 (2000): 425–434.

9. D.L. Fravel, R.G. McRoy, and H.D. Grotevant, "Boundary Ambiguity and Adoption Openness, Birthmother Adjustment Eleven to Twenty Years After Adoption: A Longitudinal Study," forthcoming.

10. Ibid.

11. It is not always the case that both birthparents participate in adoption planning, and the unfortunate reality is that most adoption research to date addresses only the experiences of birth*mothers*. For this reason, we use "birthmother" for accuracy in discussing matters related to results of research studies. Whenever possible, however, we extend our thinking to include one or both

birthparents and other members of their family who may or may not be involved in the adoption. The term "adoption triad" includes the adopted person, the birthfamily, and the adoptive family.

12. Ibid.

13. Ibid.

14. K. Daly "Toward a Formal Theory of Interactive Resocialization: The Case of Adoptive Parenthood," *Qualitative Sociology* 15 (1992): 395–417.

PART II

Focus on the Adopted Person

CHAPTER THREE

Growing Up in Closed Adoption

I remember thinking when I was young that I must have come into this family because it was where I was supposed to be. My sense of loss came about mostly because of the secrecy. I wondered what was so bad about me and my background that I wasn't allowed to know about it.—Betsie

Adoption is a lifelong, intergenerational process, which unites the triad of birthfamilies, adoptees, and adoptive families forever.[1] The lifelong adoption experience as it touches a birthparent, an adopted person, and an adoptive parent brings with it issues that deeply touch the heart. Recognizing these issues is an important step for all members of the triad and the professionals working in the field so that mutual understanding and sensitivity strengthen family relationships. This chapter will examine those core issues as they relate to the adopted persons who grew up in closed adoption.

Growing Up Adopted

Born with brilliant red hair and a spunky personality to match, Betsie Norris joined her adoptive family when she was sixteen days old. Betsie always knew about her adoption. Reared by loving parents who understood the need to communicate with her about it, Betsie grew up feeling comfortable with the relationship. Yet within this positive, open environment, adoption still sent her on an intensely emotional journey, a fragile search for people in her past she did not know.

Also adopted as an infant, Sue grew up in an adoptive home that emphasized her chosenness, her specialness. She knew her parents loved her, and she felt intensely loyal to them. She kept the reality of adoption tucked away until early adulthood. Following the death of her parents, Sue felt free to begin her journey, to confront the intensity of her losses. She needed to find an understanding of feelings she didn't comprehend. Ultimately she made a decision not to search.

Adopted as an older child at age seven, Nancy was separated first from her birthfamily and then tragically from a younger brother who had come with her to a children's home. Nancy entered a home environment where adoption talk was strictly forbidden, her name changed to erase her past, and her feelings forced underground. Adoption set Nancy on a walk to face an indistinct past, to reconnect with those who were faint within her memory.

Making plans for an overseas trip, Robert began collecting the needed documentation for his passport. Officials at the state vital statistics department couldn't locate the most obvious one, his birth certificate. Confused, he casually mentioned the dilemma to his father whose reaction was startling. As his father stumbled around for a plausible explanation, it became apparent to Robert that a significant problem existed.

Robert's father finally told him the truth: He was adopted. Learning this at age thirty-four sent Robert on a path strewn with uncertainty, mistrust, and secrecy. Each step felt like quicksand as he attempted to discover hidden truths and find answers to questions he never would have thought to ask. The journey would reshape his life with a new meaning that seemed fleeting, unreal, and ill-defined.

Betsie, Sue, Nancy, and Robert represent a broad spectrum of the millions of adults who have grown up in adoptive homes. Some entered those homes as infants, others as older children. Some experienced openness and communication about their past, others encountered blank looks and raised eyebrows as hushed tones squelched their normal curiosity. A few stumbled into the secret of their adoptive status while in late adolescence, even adulthood, finding themselves bewildered and confused. For most, their adoption experience created questions to be answered, a past to be found, and deep-seated emotional issues to be resolved. In essence, a lifelong process, unique to each person, in an attempt to find Self.

Growing Up in Closed Adoption

Many adopted persons who were children in the '50s, '60s, and '70s felt as if they grew up under the shadow of secrecy, silence, and in some cases, shame. Others found their adoptive experience to be open, positive, warm, and fulfilling.

Cindy, adopted from a children's home in 1954, recalls her earliest memory of adoption:

I was sitting in the back yard playing dolls with a neighbor girl. I was about eight years old. She told me something that day that I didn't at first believe. "Guess what? You're adopted. My mother told me so." Startled by that revelation and not sure exactly what adoption meant, I went in to ask my mother. Hesitantly she told me that yes, I was adopted. She briefly told me a few details. She ended the conversation that day with, "You're our little girl now; you don't need to think about this anymore."

At eight years of age Cindy received a message that adoption was to be kept a secret and forgotten. She also learned it was a topic that seemed to make people uncomfortable.

"If I was in a group of people and the opportunity to mention it came up, I did. Everyone would get quiet—they didn't know what to say. Some people joked about it because they didn't understand."

Unlike Cindy's experience of secrecy regarding adoption, Jennifer met with a total lack of communication on the subject. That silence created unsure footing for her as she entered her teen and young adult years and left her with a sense of shame.

Jennifer was adopted in 1963 as a two year old. She remembers being told of her adoptive status perhaps twice prior to her adolescence. "No one ever mentioned the word adoption around me, so I couldn't ask anyone about it. By late elementary age, I knew I was different and adoption wasn't normal. I then began to wonder if adoption was bad. That sense of shame followed me into a turbulent adolescence filled with low self-esteem and feelings of worthlessness."

The power of secrecy to disrupt positive emotional development can be seen in the life stories of many adoptees. Author and adult adoptee Robert Anderson writes, "One does not build a house on a sandbar or a personality on a pile of problematic secrets. Feeling secure about oneself is difficult when basic aspects are unknown and frightening. It is all too easy to worry about what might be at the core of the secrets with the possibilities limited only by one's imagination."[2] For some, growing up adopted created memories filled with pain, disillusionment, and wonder. For others, the adoption experience brought positive emotional growth and fulfilling memories.

Dianne's adoption experience produced in her affirmative feelings. Learning of her adoption at age five, Dianne recalls warm memories throughout childhood.

I had a little ironing board, and when my mom would iron clothes, I would iron my dolls' clothes while we talked. One of the neighbors was pregnant and I asked my mom what it had been like when she was pregnant with me. Without skipping a beat, she said, "Well, I didn't have you; you were what is called adopted." I never felt out of place growing up adopted. I always felt it was very special to be their chosen one. I felt lucky being adopted into this family. They always accepted me as the adopted one but never referred to me as such. I was never given anything but love and respect and a sense of belonging.

Betsie, who grew up the only girl along with two adopted brothers, felt content with her adoptive status. "Adoption was such a normal thing in our family and my parents handled it so well." Yet, in spite of the family's openness of communication regarding adoption issues, Betsie still dealt with some issues. "I felt different because I didn't look like the others," she commented. "I had no real conscious thoughts of being different. But looking back now as an adult, I think I felt it more than I realized."

According to Michigan therapist and adult adoptee, Linda Yellin, "When one is adopted, no matter how accepting, loving, or nurturing the adoptive parents are, consciously or unconsciously there is still a blow to one's self-esteem as a result of not being kept."[3] Some, if not all, issues for adopted persons begin with a sense of abandonment and rejection. From that grow other issues that confront adoptees throughout life as they put adoption within the context of their life history.

CORE ISSUES FOR ADOPTED PERSONS

For some, the question "Why did my parents give me away?" is no more than a passing thought. For others it is an obsession that can't be stilled. Yellin sees this common thread in her clinical work with adopted persons:

Many adoptees struggle with integrating their intellectual understanding of the facts and the societal norms at the time of their release with the feelings that come with the question "Why was I given away?" They remain emotionally confused. It is more than just feeling unwanted, but wondering how anyone could give away flesh and blood. They are puzzled why no one would help the birthmother. They want to know what's behind the real story.

As adopted persons encounter adoption issues, whether in early or midadolescence (or for the first time in adulthood), this confusion leads them to deal with what many experts feel is the hub around which all other adoption issues revolve.

Loss

Around the age of ten or eleven, I really began to understand what adoption meant—I had gained a family. I soon came to realize something else—I had also lost a family in the process. Where is that family now?—John, age 33

I think I felt the losses in my life when I found my birthfamily. I had wonderful adoptive parents but grew up an only child. I didn't know my birth situation, so I wasn't sure if I had siblings. I had a strong inner feeling that I did. When I found out I had four brothers and sisters, all I could think about were the tragically lost years without them.—Marsha, age 42

Adoption is the only relationship in life that by its very existence creates loss for everyone involved. "Without loss, there would be no adoption. Loss is the hub of the wheel."[4] All those within the adoption triad—birthparents, adoptive parents, and adoptees—have experienced at least one life-changing loss.

For the adoptive parents, the subject of chapter seven, that loss is created by infertility. A portion of those losses includes loss of a biological child, loss of dreams for a family as planned, loss of status as biological parents, and loss of providing grandparents with a biological child.[5]

For the birthparents, the focus of chapters five and six, that loss begins with the termination of a lifelong relationship with their birth child and is layered by all the issues and emotions that follow the relinquishment.

For the adopted child, the list is a long one. "The adoptee experiences many losses over a lifetime: loss of birthparents, loss of a biological connection to the adoptive parents, the loss of status as a normal member of society with one father and one mother, the loss of birth family ties, loss of cultural heritage, loss of siblings, loss of genetic information."[6] For all affected by adoption, "it is these losses and the way they are accepted and hopefully resolved that set the tone for the lifelong process of adoption."[7]

For some the loss feels like an amputation that leaves them vulnerable to future losses. As she grew older and moved into her midthirties, Sue encountered for the first time a profound sense of what she didn't have. She now knows that as a young person, she kept adoption issues hidden well below ground. "Before I had my daughter, much of my adoption stuff was underground for me. When she was born, it really hit me that to my knowledge, she was the only connection in blood that I had. I was unprepared for the intense feeling of loss I experienced and still do."

Challenged with new feelings and emotional experiences at the birth of her daughter, Sue recognized she was dealing with a pervasive feeling of disconnectedness in her life. After she experienced a strong bond to her daughter, she understood for the first time what connectedness felt like. Not only did she feel disconnectedness as a loss, Sue also commented that the secrecy of her adoption left her without a history, without life in its truest context—her own reality. Her journey into the pain of loss is bringing some resolution.

Anderson, in his book *Second Choices*, comments about loss. "Life consists of a series of losses, which by themselves do not cause psychopathology. One does better to confront a loss directly; ignoring it or wrapping it with platitudes may obviate the need for grief over the short term, but invites a problem with self-esteem over the long term."[8]

In *Faces of Rage*, author David Damico states that if we fail to resolve loss in a healthy manner, it could have consequences:

- We will impair our ability to recognize and comfort others in pain.
- We will injure our ability to feel and remember, as our practice of blocking out bad times extends to difficulty in remembering good times as well.
- We will force ourselves into self-protection that will keep others at arm's length.
- We will project our own fears and beliefs into our present moments.
- We will construct walls of rage that lock the needy part of ourselves inside, away from anyone—including God—who can heal and restore us.

"Unresolved loss," warns Damico, "extends to every aspect of our physical, emotional, and spiritual being."[9]

For some adopted persons, resolution of the loss has carried them through much emotional work. Damico offers encouraging insight into this journey of loss resolution:

When we allow ourselves to experience pain, hope begins to enter. It reminds us of the loss, which always hurts. But the reminder of the loss helps us clear a path through the pain to a new shore. When we get there we will be different and so will our world. Hope brings us to acceptance. Never ignoring or erasing the loss or pain, hope teaches us to respond to and honor loss. It brings dignity to pain. It makes us strong, more authentic, and more understanding of others whose losses mirror ours.[10]

For those who are still continuing the journey through loss or have touched a point of resolution, another issue may silently clamor for recognition.

Abandonment and Rejection

Throughout my entire life, I always heard the "your mother loved you so much, she gave you to us" story. It never made much sense to me. Reality is, she left me.—Robert, age 26

I have always wondered what I could have done to force my mother to get rid of me. Maybe if I hadn't cried so much.—Katie, age 21

I grew up with the fear that some day I was going to wake up and nobody would be there. The house would be empty. They would have all disappeared. Maybe that's what happened to me in the very beginning.—Kim, age 28

The word *reject* means "to repel, to repudiate, to throw back or throw out as useless or substandard." A large shadow looming over the lives of many adopted persons is the feeling of being rejected. Rehearsing rejection and abandonment, for some, becomes a way of managing the pain.

Rejection must rank as one of life's most anguishing experiences. Especially in the vulnerable years of adolescence into early adulthood, feelings of rejection on the part of the adopted person can override the positive and nurturing love given to them by their adoptive parents. Their perceptions of rejection can spill over to affect the building of healthy relationships. Some develop patterns of pursuing acceptance but then backing away when emotional intimacy gets too close.

Cathy, the beautiful twenty-two-year-old daughter of Robert and Donna Rider, would enthusiastically call her mom and dad from college to report on her newest romantic prospect. But after a few dates, Cathy began refusing invitations to go out. Her roommates told her parents that she never went out with the same boy for very long at all. Her behavior stumped her parents.

Cathy's evasive behavior is typical of a person dealing with rejection issues. The Riders adopted Cathy when she was a month old. Their openness about how she was separated from her family gave her answers to the facts, but she repeatedly asked questions they couldn't answer. "Why did they get rid of me? Why did they leave?" Cathy's perception of rejection was so strong that in most of her relationships she rebuffed girlfriends and boyfriends before they rejected her.

In an attempt to come to an understanding of the issue of abandonment and rejection, and Roszia and Silverstein suggest questions an adopted person can ask to sort through the pain.

- How has rejection played a role in my life in response to loss?
- Have I become a people-pleaser to feel accepted? or am I an extremely angry, rejecting person?
- Have I caused significant others to reject me over time because of those initial losses in adoption?[11]

A final question: What will I now do with this perception of rejection?

As adoptees get in touch with feelings of loss, rejection, and abandonment, other sensitivities may emerge that touch deep chords of self-worth.

Shame and Guilt

I knew my birthmother was only seventeen when I was born. When I was grow-ing up, if I did something really wrong, my father would ask, "Are you going to be like your mother?" I lived under such a shadow; if they thought she was so bad, I must be too.—Gloria, age 36

I could never talk about adoption in our house. If I brought it up, you would have thought I'd said a dirty word. I grew up thinking that because adoption was a bad word, there was something terribly wrong with me.—Jackie, 38

Whenever I acted up, my mother would go into a lecture: don't you appreciate what we have done for you? I felt guilty all the time for failing to act like they wanted me to.—David, 34

"It is a very heavy feeling, this pervasive sense of shame. It is the ongoing premise that one is fundamentally bad, inadequate, defective, unworthy, or not fully valid as a human being."[12] The feeling of shame is not about what we did or did not do. It is about our very selves. It is about who we are. Shame tells us we are unworthy, horribly unworthy. "Shame is without parallel—a sickness of the soul."[13]

Adoption exposes a person to this invisible sense of shame. Why? Be-cause the most conspicuous way for parents to create shame within a child is to turn their back on him, to fail to take responsibility for him, according to Lewis Smedes in his book *Shame and Grace: Healing the Shame We Don't Deserve*. Adoption, by its mode of creation, constructs this per-ception within a child that translates into shame.

Kristy, twenty-eight, felt disowned by her birthmother, the woman who gave her life and then gave her away. Kristy knew intellectually that having been given up for adoption as a baby had absolutely nothing to do with her as a person. However, it was not what she thought that drove her spirit but what she felt. Her feelings told her that if she had been worth it, her mother would have moved mountains to keep her.

Another source of shame for many adopted adults is the feeling that they never were what their adoptive parents had hoped for. They never measured up to the child their parents could not conceive. This left them with the awesome pain of not only never "being" that dreamed-for child, but never "doing" the right thing.

Guilt for the adoptee is rooted not only in a sense of never doing the right thing—never measuring up within the adoptive home—but in feeling that even as a small child he or she caused the breakup of the relationship within the birthfamily.

For Nancy, that feeling of guilt followed her throughout childhood. "I never really felt like I fit in, and I always wondered why I was taken away. What had I done wrong?"

Feelings of guilt and shame overlap. They are fluid feelings that never stay in their own place quite the way our labels want them too.[14] One feels guilty for something one has done, and another feels shame for being the type of person who would have done it.

As an adult, facing feelings of shame can be a freeing experience. Smedes suggests three self-discoveries a person can make:

- I am someone to whom someone made an unconditional commitment from the beginning.
- I am someone whose parents consider me worthy of the love they give.
- I have the power to own myself: I take responsibility for my life, I am proud to be who I am, and I have joy in being myself.[15]

Core issues such as loss, rejection, shame, and guilt often confront adoptees as they face gnawing emotional pain. Another core issue usually wells up in adolescence and seeks resolution well into adulthood.

Identity

"Who am I?" "Who do I look like?" "Who do I act like?" These questions are wrapped up in identity formation. Adoptive identity development concerns how the individual constructs meaning about the adoption. For the adopted person, understanding occurs as one examines three aspects of identity: "How do I see myself, how do I see myself in the context of my family, and how do I see myself in the context of the world around me—friends, community, school, job, etc."[16]

The importance of adoptive identity differs from one adopted individual to another. "While some individuals engage in a great deal of intense reflective thinking about their status as adopted persons and the meaning that identity hold for them, others devote relatively little thought to their identity and its meaning."[17] How adopted persons deal with identity appears to fall on a continuum from showing little interest to preoccupation with exploring their roots.

Growing up with a clear narrative of their adoption story, getting solid information about their birthfamilies, or making contact as adults aided some adoptees in integrating their two identities. For others, it can lead to more questions because of the vast differences between the adoptive family and birthfamily.

Preoccupation

Meeting my birthmother is a lifetime dream for me. I often think about her and even dream about looking in old high school yearbooks to see if I can recognize her. I am much more interested in meeting my birthmother than my birthfather. Maybe that is because I am not real close to my adoptive mother and am with my adoptive father. I talk with my parents about my adoption and ask them for more information about my birthmother. I remind them how close I am to the age when I can look in her file at the agency. I wish for contact with my birthparents, but I would understand if they didn't search for me, because it would be a "hard" memory to bring back.—Melanie, age 19[18]

Feeling Different

Kim, a twenty-five-year-old adopted woman from Korea, encountered almost daily a feeling of being different. "When we went to a restaurant, grocery store, just about anywhere, I could sense people turning their heads to look at us. I knew they were wondering where I came from. I was born in Korea and it's obvious that I'm adopted."

Penny also grew up with a feeling of being different, wondering who she was and where she fit in. When she joined her family at the age of two, she was the only child. Soon to follow would be three children born to her adoptive parents. She grew up in a loving, nurturing family of very light-complexioned blondes. Her sisters and brothers all towered over her in height. She felt like the only "short and fat" one in the house. Her own perceptions of these major differences created a sense of confused identity—"Who am I really? I don't fit here."

Something Is Missing

People ask me, "Don't you hate your mother?" "No, how could I ever hate somebody I don't know? How could I love somebody I don't know?" I just have a million questions: Did you ever think about me? Did you ever try to find me? Were you ever curious about how I grew up? My adoptive parents are my parents—I love them to death and I don't want to hurt them. But I've always had the feeling that something was missing. I don't know how to explain it. It wasn't anything my (adoptive) parents did wrong. It's just something that's always been there.—Nanci[19]

Carole, a thirty-three-year-old adoptee experienced the same feelings. "I love my parents dearly. They raised me with good moral values, a sense of family, and a lot of love. But still, I needed to meet the woman who gave birth to me. As much of a cliche as it may seem, I needed to find that missing puzzle piece."[20]

In moving toward resolution of the issue of identity, Carole discovered a secret. "Much of my adolescence was a furious search for identity, natural for that age, but was intensified by my preoccupation—almost an obsession—with being adopted. As I grew older I grew calmer. The obsession dwindled to a desire. I learned that my identity was what I made myself. I started to define myself based on me, not on what might have been if only I had known my birthmother."[21]

WHAT LESSONS HAVE WE LEARNED?

Listening to those who now view adoption from the other side of childhood offers an opportunity to improve the experience for all whose lives are touched by the experience. What advice do these adults give?

If I could change something, it would be that I was told sooner and that I felt free to talk about it.—Julie, age 47 (She found out by accident at the age of fourteen that she was adopted.)

I wish I could change how my parents understand my need and desire to know the truth. I don't want to hurt them. It's about me, not them—Thomas, age 43.

We were taken from our parents when I was around seven. I wish my adoptive parents had communicated with me and given me reasons for what happened. I wish my brother and I had not been separated. I had cared for him but I was never permitted to see him. I also wish that someone had guided me through the whole experience from day one of separation from my birthfamily.—Nancy, age 61

If I could change something, it would be that my parents hadn't so emphasized their view of what was positive—that I had been "chosen"—rescued almost. I would like to have been allowed to talk about some of the negatives—like feeling so different from them.—Sue, age 45

Preparation and Reflection

The precious gift you gave to me,
Is the decision you made to set me free.
You gave me something you could not give,
The life I lead now, the life I live.

But you made that choice, unselfish and true
It was your decision no one made you do.
When you gave me my future and let me go,
You gave up the right to watch me grow.

Another stepped in and picked me out
I was the one, she had no doubt.
She watched me grow up through the years
She was there through laughter and tears.

I fell down, she dusted me off.
She was there to cure colds and my cough.
My first heart break, she held me tight,
She let me know everything was alright.

She's been there for me through thick and thin.
My family taught me blood does not make kin.
But if you wonder if I ever think of you,
Ease your mind, time to time I do.

You hold secrets only you would know.
You possess things only you could show.
My personality, features, and medical history,
brothers, sisters, grandparents, only you could tell me.

I'm taking this time for preparation and reflection
Some say I am just scared of pain and rejection
But for now I am happy and don't care to see,
Why 19 years ago you decided to abandon me.

Maybe in the future our paths will meet.
Through an agency or passing on a street.
If this should happen please don't hesitate to say
I knew we would meet, I've been looking forward to this day.
—Reneka Howell, January 30, 2001

A Word from Betsie

I love my adoptive parents and I'm grateful I had the opportunity to be raised
by them, but that doesn't make me grateful I was given up for adoption. I can't
say it would have been better this way or that way. I do think it helped contribute
an aspect to my personality that maybe, otherwise, would not have been there.
I think adoptees have to be flexible and perceptive to grow up in a family they
are not biologically connected to. We have to figure things out as we go along.
I don't think we know internally what the rules or standards are as much as
someone intricately connected biologically.

Growing up adopted in a closed system, for many persons, sets them
on a peculiar and unique journey as they begin to put their lives in
perspective. It's a journey to discover something about themselves—a
journey to reconnect a broken cord. It's a journey to embrace what one
has been given, to grieve what one has lost, and to build upon what one
has discovered.

NOTES

1. Sharon Kaplan Roszia and Deborah Silverstein, "The Seven Core Issues of Adoption," www.adopting.org.

2. Robert Anderson, *Second Choices: Growing Up Adopted* (Chesterfield, MO.: Badger Press, 1993). 21.

3. Personal interview with Linda Yellin, therapist and consultant, reunited adoptee, January. 1994.

4. Sharon Kaplin Roszia and Deborah Silverstein workshop entitled "The Seven Core Issues of Adoption, 1988." Roszia and Silverstein developed "The Core Issues of Adoption" in the mid-1980s. They have presented the subjection nationally and internationally, have multiple audio recordings and a video presentation. They both reside in California.

5. Jayne Schooler, *The Whole Life Adoption Book* (Colorado Springs: Pinon Press, 1993), 201.

6. David Brodzinsky, Marshall D. Schechter, and Robin Marantz Henig, *Being Adopted: The Lifelong Search for Self* (New York: Anchor Books, 1992), 142.

7. Roszia and Silverstein. "The Seven Core Issues of Adoption."

8. Anderson, page 31.

9. David Damico, *The Faces of Rage*, as quoted by Schooler, 109–110.

10. Ibid.

11. Roszia and Silverstein.

12. Merle Fossum as quoted by Lewis B. Smedes, *Shame and Grace: Healing the Shame We Don't Deserve* (San Francisco: Harper and Row, 1993), 4.

13. Gershen Kaufman as quoted by Smedes, page 7.

14. Smedes, 11.

15. Ibid., 71.

16. Harold Grotevant, et al. "Adoptive Identity: How Contexts Within and Beyond the Family Shape Development Pathways," *Family Relations* 49 (2000): *379–387*.

17. Ibid.

18. Adapted from Grotevant, page 382.

19. Jodi Phillips, "Powerful Forces Lead Children on a Search for Their Birth Parents," *Houston Chronicle*, June 27, 1993, sec. A, p. 9.

20. Carole Wallenfenfelsz, "Missing Pieces," *Birthparents Today Newsletter*, (Cincinnati, Ohio: Summer 1993), 4.

21. Ibid.

CHAPTER FOUR

A Walk into the Wilderness: Learning of Your Adoption As an Adult

If I had not had my identity anchored in my relationship with God, this would have been a much more devastating crisis, because my human identity has been destroyed.—Lois, age 49

To keep a secret from someone is to block information or evidence from reaching that person and to do so intentionally. To keep a secret is to make a value judgment, for whatever reason, that it's not that person's right to possess the secret. To keep a secret requires a maze built by concealment, disguises, camouflage, whispers, silence, or lies.[1]

- Lois, at forty-seven, discovered the secret as she sat by the bedside of her elderly father.
- Jan, at forty-four, discovered the secret in a casual conversation with a relative on a family vacation.
- Marianne, at fifty, discovered the secret when her brother found his amended birth certificate and began to ask questions.
- Karen, at thirty-two, discovered the secret while enjoying a conversation with a distant cousin.
- Tammy, at thirty-four, discovered the secret from her sister who sat at the deathbed of her mother.
- Alissa, at twenty-eight, discovered the secret because a family member let it slip.

Each of these individuals stumbled onto life-altering secrets after personal identities were formed, adult relationships secured, and heritages passed on to future generations. Each represents thousands of other adoptees that grew up in the shadow of the secret. One day, at the most unlikely time, each heard the same disturbing words—"You were adopted."

This revelation changed the course of their lives. It was a secret that redefined present relationships and a dilemma that added new people and places and enlarged a family system. It was a mysterious disclosure that sent many wandering into an emotional, psychological, and spiritual wilderness. It was a crisis of the whole person—mind, body, and soul. It would require responses from the depths of their souls, which would eventually, hopefully, lead to inward resolution and outward reconciliation.

THE CONSPIRACY OF SILENCE

For many adopted persons in midlife and beyond, the fact of their adoption was hidden in an attempt to deny its reality. For many adoptive parents of the '40s, '50s, and '60s, this secrecy was a misguided decision encouraged by the paradigm of the time. Yet this action gave no thought to the long-term future of the adoptee or insight into what the consequences of such secrecy would do.

"While some secrets can bring people together by giving them a sense of intimacy and sharing," says author Betty Jean Lifton, "secrets can be destructive if they cause shame and guilt, prevent change, render one powerless, or hamper one's sense of reality."[2] Adoption, in the last half of the twentieth century, became that pathogenic type of secret requiring a conspiracy of silence to maintain it.

"Finding out the secret of one's adoption as an adult feels like absolute betrayal," says Dr. Dirck Brown, family therapist and author. "It is the most prominent, deepest sense of betrayal. It is a real blow, a psychological injury."[3]

Although the adoptee knows nothing of his family status, extended family members often do. Psychologist Mark Parel calls this type of secret the *internal* secret, which a few family members keep from another family member.[4] Even if the adoptive parents ably maneuvered through the maze of concealment with disguises, silences, or lies, the careless comment by a relative, the discovery of hidden papers in the back of a dresser drawer, or the reading of a will brought the secret to light.

"There are far more people who learn of their adoptive status at the deathbed of a parent or the settling of an estate than the general public has any idea," comments Dr. Randolph Severson. "When the truth comes out, an emotional rippling effect takes over."[5]

What Dr. Severson has observed in counseling adoptees experiencing this personal crisis is that there is both absolute shock and relief. "More people suspect it but have not admitted it, or they are unconsciously aware of it," Severson explains. "There were probably subtle hints along the way, such as a lack of pictures during pregnancy or coming home from the hospital. There were probably no stories unless they were fabricated. Some have resurrected memories of whispers at family reunions and holiday get-togethers.

"As the shock subsides, relief comes when the adopted person realizes what he thought was off base wasn't. These adults have grown up wondering, *Why do people get anxious when I talk about my birth? Why don't I look like anyone? Why do I get strange looks when this subject comes up?* As the truth emerges, there is a rhythm of shock, anger, and relief."

She Wondered All Her Life

Lois, now fifty-four, grew up an only child feeling very wanted and loved. Occasionally she would hear her mother say, "We couldn't have any children and then you came along," but the phrase had no real meaning to her.

Occasionally the kids in the neighborhood teased her saying, "You're adopted, you're adopted." A quick run home to a reassuring remark from her mother, "No, honey, you're not, and if you were you would be special and chosen," calmed her fears. These statements and many more scattered throughout her childhood were the hidden remnants of a part of Lois's legitimate personhood, her true identity. It wasn't until her elderly father let the secret slip that Lois was able to gather those mysterious pieces of her childhood together and some of the painful issues in her life began to make sense.

Looking back on her life after the adoption revelation, Lois recounts memories of her parents' behavior that were a part of the secret they felt constrained to keep. "I can remember my mother standing and watching out the window for long periods of time as if she were looking for someone. They were both paranoid about privacy and had a very guarded attitude about their personal life. My only babysitter when I was young was my grandmother." It was as if her parents lived in fear that Lois would someday be reclaimed.

Not only did Lois's parents guard her and their personal life, her father demanded something further. It was as if he could never accept the fact that Lois was theirs by the bond of adoption, not by blood.

"As I grew older, the primary situation that caused tension—an escalating tension on my father's part-was that he needed to be reflected in me," Lois recalls. "He had to see himself in me. It was an obsession for him that I be like him and think like him. As a teenager, my faith became a vital reality to me. He wanted me to forget about it. He was relentless with an ongoing verbal violation of my personal boundaries. There was a constant attempt on his part to change me. I never went through a rebellion as a teen; I tried to be a people pleaser. Now I see that my role growing up was to keep my dad from being angry. It was an incredible pressure to be the go-between with my parents. Life was a constant tap dance.

As Lois grew into adulthood, and after the sudden death of her mother, she became even more keenly aware of the unhealthy nature of her relationship with her father. But she had no clue as to what could be the problem. "After my mother died July 4, 1990, I found myself saying, 'I cannot grow up. I can't go on.' My relationship with my father felt like a rubber band that kept us attached. I went into counseling to help sort out the blockage I felt with him. I did everything the counselor suggested to break his hold on me, but there was something, a heavy black cloud, that I couldn't see through."

In 1992 Lois's eighty-four-year-old father became extremely ill—a fast-moving case of dementia—and he was moved to a nursing home. As Lois visited with her father, each time she entered the room he would ask the same question, "Are you adopted?" Puzzled, she finally contacted an uncle she had not seen since she was ten years old. He confirmed the truth, as did other relatives and friends of her parents.

For Lois, the revelation brought instant relief. It also left in its wake shock and emotional upheaval. It propelled her into the wilderness, a dry barren place of the unknown. "When I learned of my adoption, it brought a tremendous sense of relief—emotionally and physically. Most of my adult life I discerned something was amiss, and this explained it all. It explained the actions of my parents. It explained the harshness and demands of my father and the incredible hold he had on me."

This knowledge brought relief, but it also brought shock. "I was incredibly shocked that Mother never told me. I felt close to her. But I understand why she did it. I think it was my mother's desire to be a wonderful mother. She died in my arms right after a heart attack. As we were frantically waiting for the ambulance, I administered CPR. I kept thinking, 'You gave me life, let me do this for you.' It's a tragedy, for her sake, that she died never revealing the truth."

Although Lois has yet to experience a great deal of anger, she believes that "the anger isn't over for me yet. I don't handle anger well and the focus has been on absorbing the shock."

On one hand, I feel like I'm in transition. I know what the truth is. The horrible tension is gone. I've had conversations with Dad and told him I knew. He wept and there was a lot of healing that happened for me.

On the other hand, I have questions—I feel a sense of abandonment. I feel like the whole world is on the inside of a glass and I'm on the outside. My prevailing emotional feeling is that everybody marches along to a family rhythm and I don't know what mine is, and now it's too late. I should have counted somewhere enough to be told the truth.

When Lois learned of her adoption, she felt like she'd been thrown into the undertow of a fast-moving river. However, this time she had a life preserver—the truth. It validated what she had felt deep in her heart many years ago. The truth rescued her.

Jan Always Suspected It

Discovering the secret of her adoption at age 44 confirmed for Jan a lifetime of suspicion.

The reality, of course, never hit me as a child because it was kept a secret from me. But I always felt out of place for several reasons. I looked different from the rest of the family. I was darker complexioned with dark brown hair. They were blond with gray-green eyes. One grandmother even had red hair. In my teen years, I became aware that it wasn't just my appearance that was different from my parents. My personalities, my interests, my talents, my spirituality, were all very different from theirs and they did not particularly appreciate those differences.

Suspecting the secret of one's adoption generates feelings of bewilderment, some adoptees report. Learning the truth pushes them to an entirely different level of emotion. It sends them into the wilderness.

"There are no easy steps to take in dealing with this crisis of the self," said Dr. Severson. "This crisis moves one into the desert of the soul . . . a wilderness of the heart. There will be changes. One will never be the same. How one comes out of the wilderness can't be predicted."

This journey is a walk into a wasteland, laid bare by silence and what feels like utter betrayal. It's a walk one begins alone. How one returns from the wandering has everything to do with time, process, support, understanding, and forgiveness.

HOPE FOR RESOLUTION

How does a person manage the past mismanagement of the most intimate detail of life—one's personal identity? How does a person regain a sense of self and stand on solid emotional and psychological ground? How does one face the people in life who often unknowingly and without harmful intent created the maze of secrets and maintained it at all costs?

For each adoptee who uncovers the reality of his or her adoption as an adult, the circumstances are different, the pain is unique. For some, still in the early stages of discovery, emotional balance and freedom from anguish feel completely out of reach. Others find themselves on a road leading out of the wilderness, heading toward resolution and reconciliation.

The following stories portray real circumstances, real people, and real suffering. If you identify with them, their stories may give you guidance and hope.

Marianne's Story

Marianne and her older brother grew up with a unique identity—that of the American Indian. It was a heritage and culture she was raised to respect and preserve.

On a spring day in 1993, three months before her fifty-first birthday, Marianne received an unsettling call from her fifty-two-year-old brother.

"Marianne, are you sitting down?" he asked. "I have something to tell you." James then began to explain that he had sent his birth certificate to the Chickasaw Nation Bureau of Indian Affairs to verify his Indian lineage, in order to establish a small business minority status. A staff person found a problem and told him she could not verify he was Indian because his birth certificate had been altered.

"Sir," she told James, "either one or both of your parents' names have been changed or you are adopted. We can't verify your Indian ancestry."

Unable to reach Marianne at work, James called an aunt and asked her if she could verify his Indian heritage. Did she remember his birth? She told him she did not know much about his birth, but she remembered being told, "When they adopted you and Marianne, they told us you were Chickasaw and they didn't know about Marianne." This confirmed what the Chickasaw Nation Bureau had said.

Shock engulfed Marianne as her brother continued to relate his findings. "We are both adopted and we are not biological brother and sister."

The revelation of Marianne's adoption happened on May 5, 1993. James came to Oklahoma City and by 1:00 P.M. on the afternoon of May 13, 1993, both Marianne and her brother obtained a court order that would enable them to get a copy of their original birth certificates and adoption papers. By 4:30 P.M. they had found out who their mothers were. James's was a Chickasaw woman, father unknown. Marianne's was her adopted mother's sister, a woman she had known all her life as her aunt. Her birthfather was Hispanic. By 9:00 P.M. they were sixty-five miles away and in James's birthmother's home. Marianne's birthmother was traveling, and it was the nineteenth of May before they could contact her.

"Both birthmothers," Marianne related, "never wanted their secrets known. They had both married, both had four other children and had never told them. Both of their husbands had died and had never known their wives had given up a child."

Marianne's harsh and jagged walk into the "desert" caused by the tightly held secret of her adoption was compounded by multiple tragedies.

Eleven years before the disclosure, Marianne's delightful seven-month-old grandson drowned in a bathtub accident. Shortly after the sixth anniversary of Johnny's death, Charles, her only child and the one person she always felt connected to, committed suicide. He had never recovered from the death of his son. Seven months later, Marianne's father died following a lengthy illness and eight months later, her mother died from a sudden illness. Two years later her husband's life was severely threatened with two heart attacks and life-saving bypass surgery. These tragic events sent her free-falling into deep depression and despair. She was just resurfacing emotionally when the news of her adoptive status hit her.

"As an R.N. and a grief counselor, I'm aware of the issues that surface when death comes. I experienced them significantly with the deaths of my son, my grandson, and my parents. With their deaths, my future belief system was shattered. I didn't have anything left to link me to the future. I was left struggling with a major identity crisis, for I had been a daughter, a mother, a grandmother. My future was tied to these roles. With the deaths of my family, that future was gone," Marianne anguished.

Continuing, she said, "When the news came that I was not who I thought myself to be, my whole past belief system shattered, too. I wasn't American Indian, not at all. My heritage was Mexican. I had no future—it had died. I had no true past—for it had all been a lie."

It has been nine years since the unveiling of the secret. Where does Marianne find herself in the process toward emotional, physical, and spiritual healing?

Early in the journey, I struggled every day. I had to work really hard at just being here. I was not so angry at the decision that was made fifty years ago as I am that as times changed we were not told and never would have been told. This is what has devastated me today. I'm angry at the lies and the betrayal and the fact that I now cannot get answers from those who could have told me. I struggled with the bitterness because this was all so preventable.

Over the years time and support activitated the healing process so that she is able to extend to others words of advice.

The first thing you should do if this happens to you is seek the support of those who have walked a similar road. My husband, of course, supports me, but my brother, even living in Florida, was a tremendous help, for he understood what it felt like. Second, find a group that deals with adoption, loss, grief, some group that can help you through the recovery process and get professional counseling. I've lost a part of myself. I'm trying desperately to find out who I really am.

Karen's Story

In the summer of 1990, Karen, age thirty-two, and her family made plans to attend a family reunion in Arkansas. She had no idea the visit would alter the course of her life and relationships forever. The experience was so traumatic that, in order to put the pieces together, Karen reconstructed a journal of the events of the week that shoved her into a wilderness of personhood.

Remembering June 16, 1990

I went to the family reunion in Arkansas. As I was looking about at all my relatives, I noticed how much the family resembled one another. Steve (my husband) made the comment, "You are the prettiest one here; you don't look like the rest of the family."

I wanted to come to this reunion for two reasons. First, I did it for my dad, and second I was extremely interested in tracing my roots. I had found out about an Indian Chief, Red Eagle, who was an ally of Andrew Jackson in the 1820s. That was of great interest to me. I went around asking questions of all the older people at the reunion. I looked at pictures and found some of my father when he was a little boy. I studied his face intently trying to find some resemblance in me or my children. I had always wondered why I was so different from everyone in my family.

At the end of the day an older cousin came up to Steve and me. His wife said, "Oh, I remember you when you were just a little bitty thing right after Clyde and Betty got you."

When they walked away, I said to Steve, "Did you notice anything strange in that conversation?" He replied, "Yeah, got you from where? Under a rock or what?"

That evening, at my mother's home, I pored through the pictures with intense persistence looking for anything that might give me the truth without asking Mom. I was fearful of asking her. I have had too many negative confrontations with her in my life and wanted to avoid a scene.

I spent five hours looking at a chicken crate full of pictures of me growing up. One of the last pictures I looked at caught my attention. It was a picture of Mom holding me when I was one week old. She was in a form-fitting dress and was shapely. I really knew at that point that I was adopted, but I needed it confirmed.

Remembering June 17, 1990

The next morning, Father's Day, I couldn't stand not knowing for sure. I went back to Mother's house and went into her bedroom. I told her what my cousin had said. I then asked her, "Mom, am I adopted, too?" She said no too quickly. I replied to her, "Mom, if I am, please tell me. You are my mother and always will be, but I have the right to know." She still denied it.

Knowing the truth, I pulled out the picture I had found the night before. I said to her, "I'm sorry to hurt you like this, but in this picture of you and me you look too good. I've had two babies and I know this is not a picture of a woman who recently gave birth to a baby." She began to cry and then said, "You were adopted at birth."

She told me that as long as I didn't know, I was hers. She said things would never be the same between us again. I tried to reassure her, but it was no use. She dismissed me saying, "Now you'll go and find you have a pretty mother and you won't love me anymore." I was hurt, shocked, and angry.

We left for home. I cried all the way. I felt betrayed, crushed, devastated, confused, hurt, and stupid all rolled up into one. It was a horrible day. I cried myself to sleep that night. Steve was very supportive and felt badly because he could not cheer me up as usual. Just as I got to sleep, Steve shook me and shouted with excitement. "Brian's not going to be bald." (My father has been bald since he was twenty years old.) Leave it to my dear Steve to brighten up any dark situation. That was the only laugh I had that day.

Remembering June 18, 1990

When I woke up, I was driven to search for the truth. I felt desperate for knowledge. The rug had been pulled out from my neat and tidy little idea of who I am. I called the Department of Vital Statistics to find out how I could get a copy of my original birth certificate. The man told me to "just go down to the courthouse and get a court order. We will release them to you."

Remembering June 19, 1990

My best friend, Anita, went with me to see the judge. I was not prepared for the question of why I wanted to know. My request was denied without medical reason. That evening I called my aunt thinking my mother's sister might know something. All she knew from family gossip was that my birth mother had been married at the time of my birth with several children already. That certainly didn't make me feel any better. I thought if she was married with children already, then what was wrong with me? I felt rejected and unwanted.

For Karen, the day she found out about her adoption and the confusion of the weeks that followed is branded into her memory. As time progressed, the revelation resulted in serious trauma that sparked both emotional and physical upheaval.

After the secret came out, I became physically ill. I developed hypoglycemia and gastrointestinal problems. I became extremely tired—incredibly fatigued. It was not just the revelation of "being adopted" that triggered the emotional and physical stresses. It was a blessing to finally have my questions answered. It explained so much about who I am, why I have certain personality traits and physical characteristics.

What triggered the problems I am experiencing is the betrayal of trust. Adoption was not a new term to me. I have a sister, Margie, whom they adopted when I was fourteen. It was because of me that she has learned of her adoption. I told my mom when she was born that we had to tell her. It was her right to know. How ironic!

Following the revelation of Karen's adoption, Karen took steps to deal with her trauma.

What I did right away was a flurry of activity. I searched for my birth mother and found her. My adoptive mother rejected me because of the search. After an eighteen-month growing relationship with my birth mother, the revelation of another sister and my search for her ended our communication. I have been rejected by both of my mothers. I struggle with feelings of being detached and unloved.

I advise anyone in the same situation to seek support right away from someone who has been in similar circumstances. First, I started helping others in their searches. Looking back, I think all that activity was an effort to deny or avoid my own pain. I thought I was coping by helping others, but again I was pushing aside my own needs. I would advise others in this situation to get into counseling right away. Adoption support groups are a great place to begin.

Tammy's Story

On April 27, 1991, Tammy received a call from her sister, Lisa, who was noticeably upset. Tammy immediately thought that because her mother was critically ill the worst had happened. But that was not the reason for the call. It was something almost as traumatic.

"Tammy," Lisa said. "All day today, Mom has been calling out for us—she has been calling out her adopted daughters. I really didn't think much of it until tonight when I happened to mention it to our aunt. You won't believe what she said. She asked, 'You mean you girls don't know?'"

Tammy, stunned by the news, told her sister she would handle this. "I will call Dad," Tammy reassured her. "He'll tell us the truth."

Immediately Tammy dialed her father's number. He was at his farm-house in southern Ohio. Tammy's parents were divorced and both had remarried. When he picked up the phone Tammy said, "Dad, I have a question for you. Are we adopted?"

There was total silence on the other end, and Tammy repeated the question. All her father kept saying was, "I love you." Soon he began to cry. He rarely did this. All he could say was, "I love you."

Tammy repeated her question again, already knowing in her heart the truth. She felt the need to comfort her father, assuring him that no matter what, they would be okay. He finally told her that both girls had been adopted, Lisa in 1957 and Tammy in 1959.

Tammy's mother lived just two short weeks following the revelation. Tammy was only able to talk to her one last time. "I had to tell her I loved her anyway," Tammy commented. "But that wasn't enough to get her to talk to us about it. She didn't respond."

After her mother's death, Tammy learned that had her mother never uttered those words, the truth would have surfaced at the reading of her will. The girls were referred to as "adopted daughters." What followed for Tammy was incredible emotional trauma.

Tammy realized early in the experience that she could not bear the pain alone. The first thing she did was contact an adoption support group in her area. The group helped her not only to deal with the emotional and psychological injury, but to take practical steps in locating birthfamily information. "I knew I needed help to handle this. I felt like I was losing my mind. All I had established my life upon had been ripped from me. All of a sudden I had no true heritage, no medical history, nothing. One of the most helpful things I did in counseling was to talk. I mean talk and talk and talk. I talked about my family, my anger, my fears, everything. I talked until it was all out."

A year after the secret was disclosed, Tammy made a decision to locate her birthmother, which she did on June 8, 1992. The reunion has been positive and exciting for her. "I've been blessed in finding my birth mother and three half-siblings. Even though they live quite a distance way, I've spent time with all of them."

Over time, how has Tammy processed this traumatic, life-jarring event? "I have periods of anger still today," she offered. "But I'm an optimistic person and a survivor. I determined that I would not get stuck in anger. Sometimes I want to cry out, 'If you could have trusted me enough to love you, this wouldn't have happened.' I can't get into the blame game or make judgments. After all, I haven't done too badly in my life. I realize but for the grace of God, there go I."

Alissa's Story

"I guess I should have caught on a lot earlier," Alissa said of her adoptive status. "But I didn't. I must have blocked out all the cues."

Alissa's adoptive circumstances vary somewhat from that of most adoptees in this book. Her biological mother and the man she thought to be her biological father raised Alissa. Quite by accident, one rainy afternoon four years ago, an aunt let the secret slip.

We were sitting in her living room discussing the situation of a little neighbor-hood youngster. A relative was raising her with no contact from her birthfather at all.

"I wonder," my aunt asked me, "if Becky will question anyone about her birthfather? By the way, why haven't you ever pursued it?"

My mind went blank with her question—it stunned me so. I stammered a minute, asking what she meant and pretending I just didn't understand what she was saying. I was in shock. All I could do was mumble some excuse and leave. I had to ask someone who knew—my mother.

After hearing from her mother that the man who raised her was not her biological father but her adoptive father, Alissa still had great diffi-culty processing the news. As she began to mull the whole thing over in her mind, she recalled situations and comments along the way that should have given her a clue there was something different about her. "I felt like one of those little dinghies tied behind the big boat. Suddenly the dingy is cut loose to drift out to sea. Waves of fear, loneliness, and anger washed over me, depending on the day and the time. Mostly, a feeling of extreme isolation engulfed me. Suddenly I felt I didn't belong anymore. I wasn't fully a part of any family."

As time progressed, Alissa's feelings, especially that of anger, deep-ened.

My anger was not so much with my birth father, whom I met two months after the secret came out. He acknowledged he had been wrong. My anger was with my mother and other family members who held on so tightly to the silence. The hurt I felt because of the broken trust was far more intense than the fact that my birth father abandoned me.

Sometimes it felt like a dream—like this could not have really happened. I've talked with my birth father on several occasions, but my family—my mother, my brother, and sister—haven't allowed me to discuss this since the initial con-versation. I feel like I have to pretend it didn't happen. My pain has not been acknowledged. My mother has never said she is sorry, and I guess that's what I really want to hear.

As Alissa realized she was walking deep into a wilderness, walled off by anger and bitterness, she knew she had come to a significant cross-road. She could choose to stay angry and bitter or turn and walk out of that dark, desolate place on to a road that would lead to healing and inner resolution.

I decided when things broke loose and I felt so intensely angry that I would not, I could not, stay in that emotional whirlpool. I would move past it. Having made that choice, I've tried to extend forgiveness—not so much for their sake, but for mine. God showed me that forgiveness is not just getting rid of angry feelings;

it's accepting that they owe me nothing. I can't sit and wait for lost days to be made up and keep track of "nice" gestures. I will not keep score.

I've also been able to find meaning in all of this. I have a better understanding of people because of the trauma and depression I experienced. I have a better understanding of myself, because I know I've learned much. I also have a deeper relationship with God because He enabled me to extend forgiveness—it was not of myself.

CLOSING THE WOUND

According to Dr. Severson, finding out one's adoptive status as an adult strikes intensely and deeply at one's sense of reality. What develops for the adult adoptee afterward is determined by several factors. All play a significant role in the heart and mind of the adopted person as she goes about the business of redefining who she is.

First, where that person is in her life span is a critical factor in regaining balance, Dr. Severson feels. Is the person married? Does he or she have children? Maybe even grandchildren? Another consideration is the age of the birthparents should a reunion be pursued.

Second, regaining one's equilibrium has a lot to do with one's personality type. Dr. Severson comments, "If the adopted person is an understanding person, he will deal with the issue and go on. If his personality is highly sensitive, or he is emotionally vulnerable, his world may turn upside down. A person doesn't have to become impaired by this revelation. He may have trouble committing to other relationships or trouble trusting people in general, but it can be worked through."

In any transgression there comes a time when we must decide what to do with the anger, resentment, and bitterness that consumes us. To consider forgiveness can seem almost inconceivable. Don't we have a right to consider some offenses unforgivable?

As much as we may deny it, a lack of forgiveness may signal "something more is going on besides our rightful and understandable refusal to forget what has been done to us."[6] There are several reasons why an adopted adult may actively or unknowingly avoid forgiveness.

Why We Choose Not to Forgive

We may choose not to forgive our parents for the secret they kept from us because our unforgiveness can be used "to punish them." Conspicuous absence at special family gatherings, avoidance of phone calls, "forgetting" special occasions, all are passive ways to pay back our parents for the "crime" they committed.

We may choose not to forgive our parents because by "denying forgiveness, we allow ourselves to feel power over them," a power that was originally denied us.

We have been victims of lies, deceptions, and even reality. Once the secret is out, we may sense a feeling of power over those who previously owned it.

We may choose not to forgive our parents because it may seem like we condone what they did. It will let them off the hook.

We can choose to stay angry and distant due to the incredible sense of betrayal. Doing so assures us the walls will stay up; the distance will be maintained. We can continue to inflict pain on our adoptive parents as a long-term, ongoing reminder of their wrongdoing.

We may choose not to forgive our parents because forgiveness is difficult work. It requires us to walk on a road paved by uncertainty and to face personal issues of our own honesty and intimacy—all without any guarantee of mutual receptivity.

Extending an open hand of forgiveness places us in an extremely vulnerable situation. Seemingly irreparable damage may have been done through words and actions motivated by hurt and betrayal. Our work then becomes to evaluate if taking the risk by admitting our own wrongdoing is worth it.

Dwayne's Story

While preparing for a trip overseas, Dwayne attempted to get his birth certificate. Weeks of confusion and misinformation created a suspicion that something just wasn't right. Late on a Sunday afternoon, Dwayne went to his parents' home. He had to ask them a question: Was he adopted?

That afternoon, after moments of silence, his father confirmed Dwayne's suspicions. They had chosen not to tell him; they thought it was best, and they were told it was best. Dwayne's anger and rage at the betrayal sent him out of the house with promises of permanent severance of their relationship.

For weeks Dwayne refused their phone calls and avoided seeing them in familiar places, determined to find a balance to the chaos that raged within him. Finally, at the advice of a friend who had listened to his pain, Dwayne decided to call his parents. He was tired of being stuck in such a destructive emotional storm.

I didn't want to call them that evening, but I could no longer live like this. Yes, they had betrayed me. Yes, I could not think of anything worse one person could do to another. But yes, they had also loved me and I them.

When Dad answered the phone, after the silence, I could hear the deep sorrow in his voice. I could hear my mother's plea for forgiveness through strained words and muffled tears. My father told me he had no idea a choice they made so many years ago might cost him the love of his only son.

I chose at that moment to say, "I forgive you." I chose at that moment to close the wound. Instead of staying separated by walls of anger and unforgiveness, we are now free to talk about what happened to us and to begin rebuilding a relationship ripped apart by a decision made in ignorance.

WHAT LESSONS HAVE WE LEARNED?

Adults who have made this difficult journey through the wilderness of betrayal and mistrust to forgiveness have discovered powerful, healing principles. Dwight Wolter's and Jan's viewpoints are valid here:

Walking around angry at my parents squanders my precious energy, confuses my emotions, and depletes my physical health.

To forgive is to clear a space for change to occur. Plants need to be pruned so that light can filter through the remaining leaves and reach the soil where new life is struggling to grow. The secret is like those dead leaves. I can keep watering and watering them, but they will not spring to life.

Forgiveness does not happen by reading a book or by doing any one thing. Any wound, any rip in the fabric of a relationship takes time to heal. And it takes work. Festering wounds need to be opened and drained, cleaned out and exposed to fresh air and light. I've learned to accept that the journey toward forgiveness begins in pain. And I've been able to see that these uncomfortable feelings do not last forever. Time—and work—can heal this wound.[7]

I am not sure that the goal of modern therapy is forgiveness or reconciliation. Instead, therapy often helps us to justify our anger. That's unfortunate, because we must get beyond our anger if we are to experience the depth and fullness of life in relationship with others. A part of taking care of myself is the work of reconciliation—forgiving those who have wounded me. And I can't do that in the privacy of a therapist's office or by reading a book or by wishing things were better. Reconciliation cannot happen in a vacuum. It can only happen in the encounter between two people. Therapy is usually aimed at the health of the individual, but it sometimes fails to take into account that we must live in healthy communities, healthy relationships, to be happy and at peace.—Jan, age 50

A Word from Betsie

The best advice I can give an adult who has just found out he or she is adopted is, allow yourself time. Take time to let this new status settle in, to process what it means in your life, to adjust to this new "identity." Now is not the time to make potentially life-altering decisions. Until you've lived with this new information for a while, don't rush into a search or cut off the people who deceived you. Deal with one thing at a time. Searching immediately will not heal your open wounds; it may complicate an already overwhelming situation.

NOTES

1. Jayne Schooler, *Searching for a Past* (Colorado Springs: Pinon Press, 1995), 105.

2. The conspiracy of silence was originally coined by prolific author and adoptee, Betty Jean Lifton.

3. Dirck Brown, personal interview, June 13, 1994. Used with permission. Dr. Brown is the coauthor of *Clinical Practice in Adoption.*

4. Betty Jean Lifton, *Journey of the Adopted Self* (New York: Basic Books, 1993), 23.

5. Randolf Severson, personal interview, April 1994. Used with permission.

6. Dwight Lee Wolter, *Forgiving Our Parents: For Adult Children from Dysfunctional Families* (Center City: Minn.: Hazelden Foundation, 1989), 49.

7. Ibid., 63.

PART III

Focus on the Birthparent

Birthmothers and Birthfathers—The Lifelong Journey Begins: Discovery, Disclosure, Decisions

It was my first day at the maternity home where I would live, deliver and ultimately give up my baby for adoption. One of my four roommates volunteered to show me around the home and we'd started on the top floor where our room was one of many. We went down to the basement to see the laundry where some of the pregnant girls worked and to the first floor to see the kitchen where more pregnant girls worked. As we climbed the stairs to the second floor, she said that was where the labor, delivery and recovery rooms were. As we entered the hallway the first thing I saw was a large window to the nursery so I hurried over; I'd been hoping to see the babies since before I arrived. There were three rows of clear, plastic bassinets on metal stands. Most of them were empty. In the front row was one sleeping, round-faced baby with no hair and protruding ears. In the back row were three more babies. My roommate tapped on the glass with her long nails and said, "This is an out-patient's baby here. Real married women come here to deliver sometimes. They're usually poor and live out here in the country. We're not allowed to have any contact with them, though. 'Cause of who we are. Our *babies* aren't to be seen by *anybody*. 'Cause they're bastards, ya' know. Those are the ones in the back row." Even though the remark was sarcastic, my throat constricted with wanting to cry. "Why don't we go sit down for a while. You look like you could use it." My lips tried to smile but twitched instead so I looked away from her. We stopped at the drinking fountain and swallowing the cold water helped ease my throat. . . . (Linda, her experience in a maternity home, 1965)[1]

Who are birthparents? A birthmother may be the person who occupies the same cubicle at work as you and never mentions much about her family. A birthmother may be the gracious woman next door who eagerly participates in many social functions, but avoids neighborhood baby showers. A birthfather may be the businessman, looking assured and confident as he closes a deal, yet filled with undefined pain. A birthfather may be the man who always volunteers for community work, but seems to wear an unexplained cloak of sadness. Birthparents are teachers, librarians, school superintendents, homemakers, social workers, construction workers, doctors, nurses, and preachers. They are in the mainstream. They live right next door.

Birthparents are the often forgotten members of the adoption triad. Not so very long ago, there was a time when birthparents were routinely counseled to go on with their lives as if nothing happened. "Just forget about this," they were told. This advice, in many cases well meaning, was nevertheless costly. It has taken a tremendous toll on the emotional, psychological, physical, and spiritual health of birthmothers and birthfathers.

Until the recent media explosion about adoption, with more attention than ever on the realities of the birthparent experience, a typical birthmother might wonder if she was alone with her pain and unexpressed grief. Was she the only one who did not fit the mold that was expected—to forget and act as if it never happened? If not, why was no one else talking about it? Why was everyone pretending nothing happened? Where were the other girls with whom she'd shared time, but of course not names, in the home for unwed mothers? Somehow society has seemed to ignore that for every adoptee (of which there are an estimated five to eight million in the United States) there are, in fact, also two birthparents.

For most birthmothers and many birthfathers, the loss of their child through adoption has overshadowed the rest of their lives. They have suffered largely in isolation, living with their lonely reality—a child was born to them, whose whereabouts even as a adult may remain forever a mystery. Because of the stigmas associated with being a birthparent, even those friends and family who know about the baby rarely bring up the subject. This conspiracy of silence and secrecy, which began at the moment of the discovery of pregnancy, continued through to circumstances of the birth, to relinquishment, and afterward. It created an environment that prohibited many birthparents from the opportunity to deal in a healthy and healing way with the tremendous feelings of loss, grief, guilt, shame, and failure. For many, "relinquishment was more than merely a life-altering turning point. It became an invisible barrier separating them from the bulk of humanity."[2] Many still today live with this invisible barrier and are serving, what they believe to be, a lifelong sentence of silence and secrecy.

In recent decades two critical questions have emerged into public discussion about adoption. One is a painful, because it examines social work practice of another time that devastated many lives. The second is one whose answer continues to reform the practice of adoption and the treatment of birthparents today. The questions are:

What have been the lifelong effects of relinquishment and secrecy on the birthmother and birthfather?

What can we learn from the life experiences of birthparents of a different time that will impact adoption practice today?

To attempt to answer those questions, this chapter will journey back in time to visit the experiences of birthparents from the moment of the discovery of pregnancy, to the disclosure of the secret, and through the decision-making process. Chapter six will continue to look at the journey from the vantage point of the birth experience, through the trauma of relinquishment and the lifelong impact.

REMEMBERING THE DISCOVERY AND DISCLOSURE

Circumstances surrounding an unplanned pregnancy are as varied as the story of each birthmother and birthfather. However, each birthmother and birthfather faced similar tasks: They would have to share the secret.

For the birthmother, even prior to disclosing the pregnancy to the birthfather, the first challenge was to deal with reality of the pregnancy. From the first frightening, suspicious moment, a birthmother's life was forever changed. Her pregnancy crushed her future plans for education or career and threw her world into chaos. She was having an unplanned baby at a devastatingly inopportune time, and under utterly unsuitable conditions. She was pregnant by a man whom she might not love or even like. If love was shared, this event would greatly alter their already uncertain future. What erupted within those early days of pregnancy for many unwed women was shock and disbelief.

I tried to deny it to myself, at first. This couldn't have happened to me. I'd wake up in the middle of the night thinking I was having a bad dream, but then reality hit me. I would be sick every morning, and lived in fear my parents would hear me.—Janet

I denied my pregnancy for many, many months. I didn't gain much weight in the first several months and easily disguised it with loose fitting clothing. I wouldn't allow myself to think that this could have happened to me.—Kristin

Once the reality of the pregnancy was fully realized, another task confronted these women. It was the disclosure to the birthfather. The reaction of some men threw them into a wilderness of isolation and humiliation. Others experienced support from the birthfather, but were denied access to him.

Disclosing to the Birthfather

I was already a single mother in 1957 when I found myself pregnant again. Scared and bewildered, I confided the pregnancy to my boyfriend. When I called him the next day, I was told by his roommate that he'd been injured in a serious automobile accident. Searching area hospitals, I was unable to find him. Later that day I went to the bar where we went frequently, heard the laughing and heckling of his friends, and found him hiding from me in the phone booth. I was totally humiliated. I moved to the other side of town to quietly endure my pregnancy and release my son for adoption. Today, over forty-five years later, that humiliating experience was so traumatic, I do not remember the birthfather's name.—Jeanne

I was 24 and in graduate school studying art history. I had dated what I thought was a wonderful man, an attorney, for nearly a year. I told him that I was pregnant on a Friday night in our favorite Italian restaurant. I thought he would be a little upset about it, but I was sure that he would marry me. What followed devastated me for months to come. First, he dropped my hand and said, "Tonia, this is your problem, not mine." Then he said to me, "I cannot marry you, because I already am married." How could I have been so blind and stupid? We didn't even finish dinner. He paid for it, took me home, and I never saw or heard from him again. Now, 26 years later, the man doesn't know he has a son out there somewhere.—Tonia

I told my boyfriend I had missed my period. He was in agony and kept saying, "It was only one time. I'm so sorry!" I walked to a nearby doctor during my high school lunch hour. The nurse was in the examination room, and the doctor's diploma was from a Christian college. I feared they would tell people in my church. So when he asked more than once, "Could you possibly be pregnant?" I denied it, and said "No." I kept up the ruse at school, telling the gym teacher "observing," when it was time to be excused from showers for menstruation. I remember she looked up quickly at me, realizing from her check-off chart, that it would not be a regular time for me to be "observing." She said nothing.—Margie

I was 18 when I became pregnant. When I found out, I was in complete disbelief. I told the father before my parents. He picked me up at my house as he did every other day. I got in the car, told him I was pregnant, and his first comment was, "Are you sure it is mine?" Horrified and crying I said, "How can you ask me such a question!" His next statement was that I would have an abortion. My reaction was that I would not. He drove around the block, dropped me off, and I never heard from him again.—Lisa

Upon Learning of the Pregnancy—Birthfather's Response

Julie was four or five months pregnant when I heard from a cousin of hers. I was stationed in the Army out of state. I do not speak for all birthfathers, but I was scared and only 21 years old. I didn't know what to do, so I did nothing. I didn't take responsibility at all, at first, and then I began sending her money. There were things I should have done, but didn't. My last communication with her was to send her money for the hospital costs. She would never tell me if the child was a boy or girl, but in my heart I always felt we had a daughter.—Howard

I was crying a lot, so after a couple of months, I drove to the city where my girlfriend had gone to have our baby. I rented a room in a boarding house. We would never have thought of "living together." Although only 17, I had a trade and found a good job. I was there to encourage her and help financially. We were both scared, but enjoyed drives into the countryside. We knew we could not marry, because we were under the legal age, and afraid to tell our parents. Our secret paralyzed us. So regrettable!—Dean

Telling Their Parents

In some relationships, both saw the pregnancy as an equal responsibility. However, another very difficult task faced them. They would have to share the secret with their parents. It would be a secret that would have lasting implications for all whose lives it touched.

When Carla told me she was pregnant, I told her not to tell her parents until I figured out what we were going to do. I was 20 and she had just turned 18. After three or four days, I decided we should meet with her parents. I went to her house and asked to speak to her father privately. He became outraged and threw me out of the house. He told me never to come near their daughter again. I was so scared, I did just that.—Jim

I was always my dad's little princess and could do nothing wrong in his eyes. On the night we told him about my pregnancy, something left him—as far as I was concerned. He just sat down, like he was stunned into silence. The silence was deafening to me. We talk today, of course, now 18 years later, but the cloak of silence about the baby he put on that day still remains.—Rosanne

I was 23 and unmarried when my son was born in 1968. My out-of-wedlock pregnancy was the most shameful thing that could happen, sinful in my mother's eyes. In fact, my mother would have been happier if I were an ax-murderer; anything would have been better than being pregnant outside of marriage. I went through my life thinking that the worst thing I've ever done is place my child for adoption. Both my mother and I felt like it was a huge mistake, for different reasons. To me the mistake was signing the papers and placing him, being separated from him. To my mother though, the mistake was that I had had sex. The only counseling I received was from the social worker at the adoption agency, and the focus was only to be sure I'd place my baby with the agency. There was no discussion of how I felt.—Charla

I did not tell my mother, who had recently remarried and was recovering from surgery. My father had died six years before. I had no siblings. I did not want to be a "bad testimony" by telling people at my church and school, or to bring my boyfriend up for shame and punishment because of rape (although I had never heard that word). Because I was a strong Christian, I felt I could "do all things through Christ Who strengthens me." I obtained a newspaper from a faraway city and found an ad for an "unwed mothers' home." I told everyone I was going to that city to pursue a career.—Margie

Once "the secret" had been disclosed to those most intimately involved—the birthfather and parents—the process of decision making began. Something had to be done about "the secret." For many birthparents and their families, a sense of powerlessness overwhelmed them as they began the process of coping with the pregnancy. The only asset, strength, or bargaining tool available to deal with their turbulent emotions and loss of control was the power of secrecy. Secrecy then became the coping mechanism for the family to regain a sense of balance.

For most birthparents, because of the controlled secrecy, there were no decisions to be made, no options to explore. Decisions would be settled apart from the birthmothers' feelings or wishes. Many birthfathers were driven away from any opportunity to be part of the process.

REMEMBERING GOING AWAY, OPTIONS, AND DECISION MAKING

Going Away

When the secret of the pregnancy was disclosed, a vast majority of women were sent away—some to relatives, some to work as "nannies" for families in other cities. Some made their own decision to leave, even at very young ages, to spare their families any dishonor.

I made all the plans, and boarded a train late one winter night. Everyone thought I was leaving to work in a distant state. I arrived in a snowstorm and found a room at the YWCA. The next day I saw a notice for a live-in baby sitter and was hired. I slept on an uncomfortable cot in the preschool daughter's room, my limited wardrobe hung in a hall closet. Each morning, I took the baby from his bed in the parents' room, changed, and fed him. I had never cared for a baby before. I found a good job as an office clerk and sent "happy" letters back to family and friends. Actually, I walked several blocks in the cold winter wind to wait for an early bus to take me to work. At night, I cleaned up the kitchen after the extended family's evening meal. I had never before used or scrubbed a broiler. Then I would tend to the children, holding back tears as I thought of my vanished high school life. When I went to church, I would sit in back and speak to no one. I was fired when my office supervisor suspected I was pregnant. (In the 1950s, pregnant women did not work in public.) The baby-sitting job ended for the same reason. I found an upstairs room to rent, and typed address labels 16 hours a day there, to earn money for monthly payments to Bellhaven. My first week in town, I went to see Miss Bell, who owned the maternity home, but told her I did not want to live there or to talk with other girls. She gave me the next false name in her little book, which I was to use at the social worker's and doctor's appointments she made for me, at the hospital, and on the false birth certificate. As I was only 17, the county social worker was legally required to contact my parents. She agreed not to do so, commenting I seemed "mature" in making decisions.—Margie

While some went to relatives, or fled to fend for themselves, others were taken to maternity homes that existed during the decades of the '50s, '60s, and most of the '70s. Women, at an extremely difficult time in their lives, were sent off to maternity homes that were often far away from familiar people, places, and friends. They lost their homes, any sense of support and caring, and their identities.

Despite the term used—"home," for many it was a far cry from the emotional and psychological safety one experiences when thinking of "home." There was in most maternity homes an almost artificial sense of things. It was an environment were no one felt free to deal emotionally, outwardly, and honestly with this most traumatic life-altering circumstance. One birthmother said, "At the end of our pregnancies we were supposed to give up everything: our babies, our past 'sins,' and the few friends we made there. We were supposed to go on as if nothing every happened there, or as if we'd never been there at all."[3] For the protection of everyone's secrecy, certain rules were set in place. It was forbidden to disclose one's real identity. False first and last names were given in some places. In others, false first names were given, and no last names were allowed.

My memories of being in the maternity home are for the most part, okay. There were good and caring people who felt they were doing what was best under the circumstances. However, I felt so disconnected from everyone. Although I lived in Illinois, my parents sent me to a home in south Texas. I can remember vividly the first day I arrived. The woman who greeted me and gave me a tour of the home handed a basket to me. "Pick out a piece of paper," she told me. "On it you will have the name you are to use while here at the home." My new name was Ellie.—Jacqueline

Not only did the false identities perpetuate the air of secrecy, so did the cover stories created to explain the absence of women from their homes, schools, and communities. Rheumatic fever or kidney problems were popular excuses. Others were "sent abroad to study" or to help a sick family member. "The stories varied, but lent a consistent air of deceit and secrecy to their lives. Often these cover stories required other false-hoods to support them, such a false addresses and means of forwarding mail, or consistently fabricated answers to concerned acquaintances who asked about the missing women."[4]

Options and Decision-Making

To be a decision maker implies one takes an active role in the process. For most birthparents, especially birthmothers, the decision for the child to be placed for adoption was taken completely out of their hands. Birth-mothers have reported that people in their lives, from parents to medical professionals and the "unwitting agents of social norms," exerted considerable pressure on them to give up their babies. No one kept their babies. It just wasn't done.

Under the guise of helping them, these "helpers" sustained the cultural norm by conditioning the women so they could not discover what they really wanted. Given the pressure exerted on them, birthmothers felt unable to react in any way other than to surrender their babies. To meet the needs of others, they relinquished not only their babies, but their ability to decide on their own.[5]

"This style of coping under stress is not unusual, because women expect less disapproval for passive behavior and are particularly sensitive to approval and disapproval by others. Once they relinquished their babies, the birthmothers continued to feel as if they had little control over other choices in their lives. Even when they became aware of their desires, they felt compelled to act against them." In a study conducted by Annette Baran and others, "82% of the birthmothers in the study wanted a reunion with their children, but said they would not seek it."[6]

Birthfathers' Part in Decision-making Process Was Rarely Realized

She told me she was pregnant. She also told me two other things: she wanted nothing to do with me, and she was planning to have an abortion. Then she disappeared. Abortions were illegal in 1960, so I knew that didn't happen. I heard a number of years later that the baby had been born in Alabama, but until 10 years ago, I never knew if I had a son or daughter.—Kevin

We had only dated a few months, when she abruptly called off our relationship. It was not until three years later that I learned a child had been born—a son. I was devastated to learn that he was placed for adoption, and there was no hope of ever finding him.—Charles

Often when women were sent to maternity homes and separated from the birthfathers, any hope of marriage or any level of involvement with the process proved impossible. Men were prohibited to make any contact and told to go on with their lives as though the pregnancy didn't exits. Birthfathers, in fact, were often encouraged by authorities and families to date others, so that the secret could be maintained. It would keep the eyes of the community off the woman who had quietly disappeared. It also meant that the birthfathers had no power in the decisions that were to be made.[7]

REASONS FOR THE DECISION

David Howe, in his book titled *Half a Million Women*, gives several reasons why birthmothers chose adoption for their children.

- Parental pressure/societal pressure—"It's for the best."
- Best for the baby—"It is only fair to the child."
- No practical alternatives—"I had the rest of my life to think about." "How could I support the child?"[8]

Parental Pressure/Societal Pressure

In 1963, I was 19 and living away from home in my first year of college throughout most of my pregnancy. I had become pregnant with my high school sweetheart in May of our senior year and hid my pregnancy, despite being home on vacations. I was in a state of semi-denial. I had no prenatal care and even tried to think of a way to deliver alone so that I wouldn't have to tell my parents, because it was SO shameful. I went into labor while spending the weekend with a friend at a different college. My friend knew nothing, and I claimed abdominal problems. When I returned to my own campus, I realized I could not go through it alone and went to the campus health service. The doctor who examined me was stunned to realize that I was about to give birth and rushed me to the hospital where I gave birth. I didn't see my baby and was told nothing. Because I was under 21, the doctor explained that my parents needed to be notified. My father drove straight to get me when they were told the news. He took me to Jewish Family Services, where the social worker reinforced that it was good for me not to see my baby, so I wouldn't bond with it. At the agency I signed a birth certificate with the baby's footprints on it. I told them I had to know about the baby. They told me I had given birth to a healthy boy, and the papers I had just signed forever relinquished all my parental rights. My father brought me home, where our family doctor came once for a post-natal visit, felt my uterus, and with no mention of the baby or giving birth, wished me well. My mother's only question to me was, "Who have you told?" When I responded, "No one," my mother with great relief said, "Thank God! From now on we'll never speak of this again." And we haven't.—Donni

After spending eight months preparing for my baby's arrival by purchasing clothing, baby items, even making a baby quilt, my parents called me into my dad's office, sat me down, and informed me that if I kept the baby I could no longer live at home. I was sure being dead would have been easier to handle. How could I financially prepare for my child in a month or less, was all I could think, and who was going to hire an eight-months-pregnant teenager? They went on to let me know that arrangements were being made through Catholic Social Services to place my baby for adoption, something I never even considered. How could they do this? After all, this was their grandchild as well. With the strong abusive hand that I was raised with, I was incapable of fighting for my child. I was truly afraid of my father. I had no options. My brothers and sisters and I never even talked about my pregnancy, and those not living at home were away at college. My neighbor would not defy the decision of my parents. What could I do? They waited just long enough to leave me no choice. They never considered my feelings, wants, or desires, nor did they ever ask me. I didn't sleep for days. Again I went to my best friend and her mother, my safe harbor. They at least talked to me of my pain. Unknown to me and crying the whole time, my dear best friend loaded her car with all the baby purchases I had made over the months and returned each item to the store. She knew that would be something I could never do. I later learned that it made her physically sick, but she did it anyway.—Leesa

At the "home" in Canada we were very strongly encouraged to place our children for adoption. It was the unwritten rule. If one of the girls chose to keep her baby, she was never allowed to return after the birth to visit those of us who were still there. If a girl chose adoption, she was encouraged to come and visit us, so we could see just how "happy" she was about her decision.—Nancy

Best for the Baby

At eighteen, I found out I was pregnant. When I told my parents, they quickly made arrangements to send me to an unwed mothers' home. My parents and those at the home told me that I could not raise a child due to my age, lack of money, no one would ever date me again, and that the child would be forever branded "bastard." "Is this the life you want for your child?" they would say.[9] —Kelly

The woman at the home kept saying to me, "Stop thinking about yourself. Think of the baby. It should be brought up in a home where there are a mother and a father. Think of the joy this baby will be to a couple who wants your baby. They can't have children; you can have plenty more in the future."[10]—Sherrie

No Practical Alternatives

I thought adoption was the only thing to do (in 1953). I thought it would be a terrible shame for this child to later be asked, "When were you born?" and to learn it was before we parents were married. (No one told me adoptees face even harder questions!) I felt other people would be better parents. I just wanted to go back and start college, pretend nothing had happened, never having to tell anybody. Instead of going away to college, where I was afraid a roommate would see the stretch marks on my stomach, I lived at home and commuted to a college.—Margie

Even before I told my parents, I went to Family Services to find out what options were available to me. I was 19 and working, but still living at home. I wanted to know for myself. After I told my family, no other options were ever discussed. My parents told me I couldn't bring my child home to live. I had a low-paying job, with the prospect of no place to live. Culturally, at the time, it was like a death sentence for a young woman to go on welfare because of the potential of always staying there. I really, really realized, I just couldn't parent my child. —Jeanne

In the early moments of pregnancy discovery, many birthmothers and birthfathers began a life-altering journey. Perhaps numb at first, then escorted out of the mainstream of life to maintain their "dignity," and eventually muted by the conspiracy of secrecy and silence, birthparents were just starting to experience the early feelings of alienation, isolation, fear, and inadequacy. No matter what the circumstances were prior to the birth of the child and relinquishment, few were prepared for the broad spectrum of the invisible, intangible losses brought on by the adoption of their child.

A Word from Betsie

The reality of the birthparent is the biggest "unspoken" in adoption. Maybe it needed to be this way for us, as a society, to create and support the closed system of adoption for so many years. As an adoptee, I remember wondering as a child if my birthmother remembered I existed. Now I know how ludicrous this was, and how out of touch I was—but that's all I knew. Getting to know the reality of the birthparents has impacted my understanding of adoption more than anything else.

NOTES

1. Jonelle Blair, "Illegitimate Business." (Unpublished novel based on real-life experience birthmothers in a midwestern maternity home.)

2. M. Jones, *Birthmothers: Women who Relinquish Babies for Adoption Tell Their Stories.* (Chicago: Chicago Review Press 1993), vii.

3. Ibid., 45.

4. M. Weinreb, and V. Konstam, "Birthmothers: Silent Relationships," *Affilia* 10, no 3, (fall 1995): 317.

5. Ibid.

6. Jones, 45.

7. D. Howe, P. Sawbridge, and D. Hinings, *Half a Million Women: Mothers Who Lose Their Children by Adoption* (London: Penguin Books, 1992), 62.

8. Ibid.

9. L. Ferree-Dean, "Through the Looking Glass: Birthmothers break the Silence Surrounding the Relinquishment of Children through Past Adoption Practices" (MA dissertation, Prescott College, 1998).

10. Howe, 65.

CHAPTER SIX

Birthmothers and Birthfathers—The Journey Continues: The Lifelong Impact of Relinquishment in Closed Adoption

My own family never spoke of the relinquishment. Six months after my son was born, Christmas 1982, I lay in my bed sobbing. My mother came in and asked me what was wrong and I would not answer her. She asked again and I shouted, "I miss my son!" Her response was, "I would have thought you would be over that by now." I will never forget that moment, and never had it been any clearer to me that this was something that would not be discussed. I spent many nights crying myself to sleep. Relinquishing my child has never ever been mentioned.
—Sylvia

UNDERSTANDING THE BIRTH EXPERIENCE: TO SEE OR NOT TO SEE

When labor pains began, the experience for many ill-prepared birthmothers was frightening and traumatizing. Many found it to be both debilitating and disorienting.[1] Counseling and birthing preparation were generally not a normal part of the services offered to birthmothers. Education about the process was done informally, with the young women imagining an event none of them had yet encountered. Some were frozen in fear of impending danger, pain, and possible death. It was not only an experience of extreme physical pain, but also of psychological wounding.

Couldn't See

When I went into labor, I knew nothing about it except what I had been able to glean from others. We begged for information. For some reason, in the home I was in, the most represented profession among the birthmother population was nurses, so we asked them a lot of questions. When labor started, I was placed in a room all by myself; no one was allowed in with me. A staff nurse would come and check on me if I rang a bell. I remember ringing the bell after my water broke. It happened in the middle of the night, and the nurse berated me terribly. (Even though they were on night duty, they slept.) She checked me and begrudgingly moved me to the delivery room and summoned a resident. (We never had a doctor, just students.) I begged for some pain medication, but the nurse seemed to "not hear" me. Just before my son was born, I was put under and awoke in a room at the end of the maternity ward. They told me I couldn't see him.—Sylvia

Wouldn't See

It was Saturday morning, sunny and bright. I was at K-Mart with my mother and felt as if I needed to use the bathroom, but it turned out to be labor. Within a few hours I was packed and on my way to the hospital. My labor was short and my sister was with me. My mother came in through a lot of it, but she had her work responsibilities. Because my hand was forced to relinquish my child, I thought if I didn't see the baby or know the sex, somehow it would be easier. So once the baby's head crowned I was put to sleep.

By Monday morning when my doctor came in, I told him if he didn't release me from the hospital I would jump out of the window. And I would have. I had never felt such pain and loss in my life. They released me, and at that time I don't think I had any idea of the impact that I would experience for the rest of my life.—Lois

Cut Off and Rebuffed

From the moment I entered the delivery room, the whole process was blocked from me. I was given a spinal tap and draped with a sheet. I couldn't feel or see anything that was happening. When my baby was born, I heard crying and asked the doctor if the baby was okay. I asked him if the child was a boy or girl, and his response was, "It shouldn't make any difference to you—you're giving it away, aren't you?" They wouldn't let me hold or see the baby, and it was only by a slip of the tongue of a nurse's aide that I found out I had a girl. They kept me drugged my whole time in the hospital, so I wouldn't get hysterical.—Lynda

Allowed to See

The hospital put me in an isolated, private room after my anesthetized delivery. Several times I asked to see my baby, and on the third day an aide brought her in for me to hold in a chair. I had a camera with me, but was too petrified to lay her on the bed and take her picture, fearing the aide would come back, and it would somehow be forbidden. When the birthfather came to take me back to my apartment, we went to the nursery window and looked in, so very, very sad.—Marie

THE TRAUMA OF RELINQUISHMENT

What was never discussed with the birthmother as she moved through the relinquishment experience was the aftermath of physical, emotional, and psychological turmoil, both short-term and long-term. Hormonal changes, milk production, and postpartum depression were not addressed. Birthfathers who knew of the child and were kept out of the loop also felt the anguish of loss and being regarded as insignificant. In the decades of the '50s, '60s, and '70s, a woman who experienced a relinquishment was treated in the very same manner as a woman who lost a child to death at birth.

- No one talked about the baby or the death.
- No one talked with the mother about her feelings of loss.
- People carried on as though nothing of real significance ever happened.
- Family and friends, who failed to recognize the child's existence formed no attachment to the child and did not understand that the mother had become attached to her baby.[2]

The similarities between mothers who lose a child by death or by adoption are striking, according to Robin Winkler and Margaret van Keppel in their research titled *Relinquishing Mothers in Adoption: Their Long-Term Adjustment*. The baby was often removed right after birth, with no opportunity for the mother to see the child. Occasionally, birthparents were falsely told the baby was born dead.

It was not unusual for doctors, midwives, and social workers to discourage mothers from thinking there was any type of bond with the child. Mothers reported that they felt as if they lost a part of themselves, but no one saw it as such. All who were involved, believing that it was best not to talk about the child, whether lost by death or adoption, created a conspiracy of silence. They believed that it would make it easier for the mother to forget the whole experience and go on to make a fresh new start.[3]

The mother who lost her baby by adoption, the researchers point out, dealt with additional factors that further disturbed and distorted her ability to grieve. There were shame and guilt attached to a sexual relationship outside of marriage and ensuing feelings of failure for being unable to care for the child. "Having got pregnant under morally censured circumstances, the unmarried mother compounds her crime by not bringing up her own child. A climate of punishment and censure often seems to surround the mother who surrenders her child for adoption."[4]

"Like the mother who suffers a perinatal death, the birthmother also feels responsible for what has happened, but to a much greater degree—

her loss is self-inflicted. In spite of the loss, the child continues to exist, although adoption practice generally denies the mother any knowledge about the progress and welfare of her child. The child's continued existence confuses the grieving process."[5]

Randolph Severson eloquently writes about the difference between a death and a disappearance. "If someone close to you dies, it is very painful, you cry, you talk, you go to the graveyard, and you spend time looking at old pictures and revisiting old memories. At first, the loss is all that is on your mind, but eventually, you begin to think about it less and less and hurt a little less. But it is different with disappearance— there is no real end to the wondering."[6] For birthmothers, their children disappeared, often without their "real" permission, and the wondering never ceased.

From the time of the early days following relinquishment, many birthmothers described the experience as a freezing, a wound that never stops bleeding, as arms eternally aching to hold the lost baby, or as a limbo loss similar to that felt by families of soldiers missing in action.[7] These birthmothers entered a tunnel of grief while numb, frozen emotionally in time, unable to find their way through. Some were unable to begin or complete a process of grieving. For others, resolution was not to come for many years.

LIVING WITH GRIEF AND LOSS: ITS LASTING IMPACT

Many researchers have studied the general process of grieving in relationship to life's losses.[8] With a focus on the grief experiences of birthmothers in adoption studies at Rutgers University, Anne B. Brodzinsky, working with husband David M. Brodzinsky, monitored four variable stages:

1. *Early grief*: shock and numbness; alarm and retreat; denial and disbelief.

Sometimes now I think, "Did it actually happen to me?" I find I can't believe it, even though it really happened—Jessie

I have absolutely no memory of signing the documents. I apparently blocked it from my memory.—Leesa

2. *Acute grief*: realization; protest, anger, and crying; expressions of outrage, guilt, and shame.

Nine months after my son was born, I ran into his father one night. We had never spoke since I told him I was pregnant, and it was then that I understood "temporary insanity." I was at a local bar with my friends when I spotted him across the room. I picked up my beer bottle, cracked it over the bar, and went after him. Needless to say, we were both thrown out. According to my friends, because I really do not remember this clearly, I chased him outside and tackled him in a gravel parking lot. I began to strangle him until my friends pulled me off his body. He is still alive, and I have never seen or spoken with him again. Today I don't think I would go into such a rage. I hope I have matured and healed a bit and could maintain my decorum.—Gina

After a while, instead of crying, I seemed to be screaming all the time. I was so mad, angry, you know, that this had happened to me, that other people had decided my baby was going to be adopted. I remember yelling at my mother, "It is all your fault!" She said it was typical of me to blame it on her, when it was I who had got into trouble and brought shame to them all. And I thought, "She still doesn't understand; she still doesn't see what's happened."[9]—Julie

- yearning and pining; sadness and emptiness; repeated review of circumstances of the loss; searching; scanning groups of people for the lost one; returning to places where the child previously could be found; feelings of powerlessness, despair, and low self-esteem

Often I would be in stores and watch parents with blond-haired little boys. I always wondered, "Is that my David?" That was the name I had given him and always called him in my heart.—Bea

Living with the truth of the relinquishment of my son only further enforced within me what an awful person I must be, what a weak person I must be, and how undeserving I am of happiness.—Miriam

3. *Reorganization* is a critical turning point in how the grieving person sees herself and the loss. Increasing self-esteem, a sense of personal control, and reordering her life in ways that do not include the lost individual emerge. However, to achieve the reorganization state and an adequate adjustment, it is necessary to have an opportunity to grieve. For birthmothers, rituals and talking about the experience were opportunities not given to them. Until support groups like Concerned United Birthparents (CUB) began to form, there was not the slightest opportunity to deal outwardly with the incredible loss. For many birthmothers the reorganization process is not realized for many, many years, perhaps not until search and reunion, when new relationships are integrated into the self. Fresh aspects of grieving will arise, over the lost years or the discovery of negative events, but questions are finally answered, and there is a subsiding of the original acute phase.

4. *Subsiding grief* is evidenced by restoration and enhancement of self-esteem. Through self-help groups, public speaking, and sharing her experiences, a birthmother may seem to blossom. She looks to the future, tries new things, goes back to school, and is concerned for the well-being of others and herself. She may write or be active in legislation and reform of adoption practice. It is as though her life picks up again, from the

time before she became pregnant. She feels released from the prison of being emotionally stuck in life-impacting and function-altering grief.

The pathological nature of birthmothers' grief

A study conducted in 1985 examined the ways in which the bereavement process was delayed or distorted in twenty birthmothers who were seen in the counseling environment with other presenting problems.[10] The researchers cited the special problems of trauma that delay or confound a birthmother's grief, making it pathological.

The actual existence of the child somewhere interferes with her acceptance of finality. "A birthmother's continued sense of loss and weakened ability to adjust are in part related to her lack of knowledge about the child's development, and her inability to let the child know that she still cares and thinks about him or her. That the child continues to exist and is growing up without her, and she is forbidden to know anything about what is happening, means that her ability to grieve in any normal fashion is greatly impaired."[11]

Other losses, in addition to the loss of a child, are incurred—perhaps her home or societal support. The working through of anger and guilt is impeded because of the secret, shameful nature of her experience, and the bitterness she feels toward others (social workers, parents, or society in general) may be justified.

The loss of self and the identification phenomenon, as commonly felt after the death of a loved one, are complicated and confounded in adoption loss. This is because of the physical and emotional bond created during pregnancy. "I felt like pieces of a person, instead of a whole person," said one mother. Another said, "I sometimes feel I will never be complete."[12]

Revisiting the Secret: Triggering Feelings of Loss, Shame, and Guilt

As demonstrated, a birthmother may be stuck in one aspect of her grief, or she may cycle between the stages throughout her life in an ongoing, nonlinear process of integration. She may not feel her grief initially, but will find it surfacing later in her life at major milestones. "The grieving never stopped. It only went below my threshold of awareness for periods of time," said Carol Schaefer, a birthmother and author of *The Other Mother*.[13] Birthfathers have not been immune from the grieving process as well. For many birthparents even seemingly innocent events may trigger feelings of loss, shame, and guilt. However, many of them live through those events or encounters still shrouded by the "secret."

What are some of those major triggers?

• Wedding day

Three years after I relinquished my son, I met another young man and we married. My father told me that he would not pay for a big wedding, because he couldn't walk me down the aisle if I wore a white dress. We ended up eloping.—Elna

• Seeing friends and relatives with babies and children

I couldn't talk about my relinquishment experience. The societal expectation was to keep a lid on it. After my marriage (not to the birthfather, but years later), we encountered infertility problems. It was very hard to be with friends, especially at baby showers, when everyone would share stories about their childbirth experiences. I couldn't share mine, of course. I felt like an involuntary outcast. —Eve

A year after our firstborn was relinquished for adoption, I married the birthfather, and we had three other children. Every time a new acquaintance asked me how many children I have, I always said three. Of course now, after our reunion, I proudly say—four.—Debbie

• Milestone events and birthdates of relinquished children

I always thought of my son on his birthday or holidays. I kept track of the year he would have started kindergarten, then junior high school, and would have graduated from high school.—Hannah

I feel bad on his birthday. I still feel guilty. I couldn't allow him to be mentioned for years. He was born in the spring. I hate spring.—Caroline

• Milestone events of other children

My other children were in their late teens when I told them about their older sister. They had no idea that when they accomplished a "first," my firstborn always came to mind. I always wondered about her interests, her likes, her accomplishments right alongside of theirs.—Patsy

Ways They Coped

In looking at the life experiences of many birthmothers, three themes emerge:

• the emotional pain of isolation and shame
• self-blame and stigmatizing
• perceived relational failure and depression.[14]

An important question resonates: How have birthmothers whose lives have been forever altered by the adoption experience coped?

Some coped in destructive ways

I coped by shutting down. Relinquishing my child has been the most difficult, painful event of my life. I became self-destructive and rebellious. I wanted to live on the edge, because I wanted the edge to pull me over. To shorten a very long story, my self-destruction landed me in therapy. I have been involved in therapy over seven years, and I attribute the quality of my life to my therapist. I was also introduced to Adoption Network of Cleveland. There I found I wasn't alone.—Leesa

I became "super-spiritual" and denied the unspeakable. I kept the secret buried for over 30 years, a method of coping that was destructive to my physical and emotional health, until I decided to search.—Marie

I entered the Army as a way of trying to forget, and married the birthmother the next year, as "the right thing to do." I coped by carefully guarding our secret, and overworking. I still am no good at acknowledging true feelings in myself or others. I was an angry husband and father to our other children.—Randall

Others found successful adjustment

The first couple of years were very difficult. I couldn't forgive myself. However, my older sisters continued to be very understanding and supportive. They affirmed their love of me—nothing had changed with them.—Katrina

I don't carry around feelings of guilt or regret. I think I owe that mainly to my parents and two brothers who stood by me the whole time and gave me their love and support.—Juanita

My greatest empowerment has come through finding my "voice" and working to educate professionals and to make legislative changes regarding antiquated adoption laws. While helping future generations know a true genealogy, I am also being healed. Before, I was a passive, secret mother. Now I don't mind being called a "social activist."—Bea

TO SEARCH OR NOT TO SEARCH AND BEING FOUND

As I pulled into the driveway of the agency, my heart began pounding wildly and my breathing became rapid. Memories came flooding back along with the feelings. I felt like I was returning to the scene of a violent crime in which I was the victim (or was I the criminal?). Once in, I was told by the social worker that I had "made my bed and now would have to lie in it." But I would not be demeaned again. I would not accept the role of the shamed pregnant teenager, although I felt strongly that was what was expected of me, all these years later. Confronting my fears by returning to the agency was one of the most empowering experiences of my life. It was important that I face my feelings and reclaim some of my own self-respect that I had lost in that building fourteen years before.—Terri

To search or not to search? and How to respond if found? are questions on the hearts and minds of birthmothers and birthfathers. For the last five decades, those touched by closed adoption have created an ever-growing network of connections and support as they attempt to locate their lost biological relatives. Local adoption triad groups, national organizations, conferences, and Internet search resources are shedding light on the motivations to search or not to search. Understanding these motivations gives further insight into the healing process.

Why Didn't They Search?

For many birthparents, searching was something they thought about, but made a conscious decision not to do. Consistent with many other research studies, Dr. Paul Sachdev noted that many of his respondents did not search, but waited to be found by their children.[15] A variety of reasons dictated this choice.

I Didn't Want to Disrupt His Life

My sister's birthday is the same day as my son's. Every year we go out together, and our discussion always turns to my son. On his 25th birthday, my sister asked me about searching for him. This prompted a year or more of soul-searching. Was it my place or not? Should I start this search or wait? At the crux of my internal struggle was the fear that I would be disrupting something, that by taking an active role in searching for him, I might some way cause him harm. In the end, I came to a resolution: I would not search. I would instead wait to be found. I remember this as being a very "theoretical" decision. I did not even think to reach out to register at any of the many available reunion registries—I didn't even know of their existence. I didn't even think to call the adoption agency to express my willingness to be contacted.—Donni

(Donni was found by her son the summer after his twenty-seventh birthday.)

I Didn't Want to Intrude into the Adoptive Family

I didn't want to upset anyone, especially the adoptive parents or my child. I think adoptive parents live in fear of the "real" mother showing up at their door anytime, which could be a terrible shock. So I always believed I would see her again, on her terms, not mine. At that time I would be sure she wanted to see me.[16]—Charlene

(As of this writing, Charlene is still waiting for her daughter to find her.)

I Feared She Would Reject Me

I always thought about the day my daughter and I would meet. But I also lived in fear that if I searched for her, she would have nothing to do with me. It has been difficult to wait, but in other ways, easier than it would have been to live with rejection.—April

(April's daughter located her. Both of them are living in the same city, only three miles apart.)

I Felt I Didn't Have a Right to Do This

When I placed my baby in the arms of the social worker, I was told in no uncertain terms that I had made a decision and it was permanent. There was no need for the agency to see me again. I was to make a new life for myself and forget all about her. I felt I had no rights and was made to feel that I had made a mistake and would need to pay for it for the rest of my life.—Ellen

(As of this writing, Ellen's daughter has contacted her by phone. They live on opposite coasts of the United States and have not had a face-to-face visit.)

We Had an Unspoken Pact—Never to Discuss the Child Again

I thought often about my son, my only child, whom I placed for adoption in 1968. I thought of searching, but came repeatedly to the roadblock of not knowing how I could do this while my mother was alive. After all, since the time of my son's birth, I had an "unspoken pact" with my mother never to discuss it again. My mother was the only family I had left.—Charla

(Charla decided she would wait until after her mother's death and then maybe start a search for her son. However, he located her in 1998.)

Why Did They Search?

As varied as the reasons for postponing a search for their child, birthparents also searched for numerous motivations.

I Have a Genetic Medical Problem

In my late thirties, I became seriously ill with a heart condition. When I learned that it was genetically connected to my side of the family, I was driven by the thought, "I must find my son before it is too late."—Dale

I Needed to Know If My Daughter Was All Right

My daughter was always, always with me—always on my heart and always on my mind. There came a time I could no longer live with the wondering. I just had to know if she was all right and what her growing up had been like. I am now experiencing a peace about my doing the right thing, but it has been over 25 years in coming.—Alicia

We Needed to Let Him Know the "Whys" of His Adoption

We always wondered what he was told about us, why the adoption happened. At our reunion, we not only connected with our son, but his adoptive parents. They have always been open and honest with him and treated our story with understanding and compassion. We are deeply grateful.—Stan and Diane (Birthparents who married one year after relinquishment.)

I Just Needed to Do This

I thought a long time about beginning the search. By the time my son was 22, I would think, "He's more settled now, he is out of school." I would write for information and just let it sit. I just was afraid of what I would find. By the time he was 28, I decided that this is something I must do and sat down to write him a letter. I rewrote this letter twelve times, before finally sending it on to the adoption agency.—Corrie

Corrie's Letter to Her Son, Travis

May 14, 1996
Dear Travis,
Last night I received information from the search group in Texas informing me that there is a strong possibility that you are my birthson. I have longed to find you for years, always waiting for the right time. I certainly didn't want to disrupt your life, or that of your family, as you were growing up, and I do not intend to do that now. It has just become a need in my life, and I hope that at your age now, you are able to understand.

When a woman gives up a baby for adoption, it doesn't end with a signature. It is never over. The regrets and hopelessness of the situation live on. Birthdays are the hardest, since that is the only thing I really know about you. I guess the most haunting question that I ask myself is, "Did I do the right thing?"

I am fifty-one now and am active with horses, dogs, and the local animal shelter. I returned to college, became certified to teach, and work as a substitute. My husband owns his own business, and we live in a small town in Ohio.

There is so much more I would like to share, but I know that this may not be a turn in your life you wish to take. I understand that you have a mother and father. They raised you, and my contribution to your life was very small. I do have one request. Would you respond with some type of information that would confirm (or not) that you are my birthson. If you aren't, I will continue my search. If you are, it may serve as some kind of closure to unanswered questions that have created this void in my life.

Sincerely,
Corrie

(Travis responded positively to this letter. Corrie and her entire family have been reunited with him and also enjoy a warm relationship with his adoptive parents.)

WHAT LESSONS HAVE WE LEARNED?

What we have learned is that the relinquishment experience for birthmothers and birthfathers has had a lifelong impact, and in many, many instances that impact has had a negative effect on healthy emotional development and stability. Current research in the field provides a model. When followed, it will not entirely ease the pain and loss related to the experience of relinquishment, but does provide a path toward healing and emotional and psychological wholeness. What has research taught us?

The Level of Openness Impacts the Lifelong Experience for Birthparents[17]

Research demonstrates that the type of adoption directly influences the birthparents' response to the loss. Birthmothers in time-limited mediated contacts and in traditionally closed adoptions have significantly worse grief resolution than mothers placing a child in ongoing mediated contacts and fully disclosed adoptions. Opportunity for contact in ongoing mediated arrangements and in fully disclosed adoptions seems to help some birthmothers feel "less empty" and be more readily able to see the child in relation to another family.

The Availability of Support through the Adoptive Grieving Process and Beyond Greatly Increases Birthparents' Opportunities for Moving Forward in a Healthy Way

Lifelong grief resolution is also affected by the availability of support at the time of relinquishment and beyond. Supportive environmental factors most noted include:[18]

1. A safe place to be (not only physically, but also emotionally)
2. Freedom to express feelings
3. Proximity to, and empathy, and warmth of loved ones who can express "some measure of knowing what has occurred"
4. Rituals of passage as the child moves from the care of the birthmother into the care of adoptive parents
5. An opportunity for reorganization, in which an understanding of the situation and roles of everyone involved is eventually gained.[19]

A Word from a Birthmother

I'm a different person today. Being found 2 years ago by the son I placed for adoption in 1968 has made all the difference—it has transformed me. I don't have this deep, dark secret anymore, it's such a relief.

I always thought others would judge me the way I judged myself. I've now found that, in my own eyes and in the view of others, being a birthmother is not such a horrible thing. I had never been able to mourn and move forward on this issue. I may never have initiated the search myself (although of course I thought about it), but as a result of being found, I've been able to heal. I'm happy now. I didn't realize how miserable I was until I stopped!—Charla

From the Heart

A Mother's Love
May 16, 1986
Dear Betsie,
Your call has brought us such joy. I can't begin to express myself. I've written hundreds of letters to you in my heart over the years and was particularly with you for each birthday, special celebrations as I perceived it—nursery school, first day of kindergarten, graduation, etc.

I can imagine your joy at not only finding me, but also your birth father and full-blood brothers. I have wished for you so often, but have strongly felt that what was done at your birth was done out of strong love for you and our desire for you to have a normal family situation, which we could not provide at that time . . .

We have so many questions that we can't ask them all now. What do you like? Where did you go to grade school, high school; you mentioned Maine? How did you like it? How did you chose nursing? Do you like animals, and on and on and on. We've saved some.

We'll see you soon.
Much love,
You'll have to decide what to call us. Whatever you decide is okay.[20]

NOTES

1. M. Jones, *Birthmothers: Women Who Relinquish Babies for Adoption Tell Their Stories.* (Chicago: Chicago Review Press, 1993) 51.

2. D. Howe, P. Sawbridge, & D. Hinings, *Half a Million Women: Mothers Who Lose Their Children by Adoption* (London: Penguin Books, 1992) 30.

3. R. Winker, and M. van Keppel, (1984). *Relinquishing Mothers in Adoption: Their Long-Term Adjustment* (Melbourne, Austral: Institute of Family Studies, 984), 9–10.

4. Howe, 30

5. Howe, 31

6. R. Severson, *A Letter to Adoptive Parents on Open Adoption* (Dallas: Heart Words Center, n.d.), 9 [leaflet].

7. L.H. Stiffler, (1992) *Synchronicity & Reunion: The Genetic Connection of Adoptees and Birthparents* (Conroe, Tex.: L.H. Stiffler, 1992).

8. This section is adapted from *Synchronicity & Reunion* with permission of the author.

9. Howe, 72.

10. L. Millen, and S. Roll, "Solomon's Mothers: A Special Case of Pathological Bereavement," *American Journal of Orthopsychiatry* no. 3 (July 1995): 55, 411–418.

11. Howe, 33.

12. L. Millen, S. Roll, and B. Backlund, "Solomon's Mothers: Mourning in

Mothers Who Relinquish Their Children for Adoption," in T.A. Rand (ed.), *Parental Loss of a Child* (Champaign, Ill.: Research Press, 1986), 257–268.

13. This section is also adapted from *Synchronicity and Reunion* with permission of the author.

14. M. Weinreb, and V. Konstam, "Birthmothers: Silent Relationships." *Affilia*, 10, no 3 (fall 1995): 319.

15. P. Sachdev, "Birthmothers and Their Experience with Reunion." Unpublished study. Dr. Sachdev at the time of this writing was professor, at the School of Social Work, Memorial University of Newfoundland, St. John's, Canada.

16. Ibid.

17. The following information is adapted from H. Grotevant and R. McRoy, *Openness in Adoption: Exploring Family Connections* (Thousands Oaks, Calif: Sage Publishers, 1998).

18. Although research on birthfathers is omitted from this because of the unavailability of data (since birthfathers are hard to find and to interview), the same factors listed would also be instrumental in their healing.

19. Grotevant and McRoy.

20. From the first letter of Betsie's birthmother.

PART IV

Focus on Understanding Adoptive Parents in Search and Reunion

CHAPTER SEVEN

Communicating the Decision to Search to Your Adoptive Parents

I did not want to hurt my adoptive parents by my need to search. Searching was something I had to do for myself in order to be a whole person.—Betsie

For the third time that evening, Robert laid the phone back on the receiver. He had planned to be at his parents' home for dinner within the hour and he now wanted to cancel. Until tonight he had avoided something he knew he had to do. He had brushed the issue aside for months. He didn't want to hurt them, but he needed to tell them about something he was thinking of doing. No, not just thinking about, he was doing it.

Tonight Robert would tell his parents that he had started a search for his birthparents. It was a search for answers—an exploration to find connections to the people who had given him life. It wasn't about his adoptive parents; they were wonderful. The search was about him. He had delayed as long as he could to share the search with them. He had waited until the unknowing became unbearable.

In the early years in the life of a child, adoptive parents have an important task. That task is telling their child about the adoption and the circumstances surrounding it. However, when that child becomes an adult, another type of telling emerges. The second telling is the disclosure by adoptees to their adoptive parents that they have searched or are planning to do so.

Both tellings are related to the same basic element—the other set of parents. In the first telling, adoptive parents tell children that they have another set of parents; in the second telling, the adoptees confirm this by their searching interest.[1]

Communicating with adoptive parents and extended family members about the need to search presents a challenge for all adopted persons. For some, the challenge is minimal, the "telling" easy, the support present. For others, breaking silence about the people and circumstances that led to the formation of the adoptive family introduces a whirlwind of emotions, which swirls around all parties touched by the opening of a previously closed, even taboo, issue.

WHERE DOES THE SEARCH MOVE ADOPTEES? WHAT DILEMMA DOES THAT EVOKE?

When adoptees move toward search, it moves them into a whole new realm of how they view their biological family. As characteristic of the last five decades, many adopted persons grew up in secrecy. That secrecy entombed the identity of their biological parents and the circumstances of relinquishment. Out of that secrecy, many adopted persons created unreal or fantasy birthparents. The search for biological parents puts the fantasy to rest. Postsearch adoptees can no longer construct imaginary stories about their origins or the reasons for their adoption, nor can they project on to biological parents feelings that initially developed in relation to the adoptive parents.[2]

The dilemma that emerges for adoptees is telling the adoptive parents of the search and subsequent reunion, because this requires a completed reevaluation of the adoption story in light of the reality. Adoptive parents may have falsified or omitted information (guided by social workers to do so). They may have knowingly given their adopted child a history that fails to match with reality.

In one particular study, it is reported that one-third of the adoptees in the research effort did not discuss their desire to search with their adoptive parents. What were the reasons?

• We were told we were special and chosen.
• We were afraid we would hurt our adoptive parents.

What happens in many cases for postreunion adoptees and their parents is that the initial story must be redone. It can no longer focus on the "chosen" component of the adoption story. "Adoptees and their adoptive parents have to confront the true story of the relinquishment and the reality that there is, indeed, another set of parents. Many adoptees do not feel that they can do this with their adoptive parents so they do not tell them of the search."[3]

WHAT SHOULD ADOPTEES KNOW ABOUT THEIR
ADOPTIVE PARENTS?

One important piece of the triad puzzle, which adoptees should know, is that most adoptive parents agree it's a natural thing for their adopted young person to want to know about the past. People need to know their roots. However, in responding to this need, feelings emerge that are considerably complex. For some parents, cognitive recognition that this is a normal issue for an adopted person stands miles apart from the psychological and emotional impact.

Randolph Severson, author and therapist, portrays the ambivalence encountered by some adoptive parents as they move toward honesty, enduring some confusion and even pain along the way. "Adoptive parents—some with joy and some with anguish—are awakening to the fact that roots, however twisted, are as vital to the leafing of the tree as is the gentle nurturing of the sun and rain."[4]

Jill, an adopted person whose reunion is still in its infancy, encountered this dilemma with her parents. She commented: "Cognitively, my mom and dad were very supportive of my reunion. They said and did all the right things. However, emotionally my mom had a hard time. I overheard her talking on the phone. Her worst nightmare was that I would leave her for my biological mother. When we found my birthmother, my adoptive mother came face to face with her greatest fear. As it turned out, my relationship with my adoptive family has grown stronger."

Opening the door to discuss search and reunion issues with adoptive family members requires one to cross over what feels like a rickety, unstable bridge. That bridge, built by materials from an unknown past, reinforced by the circumstances of the present, yet jeopardized by the concealed issues of the future, stands shaky and uncertain.

As one nears the bridge, one knows that crossing it will alter the lives of everyone within the family circle. To gain support while crossing that span, one must take time to step into the shoes of those whose lives will be most greatly affected—adoptive parents and grandparents. A step back into the last generation and a look into the future will provide helpful insight as adoptees communicate with their family about their need to search and ask them for their blessing. How can that be done and what will it accomplish?

First, a glance back at the societal attitudes present at the time of the adoption will help adoptees recognize how the viewpoint of a generation ago shaped their parents' thinking and actions (see chapter 1). Second, a look at the intergenerational changes that have occurred within one's family's style of communication furnishes a unique insight into why parents perhaps failed to deal at all with adoption issues in the past two generations. Finally, listening to the feelings and deep concerns that fashion a parents' perception of their lifelong experience as adoptive parents will help adoptees field their future responses as the search issues become an ever-increasing reality.

HISTORICAL PERSPECTIVE

To facilitate good communication across the generations regarding the search and reunion issues, the adopted person must understand the generational context of both the institution of adoption and the perspective their adoptive parents and birth parents developed within that context.[5]—Anu Sharma

We Did What We Were Told to Do

One primary attitude adoptive parents were told to assume following the finalization of the adoption was, "Take this child home, love him, and forget that he or she is adopted." Parents were told that secrecy is best for everyone. Those simple instructions played out in how parents handled the issues that were a part of their unique parenting experience.

We Kept It a Secret

When we brought Cathy home from the hospital, nearly thirty years ago, our social worker shared our excitement. She told us Cathy most likely would look like us, with her blond hair and blue eyes. No one would ever guess she was adopted. On the day of the court hearing, our worker said to us, "Now just take her home and love her like your own. Forget about the adoption. You are her only family." So that's exactly what we did. In fact, we didn't tell Cathy about her adoption until she was nineteen. That was a horrible mistake. But we did what we were told to do. (Sherry, adoptive mother)

For Sherry, her husband, Ken, and the hundreds of adoptive parents of the last generation, adoption was cast as merely an event in time—a static one, with no reference to the future. Many parents acted on the belief that there was no hidden agenda within adoption and that keeping the event a secret was the best approach. "Pretending" was promoted as the healthiest coping mechanism within the adoption community.

Kenneth Watson, an adoption expert, remarked that "the implication of the adoption on the subsequent development of the child or the family was either viewed as inconsequential or denied altogether."[6] These perceptions—"we are just like a biological family; adoption has no reference to the future, and things are best kept a secret"—further established a precedent on how children were told about their adoption, if they were told at all.

We Made Up a Story

We were advised by our agency to tell Ryan early on that he was adopted. We were also told, in order not to damage him with a negative story about his birth parents, to tell him they had both died in a car accident. We thought that was strange advice since we knew it wasn't true. Since our worker was the professional, we did what we were advised. It turned out to be very bad advice. (David and Joanne, adoptive parents)

This family was not alone in the way they handled their son's adoption story. Many adoptive parents were directed to take that same route in order to protect a child's perception of his original family. The predicament for these parents was how to discuss adoption with the child in a way that gave them full entitlement as parents yet did not paint a negative picture of the birthparents and do damage to the child's self-esteem.

It was not uncommon for adoptive parents, acting on the recommendation of their agency, to fabricate explanations for the circumstances of their child's birth and how they entered the family. Parents used a string of stories, from a range of freak accidents to unexplained disappearances, all done with the best intentions.

Parents were told to forget about the adoption, maybe not even mention it. Those who were told to tell their child of their adopted status were not told *how* to do this. They were instructed to deny any differences adoption might create within the family relationship and to fabricate stories about the adoption. Many parents were also handed another myth—"if they did a good job, their child would never wonder about his birth family. He would never want to search."

Exposing the Myth

Years ago, while sitting in the office of our agency worker, I asked her how to handle my son's curiosity about his birth family. I was told by her, "If you are the right kind of mother, your son will never want to search." The day Kevin came to me asking help in locating his birthmother sent me through a maze of guilt and inadequacy. How had we failed as parents? Our son wanted to find his birth family. (Melanie, adoptive parent)

Carol Demuth, in her book *Courageous Blessing: Adoptive Parents and the Search*, says adoptive parents were given the message "If you were loving, nurturing parents who acknowledged your child's adoptive status early, there would be no need on his part to know anything else."

A Model of the Myth[7]

What Parents Were	*Taught*	It'll be just like a biological family.
What Parents	*Understood*	Secrecy and fables are best.
What Parents	*Expected*	Child would never look back.
Parents Discovered	*Reality*	Many adoptees have missing pieces, feel empty, and must seek resolution.
Parents Experienced	*Frustration*	Issues of adoption and search are difficult to handle.
Parents Experienced	*Anger*	Someone didn't tell us the truth.
Parents Felt	*Betrayed*	Someone really lied to us.

Demuth continues: "Parents feel betrayed. Not by their child—but by the system that perpetuated a false image of what adoption could be. Parents were unfairly led to believe they could be everything to their children that they would never need to know anything beyond what the family could provide. It was as if the adoption decree was supposed to do away with the child's birth family."[8]

One of the most dynamic ways an adopted person can tap into the historical and societal context present at the time of the adoption is simply to ask questions. Some of the following questions may prove helpful in an attempt to understand the adoptive parents' actions:

1. What was it like for you when you made the decision to adopt?
2. How did the agency or people you worked with make you feel?
3. Did you feel free to talk about the adoption with family or friends, or did you keep it quiet?
4. How did the agency advise you to discuss adoption issues with me? What did you think about the advice?

Assessing the historical context of adoption and its impact on adoptive parents is one step in preparing to communicate with them about the need to search. A second step is taking a look at the patterns of family communication that existed a generation or two ago and recognize how those patterns have changed.

CHANGES IN FAMILY COMMUNICATION

Why didn't my adoptive parents ever ask me how I felt about adoption?

Why did I get the message that I should never question anything that had to do with my adoption or really inquire about any other issues?

Why wasn't I allowed to get angry when no one would tell me anything about my birthfamily?

Being raised within a family as an adopted child by the grandparents and parents of the past two generations was quite different from today. Elizabeth Fishel, in Family Mirrors, comments that "each new generation takes the material it has inherited, makes something new, something fitting and appropriately contemporary."[9]

Today's baby boomers who inherited relatively closed patterns of family communication from parents and grandparents have refashioned those patterns. This generation focuses much more extensively on openness, expression of feelings, and removal of masks. Looking back at what it used to be like in most families a generation ago may provide clues about why issues were left untouched, feelings untapped, and questions unanswered.

A generation ago, according to author Dolores Curran, "people paid little attention to what went on inside a family—whether there was good communication, emotional support, or trusting relationships."[10] People were only concerned about how well the family functioned.

"Our parents' generation," said Anu Sharma, "was very duty minded. Not that they weren't good at relationships, but they emphasized achievement."[11] They were concerned about how the family functioned— economically, educationally, socially, religiously. Little thought was given to how individual family members related to each other or to other issues and concerns in their life.

From the past generation to the present, the emphasis of the family is changing rapidly from considering how a family functions to how members relate to one another. The language of emotions has modified as it passes from one generation to another.[12] Fishel accounts for movement in three areas that provide explanation for the question, Why didn't we ever talk about adoption in my family?

A Broader Spectrum of Emotions

As this generation of adopted persons grapples with the issues of adoption, it does so within a wider range of acceptable emotional expression. This expression of feelings allows the presence of a dark side as well as a happy, bright side. It allows for downs as well as ups. It allows for questioning of what seems to be the norm. It is unlike the experience parents of the '40s and '50s encountered while growing up and passed on to their children.

Diane, an adoptee and now an adoptive parent, expresses the difference between the past she encountered and the present she is attempting to create.

In my adoptive family, no one ever brought up negative things. If we experienced a disappointment or were afraid or didn't like something, we never mentioned it. Feeling sad and talking about it just didn't happen. In my family now, my husband and I work at getting our three children to share their feelings, knowing that we probably won't like some of them. Especially now that they are nearing the teen years and adoption issues may hit them pretty hard.

More Willingness to Resolve Conflict

The "good" family of the past was taught to hide its real issues and problems. It went even further than that. The "good" family of the past had no issues and no problems.[13] Denial was a key coping mechanism. It was used to portray an image of health, wealth, and prosperity. Dolores Curran explains:

How did our ancestors cope with the problems we know they had? They coped in a way that modern parents can't and don't want to use. They wrote off the people, owning the problem as different. Over and over in my research I came upon the term black sheep, but this flock of sheep came in many forms. The spouse who was unfaithful or alcoholic was labeled a "ne'er do well" by the community, thus sparing the family the responsibility and shame for his or her behavior. The depressed woman was "going through her time" or "in the change," and her family was thus alleviated from blaming itself. . . . A child with learning problems was "not quite right" and those who questioned approved mores and customs were "just plain crazy."[14]

Adoptees who questioned, acted out, or otherwise rocked the boat were called ungrateful or "bad seeds." Families were spared the nasty business of confronting issues by throwing them off as the fault of the adopted child.

Today's adults have taken the inheritance of denial and made something new. Today's adults show a willingness to face issues and conflicts more openly, which holds true for those adults dealing with adoption issues. They do not attempt to live in denial or sweep issues under the rug. One adoptee shares her perspective:

I knew it would be difficult to talk to my adoptive parents about my reunion with my birthmother. The need to find her began brewing up within me months ago. I just couldn't pretend it wasn't there any longer. I will tell them what I am doing and why I am doing it. Then I will have to deal with how they respond, but that's okay. (Robin, age 33)

A companion to facing issues and conflicts, according to Elizabeth Fishel, is a "greater awareness about problem solving and more ingenuity in generating a whole host of solutions to puzzling family issues."[15]

More Readiness to Solve Family Problems

Years ago a misconception existed that claimed Everything in good families runs smoothly and easily and something is terribly wrong if a problem arises. Today's families, according to family system theorist Dr. Jerry Lewis, realize problems are a part of life to be recognized and solved.[16] One adoptee's story illustrates the point:

When I was sixteen, I got in a lot of trouble. My parents tried to keep it quiet. They said I would outgrow it. We never talked about it; I was just told to shape up. Now that I'm forty, I know those early troubles had something to do with being adopted and being terribly confused. I was just plain angry. Our son comes home with trouble at school pretty frequently. I don't push it off. We're working with the school and a counselor to get to the bottom of it. He joined our family by adoption at the age of three. Now at thirteen, I know things must be going on inside . . . Jonathan, adoptive parent. (Gerald, adoptee and adoptive parent)

Allowing more emotional leeway, accepting feelings as they are, being willing to resolve conflict, and having a greater awareness of problem-solving techniques mark a keen difference in family communication across the generations.

How can you best tap into the patterns of communication your parents learned and handed to you? Again, by asking them key questions:

1. As you were growing up, how were issues and conflicts handled in your family?
2. What was your perception of how to handle feelings?
3. If you had a problem, how did it get resolved?
4. What would you change about the communication in your family while you were growing up?

Understanding the historical context of adoption and learning about family communication patterns of the past generation hopefully will aid you in coming to an understanding of why certain events occurred in your family the way they did. One final assessment as you talk with adoptive parents will also prove helpful.

WHAT DO PARENTS FEEL WHEN A CHILD SAYS, "I'M SEARCHING"?

"The whole question of search and reunion," according to therapist Sharon Kaplan-Roszia, "touches a whole range of feelings for adoptive parents. It reverberates clear back to the early issues of loss, grief, and self-esteem."[17] It also sends subtle messages of failure, rejection, and betrayal.

Unresolved Failure and Loss

Sandy wanted more than anything to support her daughter's need to find her birthmother.

I knew this was an important thing for her to do. I was surprised that I was initially devastated by her decision. Old memories of my inability to conceive a child came rushing back in, even twenty-three years later. Old, disturbing emotions about my own complete inadequacy surfaced—ones that I had thought were resolved years ago. I wanted to be helpful to her, but all I could say was "go ahead if you must." I've cried a lot about those words and wish it were different.

Inadequacy and Rejection

All that came to mind for Robert and Susan, when their son informed them of his search and impending reunion was, aren't we good enough for you any longer? "We felt we had given everything we could to our son—support, love—everything. But all those feelings of doing a good job as a parent came crashing down the day he told us of his plans. We don't know why it affected us so emotionally. We know he needs to do this, but it doesn't feel good for us. We just don't feel good enough for him any longer."

Dave and Sue encouraged their daughter, Marla, to begin her search. They supported it, helped her, and even went to support group meetings with her. Still, fear accompanied them throughout the process.

"I was afraid that someone who was everything we were not would sweep Marla off her feet," Sue related. "I was afraid we would just become old hat to her and become unimportant in her life if she met her birthmother." Dave also had fears, but of a different kind. "I have always been protective of Marla and even more so during the search. My only concern was that she was going to get hurt and, of course, I didn't want that to happen. We were prepared to go any place at any time to help her."

Three things helped Dave and Sue process their own fears.

During the search, which took two years, we saw our fears as insignificant in comparison to Marla's need. We saw her hurting; we saw her identity as a person lacking. We felt compelled to help her find the truth. Marla's reassurance of her love for us and that we would always be her parents was extremely helpful. Coupled with this was our deep faith and belief that God placed our children into our hands to be their caretakers not possessors. We felt blessed, we adored her, but we also had to let her go to do what she needed to do.

Carol Demuth, an adoptee and adoption therapist, explains that although adoptive parents know the reason for their adult child's search, for some it feels like personal failure. "Some parents ask themselves a score of questions like, What does this say about our relationship? Haven't I done enough as a parent? It calls into question one's sense of competency."[18]

Incredible ambivalence is a common response to the search. "They want it for their child, but it hurts deeply," Demuth says. "On the one hand, they want their child to be healed through the reunion encounter but are pained because they were not fully adequate to provide that for them. Some parents even question if they fulfilled their nurturing role since they, in themselves, couldn't make the pain go away for their child."

Recognizing the sensitive, fragile concerns of adoptive parents is an important step in the whole process of the search and reunion. Knowing that the question may renew painful memories of loss and failure, ignite feelings of inadequacy in the adoptive parents, or fuel fears of rejection or hurt for their child will equip adopted persons to approach your parents with sensitivity and understanding.

Dr. Severson strongly believes that an overwhelming number of adoptive parents understand.

The essential point is that every human being on the face of the earth has a right to look into the eyes of those from whom they drew life. . . . It is my belief, heartfelt as well, that no human being would wish to deny adoptees that right once they can be helped to see the human justice of it. And certainly I do not believe that any adoptive parents whose love for the child . . . is as enduring and ennobling as any love on earth, would deny that right to his or her adopted children. But if they do not see it, it is not because they are blind; it is because their eyes have not yet opened. Love and respect and understanding are the answer, not blame and guilt.[19]

To move beyond blame, guilt, and misunderstanding is a noble goal in crossing the bridge together. To explore, understand, and forgive your parents for lack of support or even misdirected hostility opens the doors to keeping the relationship healthy. In the effort to meet this goal, you may smooth out the pathway ahead by asking the following questions:

1. How painful was it for you to realize you would never have a child by birth? (if applicable)
2. Who helped you deal with that loss? Anyone?

3. What kind of feelings do you remember experiencing as I became part of the family?
4. Have you had feelings of failure or inadequacy in regard to our relationship?
5. What are your greatest fears about my searching?
6. What can I do so that we can share this experience together?

As young or middle-aged adopted persons step from behind the veil of secrecy to open doors and windows previously locked, they do so at what feels like great risk to their relationship with their adoptive parents and eventually to their relationship with their birthfamily members. Those who have walked through it can speak from their experiences with insight on what to expect from adoptive parents.

WHAT LESSONS HAVE WE HAVE LEARNED

Unfortunately, I can tell people how not to deal with their adoptive parents. I always told my parents I would search, but when I began, I hid it all from them. When my birthmother was found on the East coast and we made arrangements to see her, I made up lies as to where we were going and what we were doing. It wasn't until my lies got too big that I finally told them the truth. They were not hurt that I was searching. They were desperately hurt about the lies. The subject is rarely brought up now. I hope someday they will feel that our relationship again will be open, trusting, and honest. (Majorie, age 36)

My adoptive parents have encouraged me to try to find my birth parents for my own peace of mind and for medical information. I honestly don't believe my mom means it. I think she's worried that I will forget who raised and loved me over the years. My dad is open about how he feels. He doesn't want to know anything. He said it would hurt too much. As far as not sharing this with adoptive parents, I think one should share, no matter how they feel. If they aren't told about the search, and they find out, it could hurt them even more. In this case, honesty is the best policy. (Darlene, age 38)

I told my mom about the search for my birth parents and let my mom tell my dad. He wasn't thrilled when I began my search and our relationship was strained for years because we were on different sides of this issue. It was a very hard subject to discuss and still is. When I'm happy and want to share my happy news, naturally the first people I want to tell are my parents so they can share in my happiness. But my dad doesn't share in my happiness and I'm sad he feels hurt. I know that deep down my father was and still is afraid his daughter would be hurt and rejected. I think my parents were both afraid of losing me. I make sure that I show in my actions and words that my relationship with them hasn't changed. The only thing that will prove my love hasn't changed is time. (Mary, age 33)

I think my dad has difficulty with the reunion because he really believed that the only family I have is my adoptive family. He doesn't seem to understand the loss I've felt all my life. I think he is insecure about the reunion because deep down he fears I may choose my birth family over my adoptive family. I think he blames himself for my search—if he and Mom had done a better job I wouldn't need to search. It's as if his love should have been enough for me to forget the fact that I was someone else's daughter first. What I've done to deal with this is to visit them more frequently. I want to reinforce the fact that my reunion with my birth parents did not change anything. (Allison, 37)

During my search, I shared all the information with them as the process took place. They saw my excitement. However, the relationship I have with them didn't change. I still called them as often and visited them the same amount. I tried not to focus constantly on my search. Now I don't focus on time spent with my other mother when I am with them. (Martha, age 47)

One thing I wanted to do was honor my adoptive mother during the reunion period of my search. On the day I was to meet my birthmother for the very first time, I sent flowers to my adoptive mother, assuring her of my deep love for her and deep commitment to my adoptive family. (Andrew, age 39)

From a letter to adoptive parents following a reunion:

My dear Mom and Dad,

I hope that someday, somehow, you will understand my love for you. I never wanted to hurt you by searching for my birth family. I hope I have not done so. No matter how close I become to my birth parents, or how I accept them as "my other family," I do hope you know how important you are to me. I am "your child," but I am also the child of Daniel and MaryAnn. Each of you has given me such tremendous gifts—all of which I could never repay. Daniel and MaryAnn gave me life, and you taught me how to live it and loved me no matter what. I could never repay the debt I owe to either of you. The best I can hope for at this time is that you will accept my relationship with my birth family and know that my love for you does not diminish because of my love for them.

Lovingly, Rebecca (age 31)

A Word From Betsie

Contrary to what some people think about why adoptees search, I was able to search because my adoptive parents did such a great job rearing me to mature, well-adjusted adulthood. The foundation they laid made me secure enough to take this risk.

NOTES

1. Torah Lichtenstein, "To Tell or Not to Tell: Factors Affecting Adoptees Telling Their Adoptive Parents about Their Search," *Child Welfare* 75, 1 (Jan.–Feb., 1996), 61–72.

2. Ibid., 63.

3. Ibid., 64.

4. Randolph Severson, *Adoption: Charms and Rituals for Healing* (Dallas: House of Tomorrow Productions, 1991), 101.

5. Anu Sharma, of the Search Institute of Minneapolis, Minn. Personal interview, March 21, 1994. Used with permission.

6. Jayne Schooler, *Searching for a Past* (Colorado Springs: Pinon Press, 1993), 41.

7. A "Model of the Myth," created by David L. Schooler, MPC.

8. Carol Demuth, *Courageous Blessing: Adoptive Parents and the Search* (Garland, Tex.: Aries Center, 1993), 3.

9. Elizabeth Fishel, *Family Mirrors: What Our Children's Lives Reveal About Ourselves* (Boston: Houghton Mifflin, 1991), 51.

10. Dolores Curran, *Traits of a Healthy Family* (New York: Ballentine Books, 1988), 8.

11. Sharma.

12. Fishel, 60.

13. Curran, 292.

14. Ibid.

15. Fishel, 59.

16. Jerry Lewis, *How's Your Family?* (New York: Brunner/Mazel Publisher, 1989), 299s.

17. Sharon Kaplan-Roszia, personal interview, February 24, 1994.

18. Carol Demuth, personal interview, February 1994.

19. Randolph Severson, *Adoption and Spirituality* (Dallas: Aries Center, 1994), 17.

PART V

The Process of the Search

PART II

The Process of the Search

CHAPTER EIGHT

Making the Decision: To Search or Not to Search

I recall the times I thought of calling the agency where I was adopted for information. I looked up the number in the phone book numerous times, but the guilt was overwhelming. I felt social workers would not understand; they would think I was ungrateful. How dare I want to know my own medical history, what my parents looked like, or why they placed me for adoption.—Betsie

As she rounded the corner, her eye caught a glimpse of the house. It was an average-sized house, neatly kept, with a row of rosebushes lining the driveway. *Roses*, Jackie thought to herself, *she likes roses, too.*

Nearing the front sidewalk, she slowed her step. A rising sense of anxiety gripped her. She almost wished she hadn't taken it this far, but she couldn't quell the ache in her heart. A letter had been the first step. Then the phone calls. Now Jackie would soon face the woman who gave birth to her. What will she think of me? she wondered.

Today marked the end of Jackie's two-year search for the only person she hoped had all the answers to her questions. The search and reunion was something she had to do.

Ellen, Jackie's younger sister, understood Jackie's need to find her birthmother. She freely encouraged Jackie through the search process, but it wasn't an important issue for Ellen. Possibly someday. Maybe never. It just wasn't something she had to do.

To search or not to search? Each year, thousands of adult adoptees ask and answer this question. Perhaps you're asking it now.

What is the meaning of the search? Why do some search just for information and stop? Why do some seek a reunion? Why do some wait until midlife while others choose to do nothing? Is there a right time to search? What advice can be given to those in the decision-making stage? All these questions deserve examination.

THE MEANING OF THE WORD *SEARCH*

When the word *search* is mentioned within the context of adoption, a picture emerges in one's mind. Captured within the frame of that picture is a young man or young woman sitting at a courthouse backroom table, pouring over dusty, yellowed files. From the intense facial expression, one senses the emotional urgency to catch just a glimpse of his or her unknown past.

The word *search* for adoptees carries with it multiple layers of meaning. For some, searching means attempting to find nonidentifying information about a birthparent's characteristics or their own medical history, with no attempt for a meeting.

For others, *search* means reunion—a face-to-face meeting. For still more adoptees, the meaning and process move them profoundly deeper. The word *search* for them is not limited to its literal meaning of a physical effort to make a connection. The meaning expands to include all that is part of their quest, for it is an emotional, psychological, and spiritual journey.

Randolph Severson, in an eloquent explanation of all that resides within the quest, said the following:

Perhaps every adoptee bears within himself the imprint of a special or unique spiritual vocation. It is spiritual. It is always spiritual . . . the matter of the heart and soul . . . The mystery of adoption is that the adoptee was truly, as Betty Jean Lifton has said, twice born—first of the flesh and then again in the spirit.

If an adoptive family is anything, it is a spiritual, psychological reality whose ground is love. What's an adoptive family made of if not biology and genes. Heart and soul can be the only answer.

To be adopted then, is to be both born of the heart and born of the spirit. The life work of the adoptee, if he or she is to attain healing and wholeness is to rejoin the heritage of the flesh and the beauties of the spirit within the secret treasuring of the heart.[1]

WHY ADOPTEES SEARCH

Robert Anderson, in his article "The Nature of the Search: Adventure, Cure or Growth," asks simple yet profound questions. "This question, I believe, why adoptees search, can be paraphrased, Why are you interested in your mother, your father, your grandparents, sisters, brothers, cousins, nephews, ancestry, history, aptitudes? In short, why are you interested in you?"[2]

The Search As an Adventure

Anderson, from his view as an adopted person and psychiatrist, believes people search for a number of reasons. First, they search as an adventure. Often viewed as an exciting undertaking, it is an effort on the part of the adoptees to move life to a new vantage point, to fill in the missing gaps, and to clutch the time that remains with family members previously unknown. It is an effort uncomplicated by contemplating how the reunion will alter the lives of all those touched by the course of events.

Adoption therapist Sharon Kaplan-Roszia comments that some people, by temperament, are natural mystery solvers. Throughout life they have processed people and events, solved problems, unraveled mysteries. Being curious is simply part of their nature. So to search, she states, is the most natural thing for them to do.[3]

For those who search as an adventure, Anderson says, it becomes a "drama of individuals prevailing against great odds to finally be reunited with their biological families. It can be of heroic proportion, and it may intimate that the characters should be rewarded for their efforts, perhaps by thereafter having a joyous life together."[4]

The Search as Therapy

For most adoptees, facing the issue of the search is far more than "just an adventure." It is often a frightening decision, filled with enormous physical and emotional investment. It comes often after years of pondering, waiting for the courage to begin. It is a therapeutic step, because it confronts facts, issues, people, and feelings that were once vague wonderings. It brings most to a point of resolution regarding the complexities of growing up as an adopted child. The result of the search spans a wide continuum for each adopted person, from satisfying a need for factual information to touching the deepest level of the heart and soul with a reunion.

I'm Not Who I Thought I Was: What Is My Real Medical History?

Learning of her adoption at the age of forty-four sent Jan on an unsettling investigation. Regrouping emotionally following the most traumatic disclosure of her life, Jan wanted to know her birthfamily's medical history. The answers brought a profound change in her perspective about her future.

Initially, the main reason I searched was to find my medical history. I assumed that my (adoptive) mother's medical history was mine; she had died at forty-two of a heart attack. Her parents also died very young in their early sixties. I was very concerned about my health, preoccupied is probably a better word, from the time I was first married on. I wondered if I would live to see my children to adulthood. It came as a great relief to discover that my adoptive mother's medical history was not mine, and now I wanted to know what my actual medical history was.

Do I Look Like Anyone? Do I Act Like Anyone?

When Penny, a thirty year old with auburn hair and freckles, decided to search, her intent was to gather only information. Throughout her teens and early adulthood, Penny felt frustrated, embarrassed, and insecure because she looked so unlike anyone in her adoptive home. The driving desire to find a genetic similarity was the only thing that encouraged Penny during the ten months it took to receive information.

For the first time in my life, I felt physically attached to someone. The information I received told me that I look like both my birth father and birth mother, suffer with her allergies, and now I understand why I have such an interest in music. They both did. My reason for the search was not to hurt my relationship with my adoptive parents. I just wanted to know who I looked like and who I acted like. At this point in my life, I am not ready to meet them. Maybe someday. Right now, I am able to put the compelling search effort to rest.[5]

The Emptiness in My Heart Wouldn't Go Away

A common theme for many adopted persons is gratitude for their adoptive parents and how they handled adoption issues. To them, their parents did everything right, but they still needed something else. For Marla, it was a need she didn't even recognize until her adoptive parents touched the right chord. She says, "Even though I had a wonderful life and great parents, I was down a lot and felt empty inside. I felt I didn't know who I was or where I came from. I just didn't feel whole. My parents could see I was hurting, even when I couldn't see it myself. They talked to me about this and we decided to search."

Gwen experienced a similar positive home environment to Marla's, but found out by age thirty that the hushed but ever-present pain of her heart could no longer be stilled. "I always wanted to know facts about my adoption, but by the time I reached thirty, the need was far deeper—I had significant questions to ask. Why was I given away? The only way I could put the pieces of my life together was to find the pieces myself. I waited as long as I could until the anguish became unbearable. I needed answers from those who, hopefully, had held me even for just a moment before saying goodbye."

A Life Transition Brought Me Face-to-Face with My Adoption

For many adoptees, the decision to search emerges following a significant transitional event, such as marriage, birth of a child (giving the searchers the first contact with a blood relative) or death of an adopted family member.

"When adoptive parents die," states Dr. David Brodzinksy, "the adoptee might suddenly feel compelled to put a name and face to the phantom other parents who had been companions of his childhood fantasies. Since the unconscious knows no time barriers, losses tend to pile up, and the most recent loss drives the adoptee to resolve the first loss, the one that remains potentially reversible."[6] For one young adult, this proved to be true.

Dealing with adoption issues was something that thirty-seven-year-old Tina ignored throughout her life. From an early age she stuffed away thoughts and feelings about being adopted. As an adult she found herself standing face-to-face with old feelings left over from childhood.

"In my heart I wanted to belong to my mom and dad," Tina said. "I wanted to be their biological child. I was embarrassed that I was adopted, and I felt that if people knew I wasn't really a 'Wheeler,' they might think differently of me."

Tina's confrontation of the reality of her adoption is quite similar to some adult adoptees. Some face it early and look for answers in their late teens. Still others, like Tina, do not face it until a major life transition looms before them. For Tina, it was the death of her adoptive mother that brought her adoption issues to the surface.

"Overnight it hit me. Somewhere out there is someone who looks like me," she exclaimed. Following the death of her adoptive mother, the reality of another person distantly tied to her life emerged. After nearly thirty years, Tina faced the reality of her adoption and the implications that came with it. She initiated a search to find out as much about her birthfamily as possible.

With the help of her supportive husband, David, Tina set out on a journey to locate her birthparents. Unfortunately for Tina, the need to connect was not mutual. Her birthmother, up to this point, has rejected any effort on Tina's part to meet. Any path to locate her birthfather is also blocked. Tina's need to stand face-to-face with her birthfamily is a continual one. She simply wants to finish developing a picture that was exposed at the time of her adoptive mother's death.

It Was a Question That Has Always Been with Me

Actually making a decision to search, for many adopted persons, is a resolve made even before adolescence. One adoptee commented, "I started my search probably from the first time I realized what adopted meant. I think every adopted person searches, if only in their minds. If they are like me, they searched in the quiet darkness of their bedroom late at night. They searched by asking themselves questions no one was around to hear or questions no one could criticize, analyze, or judge."

Susan was one of those lifetime searchers.

The decision to search was not something I made a conscious decision to start. I just knew that someday I was going to need the answers. I guess the first time I thought about it was when I was twelve. I had always wondered who I looked like and why I was so different from my family. I was the only blond in a family of brunettes. I am left-handed. I am artistic, both art-wise and musically. A family member who knew my birth father told me his name when I was twelve. His name, which was a very long, difficult ethnic name, burned itself across my memory like a laser beam. I knew even at twelve that it was important and that I could not forget it.

I Needed to Connect with My Roots

Stemming from one of adoption's major issues or losses, many adopted adults initiate their search from a deep, pervasive feeling of disconnectedness, of having a piece of themselves missing and incomplete. There is a need, as Dr. Randolph Severson mentioned, to "rejoin the heritage of the flesh and the beauties of the spirit within the secret treasuring of the heart."[7] It is a compelling necessity to meet the people who brought them life.

For Betsie, growing up in an open-minded adoptive home that gave her the message, "talking about adoption in this house is okay," still left loose ends. The sense of disconnection followed at her heels. She comments about her struggle.

Where did I get my red hair? What nationality am I? These were questions I faced daily. I also knew nothing about my birth. Was it an easy or difficult labor? What time was I born; how much did I weigh? Where was I for two weeks before placement? Deeper inside me were more questions. What kind of body was I growing into? How did my birth mother feel about me then and now? Did she think of me? Why was I given up? That was the biggest question.

In order to connect the scattered pieces of her life, the only thing for Betsie to do was make the decision to find her birthparents.

As I grew up, I always knew I would search, but I never pictured it as real or as potentially leading to a reunion. Adoption was steeped in unreality and disconnectedness engendered by the closed system mentality. I got the message to pretend adoption did not make a difference that my family was like any other family. Part of me felt like an alien alone in the world. I felt ruled by fate not knowing who I was; therefore, not knowing what I could do in life. Later I heard terms like "biological alien" and "genealogical bewilderment" which described how I felt.

For those who make a decision to locate birthfamily members, there are no promises about the outcome. It could prove to be the most significant, positive event of their lives. It could also be a devastating blow to already fragile self-esteems. In recent years, some adoption search groups have followed reunion results. A group in Canada, Parent Finders of Canada, surveyed five hundred members about their reunion experiences. Here are the results it found:

Searcher	Reunited with	Favorable
Adoptee	Birth parents	92.0%
Adoptee	Birth siblings	98.3%
Male adoptee	Birth parents	92.6%
Male adoptee	Birth siblings	100.0%
Female adoptee	Birth parents	91.4%
Female adoptee	Birth siblings	97.8%
Birth parents	Surrendered children	94.0%[8]

Many adults make a decision to search for a variety of reasons. However, there are reasons why some do not make the same decision.

WHY SOME DON'T SEARCH

Why some individuals decide not to search appears to be related to a variety of causes. They are:

- no interest right now
- loyalty to adoptive parents
- carrying of other issues
- uncertainy about the right to disrupt lives
- fear of rejection

I Am Just Not Interested Right Now

Sharon Kaplan-Roszia commented that some are just not interested. "Their lives are full and busy with families or careers. Identity is not an issue for them," she added, "and it is something they don't want to do."[9]

For June, an adoptee in her thirties and also an adoption therapist, undertaking a search is not an important issue to her.

My adoptive mom has always encouraged me to look, especially after my son was born. She thought the medical information would be helpful. But I just don't plan to at this point in my life for a number of reasons. First, I feel I have a pretty strong identity. This comes, I think, from the basic personality with which I was born. I feel confident and comfortable with myself. Second, I look like both my brother, who is also adopted, and my mom. I've heard that all my life.

Another reason for not searching is how I was raised. I have never felt I was missing a piece of my life. My parents are dynamic people and I wanted to identify with them. They gave me security and a sense of belonging, but also a sense of autonomy. They would say, "Your accomplishments are yours"; they did not try to hold on to me too tightly.

I Feel a Strong Loyalty to My Adoptive Parents

At age thirty-one, Catherine doesn't plan to search right now. She feels this decision is an outgrowth of her loyalty to her adoptive family that far outweighs a need for anything else. Commenting about this conclusion, she says:

I was placed with my family at four months. To this day we celebrate both my birthday and the anniversary of the day I was placed with my parents. I have a brother who is three years older than I am. My parents adopted him a year before me. He and I have discussed the idea of searching, but neither of us has had a desire to do so.

I think the reason I'm not searching is that I don't have anything to search for. I have never felt anything was missing from my life. I am very close to both of my parents. I would not want to do anything to hurt them in any way. They are both older now. Maybe my feelings will change, but for now I'll leave the issue alone.

I Am Already in Too Much Pain

Julie grew up in what she calls a dysfunctional family. Her adoptive status was not disclosed to her until the age of fourteen, and that was by accident. She has had a lifetime of discovering painful family secrets. Her anguish is evident as she shares.

These last few years have been difficult. It has been a time of breaking silence about my father's alcoholism and dealing with "adult children of alcoholics" issues. I never really associated some of my emotional pain as being related to adoption, but I'm sure it is.

Because mine was a private adoption where my family members knew my birth mother, the information is available to me. I'm not going to pursue it because I have an idealistic mind. I know that Marian and Richard, my birth parents, are "just people," and that's not good enough. I have unanswered questions and I don't suppose I'd like any of the answers. Also, I realize this woman is now in her sixties and we've managed to get this far without contact. Why should I create emotional upheaval for an older woman as well as for myself at mid-life? What gain could there be? I have already gone through the death of my dad, and my mom is seventy-four. I don't want to find a whole new family and face aging/death issues with them, too.

Do I Really Have the Right to Do This?

Some adopted persons, according to Sharon Kaplan-Roszia, have been given a message from society or from the family that wanting any information about their birthfamily is inappropriate or downright wrong. They may have grown up in a family where adoption talk was strictly avoided and they assumed the role of the grateful adoptee.[10]

At age thirty-four, Nancy says that her need to find out anything about her birthfamily has caused turmoil throughout her adoptive family system. This turmoil created an emotionally complex tug-of-war for Nancy. She has yet to resolve the dilemma.

Do I search for me or do I not search for them? Can I handle what they will do if I decide to search? My uncle, my aunt, and even my grandparents have told me that what I want to do is upsetting my mom and dad. "Why can't I be grateful for what they have given me?" they ask. It makes me wonder if it's right for me to disrupt my adoptive parents lives. It's very hard to want to pursue this search without feeling like I'm the one upsetting the otherwise peaceful boat.

I Can't Face Rejection Again

While growing up, Sue kept questions about her adoption deep inside herself. In midlife Sue lifted those fragile feelings from the backroom closet of her heart and confronted them. As a result, she made a decision not to search for any family members or for any information about herself.

I can give you a long list of reasons why I am not searching. On the surface, they provide a great rationale for leaving the topic alone. First of all, I do not want to go through the process to find a family member dead and experience the grieving process for someone I don't know. Second, I don't want to take my family and myself on an incredible emotional roller coaster. Third, what will I do with what I find? I don't have an answer for that.

As Sue reflected on her reasons for choosing not to search, she reached deep into the hidden pain that had lain dormant for so long. "I have to admit, the main reason for leaving all of this alone is the terrible fear of rejection. I am continuing to work through what I feel is the consequence of my adoption. This emotional pain has impacted me so much that to risk more rejection is simply not worth it to me."

Adults who have taken the step to search have many positive reasons for the undertaking. For those who have decided not to search, the reasons need equal validation. To gain an objective perspective on the topic is to allow each individual to stand face-to-face with the question; for it is his decision alone. It is also necessary to allow time, maturity, and growth to complete its work and to rest with the conclusion at which the adopted person arrives. One young adoptee stated: "My birth mother made a decision many years ago to make an adoption plan for me. I was placed into a loving, warm family to whom I feel I belong. I appreciate my birth mother for her choice. I know she felt I could have a better life than what she could give to me. Yet I'm not ready to find her. Someday I will be ready."

There are as many different answers to the question as there are people who contemplate it. "It's a very curious thing, this process of search, for all adoptees at different times move along with different motivations. At some point we may be completely disinterested, almost apathetic about it. At another time in our lives each step may be fiercely compelled by the need to meet that person whose touch we may have felt but whose face we cannot remember," (Heather, age 25).

IS THERE A RIGHT TIME TO SEARCH?

After weighing the views of those who have searched and those who have not, another step is advised. Before actually activating the search with the primary and hopeful outcome of reunion, it's important to assess your readiness. According to therapist Linda Yellin, there are several reasons why an adoptee may postpone his or her search to work on emotional readiness.

"One reason for waiting," states Yellin, "is that the adoptee searches with an absolute planned outcome and unrealistic expectations. These types of searchers are not prepared for the unexpected and are setting themselves up for more difficulty." Yellin believes that it's a normal part of the search process to have some fantasies, fears, hopes, and dreams about the birthfamily. Yet there are no guarantees about the outcome. Key questions to ask yourself are, Am I ready for the unknown? Will I be okay no matter how it turns out?

Another reason you should delay a search, according to Yellin, is that you may not be emotionally ready as a result of severe unmet needs in your adoptive family. "Searching for a birth parent or birth family with the hope of regaining a parent-child relationship with the birth family is unrealistic. Some grief work must be done around what was lost in the adoptive parent relationship and the birth parent relationship. Exploring some of the unmet needs will help move you toward more readiness."

A third argument for deferring the search, says Yellin, is when it is not motivated by the adoptee, but by others pushing the issue. It's important for you to drive the search process. She adds, "From my first-hand experience as an adult adoptee who has searched and reunited, as well as from my involvement in the adoption community, the search and reunion process has been one of the most powerful experiences in my life. For the adoptees I have known, the search and reunion process provides opportunities for increased insight, strength, and healing and continues their journey of self-discovery as adults."

As Ken Burkett, a thirty-three-year-old adoptee who completed a search in 1993 expressed, "The search effort can be a great time of personal growth filled with discovery, pain, fulfillment, and healing. It is something the adoptee should only initiate himself when the time is right. It should never be another's decision."

Yellin believes that overall readiness to search occurs "when the adoptee wants to be in the driver's seat on the unknown search road of detours, bumps, roadblocks, rest stops, and curves in unpredictable weather."[11]

Facing the decision to alter the relationships and events of your life and the lives of your birthfamily members, adoptive family members, and your own adult family is an important one. Listening to good advice in the early stages can bolster your courage to do what you feel you must.

WHAT LESSONS HAVE WE LEARNED?

The best advice I can think of is not to do it until you're sure you're emotionally ready for anything, like rejection or finding that maybe they do not meet your standards. You have to be ready to accept what you find no matter what it is and deal with it the best way you can. It's important to have someone in your corner like I did, helping you talk through things during your period of anticipation. My cousin and my husband were my rocks. Bear in mind that your birth family's personalities may be so different that you will have to do a lot of bending to try to understand or be understood, and most of all, do not push and do not judge. (Dianne, age 42, reunited with birthfamily in 1993)

Be infinitely patient. Be open to absolutely *any* response; things rarely turn out the way we fantasize. Honor your birth parent's right to privacy. Respect their decisions. Do not reveal who you are to any other family member inadvertently. Give your birth parents *time*. (Jan, age 45, had contact with birthfamily members in 1993)

Don't give up. If you truly want to find out, there are ways! The process is slow and frustrating. Sometimes you go down a dead-end street and don't know where to turn. If you have patience and determination, the pieces will slowly come together. (Tina, age 33, searched in 1993)

As one who hasn't searched, I would say really think about it and think about *why* you are doing it! There is such a mix of positive and negative emotions regarding birth parents (or at least I feel such a mix) that I would need to be as sure as I could that I was searching for the good of all, not for some other need. (Sue, age 45)

A Word from Betsie

There is no word in our language that adequately describes an adoptee's need to know his or her heritage. People refer to this need as "curiosity," as this is the closest term that seems to fit. The connotation of curiosity, however, is one of wanting to know for a potentially trivial reason. It does not describe the deep need to know experienced by many adoptees. I cannot imagine going through life not having searched, not having the opportunity to put the pieces of my life together.

Deciding to search does create a sense of ambivalence for adopted persons. Determining the "when's," the "how's," and the "should's" takes an immense amount of emotional energy. Perhaps the following poem readily expresses the dilemma of those facing a decision.

The Shadow Family

Why do I fear you?
I have lived in your shadow
these years of my life.
I know you are there
but where?
Show yourself show yourself
to me.
Please don't make me find you.
Find me.
If I turn around fast, will I see you?
If I move my eyes there
can I see you?
Do you have my eyes or
are they mine?
Where is my smile
And my child's
Are they yours?
I have pieces that don't match.
I have half-longings
and
Many years of half-cried tears.
—Susan Kittel McDonald, 1990 (Used by permission).

NOTES

1. Randolph Severson, "Transformations" (presented to the American Adoption Congress, Cleveland, Ohio, 1993).

2. Robert Anderson, "The Nature of the Search: Adventure, Cure, or Growth?" *Child Welfare* 67,6 (November–December): 625.

3. Sharon Kaplan Roszia, personal interview, February 28, 1994.

4. Anderson, 625.

5. Adapted from Jayne Schooler, *The Whole Life Adoption Book* (Colorado Springs: Pinon Press, 1993), 203.

6. David Brodzinsky, *Being Adopted: The Lifelong Search for Self* (New York: Anchor Books, 1992), 143.

7. Severson.

8. Mary Jo Rillera, *The Adoption Search Book* (Westminister, Calif.: Triadoption Publishers, 1991), 15.

9. Roszia interview.

10. Ibid.

11. Linda Yellin, personal interview, January 1994.

CHAPTER NINE

Preparing Emotionally for and Initiating the Search

Once I made the decision to search, there came a great sense of relief. I had thought about it for years, but when I made a decision, there came a sense of peace.—Betsie

Judy hurriedly finished the letter she wanted to mail. She was writing the agency that placed her in her adoptive home. For months Judy struggled over the decision to search and also with discussing it with her adoptive parents. A weekend visit home convinced her it was the right thing to do and the right time to do it. Today, she began. The struggle of should I or shouldn't I was over. A deep sense of relief followed her throughout the day; even though she knew there would be bumps in the road ahead.

Making the decision to initiate the search is a critical turning point in the life of an adopted person. As he walks a path that may link unknown events and people from an unknown past to the events and people of the present, preparation is an absolute necessity, and he must face a multitude of concerns.

First, the searcher will encounter unexpected emotions that may propel him into confusion, anger, fear, even depression at a depth, which he has not yet experienced. Second, he must learn to recognize unrealistic expectations within himself and balance those with probable reality. Third, he should be aware of the people he will meet and their reactions, both positive and negative. A searcher must have a reasonable perception of what circumstances he may find regarding his birthfamily. Finally, the searcher must know how and where to gain support, for this is a journey not to be undertaken alone.

HANDLING THE EMOTIONAL ROLLER COASTER

The only thing for certain when plowing new ground is that unknown ruts, rocks, even boulders can block progress. As the adopted person plows new ground in his search, he may find himself profoundly confused at the depth and breadth of his emotions.

I Didn't Know I Would Feel So Angry

Every day I rushed out to the mailbox to see if the agency sent any information. It finally came and I was completely thrown off by my reaction. What my adoptive parents told me didn't match what the agency sent. Nothing matched! I thought my birth parents were young and unmarried. I could live with that. But as it turned out, they were married with other children. My birth father was an alcoholic and abandoned my mother. She just couldn't handle another child. After I read that, I felt such rage at everyone—my adoptive parents, the agency, and especially my birth father for being such a loser. I had never felt anything so deeply. (Jonathan, age 39)

The search process can trigger a great deal of buried anger. Blocked from expressing unwelcome feelings about the adoption as a younger person, the adoptee's emotions often vault to the surface as incredible rage.

Betsie, in her work as founder and executive director of Adoption Network Cleveland, a large support and advocacy group in Ohio, often sees that anger and believes it originates from and is directed toward many different people.

At whom or what is the anger directed? The anger may be aimed at:

- the birthmother—*Why couldn't you keep me?*
- the birthfather—*Why couldn't you support your family? Why couldn't you get your life together?*
- the agency—*Why couldn't you help my mother? Why didn't you share the truth?*
- the adoptive parents—*Why didn't you talk to me more about my adoption? Why didn't you tell me the truth?*

Whatever the source, legitimate or misdirected anger is something many adoptees face. What to do with it then becomes the issue. While often viewed as something to avoid, anger can become the ally of the adoptee. Betty Jean Lifton comments, "We must remember that no matter how painful these waves of grief and anger are, they are part of the ongoing process of mourning that comes with reclaiming one's lost emotions and integrating them into the self. Adoptees find it hard to believe at the time, but the chaos carries healing in its wake."[1]

An adopted person's anger en route to healing is best encountered with help. Adoption counselor and adoptive parent, Barbara Wentz strongly suggests the adopted person seek an open ear from a third party as anger surfaces. Someone outside the relationship who would not be affected by the venting of the adoptee's anger can best be that buffer. It could be a therapist or a trusted friend who understands the dynamics of the healing process.[2]

Anger is one emotion that catches the adopted person off guard. Sadness and depression are two more.

Why Do I Feel So Blue?

Before I made the first call to my birth mother, I was excited, energized by the upcoming reunion. After that first call, I felt overwhelmed with sadness, even depression. In fact, through the evening and into the next day, I could only sit and cry. For days afterward, I felt as if a balloon had burst. I kept asking myself, Why am I reacting like this? It was a great contact. I should be happy! (Christine, age 34)

Some adoptees may for the first time be dealing with the losses adoption created in their lives. For some, the sound of their birthmother's voice is enough to invoke the incredible sadness they kept buried within.

"When an adoptee finds a birthparent," says Dr. Joyce Maguire-Pavao, "he is often not prepared for the depression that comes with that. The better the reunion, the harder it is sometimes. One reason," she continues, "is that there is a lost history. You meet the person twenty years later and you realize you missed all of his history, all of his connections. There is a real sadness about that loss."[3]

What Am I Afraid Of?

As an adopted person steps onto the rickety bridge connecting the unknown past to the unknown future, she places herself at great peril. The perceived reality of that peril grows as the adoptee confronts the taboos connected to the desire to search. The peril broadens as the adopted person faces the risk of losing relationships—first, her adoptive parents and then, perhaps, her birthfamily. The peril feels overwhelming as the adopted person attempts to scale the seemingly insurmountable wall of the adoption system. A sense of peril creates fear.

Fear can be an immobilizing emotion. It can temporarily block or permanently stop an adopted person's attempts to locate birth family members. What do some adoptees say they fear?

Rejection Again

I was afraid of being rejected again by someone I loved. Even though I'd never met my father and didn't know him, I loved him anyway! How could I not love the one person on earth whom others told me I was so much like. I was afraid that once I finally found the one person whose biological blueprint formed my life—he would say nope, you're not like me and I'm not interested in knowing you. (Susan, age 49)

I put off beginning my search for over ten years. The thing I feared the most was that my birth mother would have nothing to do with me. My worst fear did come true at the beginning. She denied knowing anything about me. Then she said she didn't want to see me. My friends supported me through this and encouraged me to give her time. At age seventy-six, it probably really disrupted her life. About four months after the initial contacts, I received a note that opened a window to our new, yet very fragile, relationship. (Sally, age 52)

Stirring Up Painful Memories

I had to overcome the fear that I would make my birth mother remember things she didn't want to remember. Maybe the circumstances of my birth were horribly painful for her and she had buried them long ago. If I came into her life, I wondered what might happen inside of her. (Mary Anne, age 40)

Ruining a Parent's Life

It took a lot of courage for me to pick up the phone and call my birth mother. Regardless of our blood tie, she was a total stranger to me and I to her. I was afraid she would hang up or deny that she was my birth mother. I was afraid I would ruin her life by contacting her. So many people told me she had moved on with her life and wouldn't want this interruption. I was afraid they were right. But I called. And she didn't hang up or deny she was my birth mother. I didn't ruin her life; even though she had moved on, she had never forgotten me. (Dana, age 31)

Displeasing a Parent

I had a real fear that my birth mother would be disappointed in the type of person I had turned out to be. What if I was a total disappointment to her? What if the life choices I had made were not the correct choices in her eyes? I had to convince myself I wasn't a bad person before I took the plunge and decided to search for her. I kept telling myself over and over that I was a good person. The reason I had to tell myself that was because I had serious doubts that this person I was searching for would agree with me. It's amazing how much control my birth mother had over my thoughts, feelings, and emotions about myself when I had absolutely no idea who she was. (Mary, 35)

Losing Control

I had a fear of losing control of my life. I felt that once I got the call, I could no longer control the search. When you choose to search you have all the control. You have the option to stop and start before going on to the next step. The match happened so fast, within a week and a half of registering with ISRR [International Soundex Reunion Registry]. I never prepared myself for getting the call. I never had the opportunity to even consider slowing down or stopping. Some people in my search group got information and they could back out and prepare for what might happen. I had to quickly prepare to meet people whom I had never known. (Beverly, 41)

Finding Dead Ends or Death

I was desperately afraid toward the end of my search that if I didn't find my father that something would happen to him and I'd never get the chance to actually know him and find out what he's like. I guess this fear was the biggest factor in my decision to start my search again at age thirty-five. I knew his age and I knew of his early lifestyle. It was imperative I find him while he was still living. (Susan, age 47)

Feeling sadness and facing rejection, disappointment, painful memories, loss of control, and dead ends are all legitimate experiences encountered by adopted persons as they prepare to cross over the bridge leading to reunion. Facing emotional upheavals prior to and during the early days of the reunion and confronting sadness and fear will strengthen their emotional backbone. Two other emotions may catch many searchers off guard.

Barbara Wentz, in her work with all members of the adoption triad during the search process, sees this as a common problem. "I compare the meeting of the birth parents and their child to that of young people who meet and fall in love. It's like being on a high where you can never get enough of being with someone. Acting on these feelings can do much damage to the fragile relationship unless there is proper emotional preparation," she warns.

"I recommend that there is no face-to-face contact without laying some groundwork. That groundwork can be in the form of letters and/or phone calls. Figuring out one's boundaries prior to meeting will help keep emotionally charged plans from overwhelming either party," she continues.

All during the search and reunion process, in order to keep your emotional life in balance, Wentz recommends the following:

• keep the other components of your life stable, don't make other major life changes.

- maintain and keep other healthy relationships, avoid becoming obsessed with the newfound person.
- keep a journal of events and feelings so you can evaluate your progress.
- move slowly with the meeting of extended family members.

Author Michelle McColm writes:

Because adoptees have lived for so many years with little or no information about their birth family, their curiosity and their need drives them to collect so much information so quickly. Wanting to meet increasing numbers of birth family members, even though the original and ultimate goal was to meet her birth mother is evidence of the depth of the adoptee's primal need to solidify her identity. All this activity leads to depression and/or exhaustion.[4]

In one day, Randy had met his birthparents, both sets of grandparents, three birth siblings and numerous nieces and nephews. He had listened to countless stories about the birthfamily. When he got home that night, he could barely relate the experiences of the day to his wife. All he wanted was to be alone. That feeling continued for days.

Riding out the emotional roller coaster brought on by the search and reunion may bring a new level of self-awareness and understanding. Although frightening and intense, the ride is a necessary part of preparing for the reunion and of the healing process. There's another crucial preparation step.

EXAMINE EXPECTATIONS ABOUT THE NEW FAMILY

Deep longings create profound expectations. Postponed desires inflate expectations of the outcome. For the adopted person whose inmost yearning is to reconnect to birthfamily members, examining his or her hope for the reunion experience may prevent unnecessary disappointment or heartbreak.

An important step in preparing emotionally for the search is to understand what expectations other adopted persons have experienced. Betty Jean Lifton addresses three types of expectations adoptees often encounter.

"Many adoptees have expectations going into the reunion that cannot be met," says Lifton. "The adoptee expects to be immediately transformed and not to be the same person, but the wonderful idealized self they might have been if they had not been adopted. They wake up the morning after the reunion and find they are still the same."

Continuing, she says, "Some adoptees expect to be instantly healed. Like Pinocchio. He is just a piece of wood and suddenly he comes to life with all the emotions. The adoptee identifies with Pinocchio and will say

'I felt dead before, but now I feel.' The problem is, if you have never felt before, you have never really known what grief or anger is or what loss is. If you allow yourself to feel for the first time, you can be overwhelmed by the feelings."

A third expectation not always met is a surprise to many adopted persons. Lifton says, "The adoptee is shocked to find he may not have unconditional love from his birth mother. They think all other people not separated from their mothers are getting unconditional love and they should be getting that too at the reunion."[5] What they find in some cases is that the birthmother does not have the emotional strength to enter the relationship or she has constructed a life and family exclusive of the possibility that the birthchild may someday want to reenter her life. "She may not be emotionally available to the adoptee," Lifton adds, "or she might be mentally unstable or even dead."

Transformation, healing, or unconditional love is what many adoptees have hoped for as they enter the reunion with birthfamily members. What are some ways to deal with these expectations?

Realize That Expectations Change

My expectations changed constantly both during my search and after my reunion. I expected my birth parents and me to become very good friends; at other times I expected them to suddenly not want anything more to do with me. The expectations of rejection were most pronounced when I told them things about myself of which I was ashamed. I wanted my birth parents to be proud of me. I thought they would reject me if they learned of my mistakes and regrets. I was finally able to overcome this when I realized they too had made mistakes and I still accepted them, flaws and all. As friends, none of us will ever have to be perfect. (Dana, age 32)

I Tried Not to Have Expectations

I tried not to expect anything from the reunion. My philosophy is that without expectations there can't be disappointments and anything that does happen is acceptable. Of course, I couldn't help fantasizing I would find my birth mother and we would get along wonderfully and live happily ever after. (Carol, 31)

I Tried to Have Low Expectations

I never had high expectations during my search. I always told myself that if somehow I could just have a photograph of my birth mother that would be enough. Or if I could stand across the street from her and someone would say, That is your birth mother, seeing her without her knowing it, I wouldn't ask for anything else. So I really don't think I had high expectations about how things would or should be. (Shelly, age 39)

I Tried to Keep My Expectations in Perspective

I tried to look at every aspect of my search from the perspective of each person currently involved or those who would be involved in the future. What were their feelings and fears? How would this affect their lives as well as those close to them? I read a lot of literature and studied different aspects of searching from those who had found or were still involved in the searching process. This helped me keep things in perspective. (Michelle, age 27)

I Tried to Look at Both Sides of the Coin

The possibility of a reunion was too important to me to let myself get carried away with the fantasy of a perfect reunion. I just kept my mind open and tried to keep my heart out of it. I knew that if I searched and found my birth mother and things turned out badly, I would still be satisfied knowing whatever it was I learned. If I learned that my birth mother wanted nothing to do with me, okay, at least I knew. I needed some idea of what she was feeling. I taught myself to be open to anything and to accept anything. (Carol, age 30)

BE PREPARED FOR WHAT YOU MAY FIND

At the age of twelve, Robert found out that he was adopted. As he began to explore his background, he discovered a painful secret. He had been sold to his adoptive parents for a substantial amount of money. The doctor had falsified the original birth certificate, leaving him no clues as to his birthparents' identity. Robert was a black-market baby. The door to his past was forever sealed. Circumstances for other adoptees have been just as traumatic.

Finding the Records Destroyed

In the late '50s, a maternity home in a midwestern state placed hundreds of babies into adoptive homes. Eleanor, now in her late forties, was one of those infants. However, when she began her search, she was devastated to find that the founder of the home had died and the family, seeing no need for all the clutter, had destroyed the records from the maternity home. Eleanor could not talk to her adoptive parents about her need to find information, and now she felt she had no way of finding out anything.

Finding a Criminal History

Once Richard discovered his birthfamily's name, the search process went relatively quickly. His birthfather had left a lasting impression upon the neighboring community. Richard's father was easily located, for he had been incarcerated for years. Richard felt shame and embarrassment over what he had found. Eventually, knowing the truth helped Richard put his entire life into a context he would not have had otherwise.

Finding Abandonment

Tracy could hardly believe what her parents told her regarding her adoption. For years she had been told her birthparents died in a car accident. Finally they told her the truth. Tracy had been left on a park bench late one evening and discovered by a passing patrolman. No clues to her birthparents were ever found. She had not only been abandoned physically at birth, she was abandoned emotionally, historically, forever.

Finding Death

For Tina, the issue of the search had consumed her every waking moment for the last several months. Recently she learned that her birthparents were dead, an option she had not allowed herself to consider. Finding that her parents were gone was a sad discovery, but Tina was able to find conclusion to her search through contacts with other family members.

Finding difficult birthfamily circumstances presents adoptees with a dilemma—what to do with what they know. For many, although the information is unpleasant or inconclusive, it provides them with a sense of completion, a sense of connectedness to the past.

Juggling the emotions, facing the fears, weighing the overload, confronting the people and issues—what a task for one person to handle! Processing emotional issues and balancing expectations are important preliminary steps in the search process. Knowing the important steps of initiating the process are equally essential.

INITIATING THE SEARCH

Betsie's Story

In a drawer, in a bedroom in Milwaukee, there is a photograph of a baby and her mother. The camera lens does not extend to the mother's face, just her arms holding the baby to her chest. The baby is dressed in a white gown. A hood pulled down over her head reveals a tuft of red hair. A peculiar silence surrounds this picture, a silence that has gone on for twenty-five years. For reasons unknown to them, on this day they begin to open up to each other and speak of the baby they gave up those many years ago.[6]

The red-haired little girl always knew she was adopted. From her earliest memories her parents had told her how much they had wanted a child and that she was special to them. They told her of the love her birthparents shared for each other and of their lack of readiness to care for a child. They loved each other, they loved her; but they had to let her go.

Once, when she was very young, the red-haired little girl and her adoptive mother went downtown to a building in an older part of the city where they lived. The mother told her inquisitive daughter this was the adoption agency. As they walked slowly down the dim hallway, the mother pointed to a room and said to her wondering child, "This is where you came from."

Even at such a young age, the little girl felt odd about that. It was a strange feeling to think the beginning of her life could only be traced to a stone building that seemed like a cold, unfriendly kind of place.

That first trip to see the building fed the little girl's curiosity. On many trips downtown her mother would point to the building and say something about it. She wanted her little girl to know all about her adoption story.

High school graduation brought a new adventure to the red-haired adolescent as she moved out of her parents' home into her own apartment. Work and college loomed ahead of her. However, with this step into adulthood and departure from her adoptive home, she began to think more about two other people. She began to think a lot about the other mother and father. *What did she look like? Does she have red hair? Where is she now? What about her young love? Who was he and where was he? Did he just walk away from her?*

More than once she pulled the heavy, awkward city directory out of the drawer. She was going to find the agency that handled her adoption. Anxiety gripped her. Questions flooded her. What if they won't answer my questions? What if they think it strange? Am I being disloyal to my parents? Does anyone else ever wonder? And the most threatening, Do I have a right to know? She didn't dial the number. She couldn't, not yet.

One afternoon while walking through a college bookstore, a book called *The Adoption Triangle* caught her eye. Pulling it off the shelf, she realized she had made an important find, *a miraculous find*, one that would change the course of her life as well as those of her adoptive parents and birthparents.

That fall evening she stayed up throughout the night absorbing the contents of the book. She discovered she wasn't alone, for others had asked the unaskable questions. She learned that she wasn't disloyal to her adoptive parents, that she could love them deeply and still have a need to find her roots. She also uncovered a spectacular secret. It was all right for her to know.

The miraculous find paved the way to begin searching for her birth family. It told her how to find support and how to look. It told her to contact the adoption agency and encouraged her to contact a national support group, which she did immediately. From that group contact, she learned something of incredible importance. She learned that in the state where she was born she could have the key that would open the door to her mystery, her original birth certificate. She wrote for it at once.

Not long after that, a manila envelope arrived at her home. Carefully opening it, she pulled out a copy of something. It was her birth certificate. She saw a name—Victoria Faith Boyer. At first she thought it was her mother's name. After studying it further, she realized it was her very own name. *I'm Betsie*, she thought to herself, *but I'm also Victoria Faith*. For her, it was like discovering a secret passageway in a house you had lived in for years.[7] She had another name, another identity, one that had been handed to her by a woman she had yet to know.

The birth certificate told her of a place not so very far away, Wallingford, Pennsylvania, and of a street where her birthmother had lived. It told her that her mother was twenty-one, not the teenager she had envisioned all her life. She knew she had to go to Wallingford, but first she had to get the information from the adoption agency. It was the right time now. She called them.

When the agency returned her call, they told her they had her information and would mail it to her. She told them she would be right down to get it, not wishing to wait a few more days. The clerk couldn't understand her hurry, but she didn't care.

The material in hand, she anxiously read it. Your birthmother was sixteen years old and blond. She had moved to the area to conceal the pregnancy. Your birthfather was seventeen and also blond.

The young woman didn't know what to believe. The ages confused her. However, she knew enough about genetics to realize that her red hair told her this paper from the adoption agency was wrong. The birth certificate, of course, had to be right. She would follow that lead. It led her to that city hundreds of miles away.

The search became somewhat of an obsession. She made many trips to Wallingford hoping to find anything that would connect her to her birthmother. In one particular trip she went to the high school where her birthmother had graduated. Nervous, yet determined, she braved the potential questions of a high school librarian and asked to see the yearbook for 1956. Within moments she looked at the face of the young woman who had loved her, kissed her, and said good-bye. No words could describe the feeling.

With much information in hand from her birth mother's class reunion list, the young woman returned to her own city reenergized. She had found who her mother had married and where she was now living. She decided to make contact. The young woman was within moments of connecting with the woman who had given her life.

Preparing to make the most important call of her life was intensely emotional. The young woman composed a script she was determined to follow. She had to be prepared to be rejected, but she just couldn't be rejected! Part of her birth name had been Faith. She felt it was a message to her. Besides, how could someone who named her Victoria Faith reject her?

She picked up the phone and dialed the number. Three short rings and a woman answered the phone.

"Is this Edith?" she asked. "My name is Betsie Norris and I'm calling you from Cleveland, Ohio. I have something very personal to talk to you about. Is this a good time? This is a very important and private matter."

Continuing, she told her mother, "I was born in Cleveland on February 20, 1960, and placed for adoption. I am happy and very well adjusted. I don't want to hurt you or your family or disrupt your life, but I'd like to talk with you. My research about my background has led me to you. I know this is quite a shock. Do you need some time?"

Before Betsie even finished, the woman on the other end flooded her with questions. "Where do you live? Do you have red hair? What do you do for a living? A nurse? Your grandmother had red hair and was a nurse."

She enthusiastically continued, "I have been praying for this call for twenty-six years. Bob will be thrilled."

"Who is Bob?" the young woman asked.

"Your father, my husband."

Had she heard right? He hadn't turned his back. He was there all the time!

"We'll call you tonight," the older woman said. "What is your number? Can I have your address?"

My address, Betsie thought sadly. *My mother doesn't know my address.*

"Just a minute, before you go, what time was I born?" the child asked her mother.

"In the evening," came the reply. "Right at dinner time, 6:01."

The red-haired woman hung up the phone, overwhelmed to learn that her life would now embrace the lives of two families. She now had five brothers—three on one side, her birth family; two on the other. She felt very rich.[8]

Walking through the journey of the search and reunion with Betsie and her family touches a deep, emotional chord. Her story paints a vivid picture of what experiences may lie ahead for adopted persons. In Betsie's case, the search, which took six months, encountered some brick walls of wrong information, delays, and blanks. But her persistence paid off.

For every searcher, whether young adult or approaching midlife or beyond, following some basic guidelines will help put together the scattered pieces of the puzzle.

RECOGNIZE THE EMOTIONAL STAGES OF THE SEARCH

"This Isn't a Big Deal"—Neutrality

"No big deal," Michael said, at least not at first. At twenty-six, he decided it would be interesting to know something about his background. He simply wrote the adoption agency for medical and background information.

In this first stage, according to author Jayne Askin, the searcher is commonly somewhat removed from the emotions of searching. Like Michael, the adoptee often expresses the reason for starting the search in very neutral terms and concentrates on the mechanics of the search, feeling no strong commitment to it.[9]

"What—No Information?"—Anger and Frustration

As bits of information come to the adoptee, the neutral attitude is replaced with emotions brought on by encountering reality. What Michael had not counted upon was that suppressed feelings and needs about his adoptive status would surface with incredible intensity as small amounts of information emerged and other crucial pieces were not available.

As the searcher attempts to gather information and confronts roadblocks, incredible frustration and anger can surface. For the first time in the search he may realize that important personal information is not readily his simply by birthright.

Askin believes anger is a critical step in working through the stages of the search. However, she cautions the searcher not to get stuck in this stage to the degree that it prevents him from processing deeper feelings. "Rage may cover feelings of rejection, insecurity, and guilt that have started to surface, or may sharpen them in instances where the searcher was already aware of his feelings."[10]

"It Consumes All My Thoughts and My Time"—Obsession

Once a searcher finds himself in the midst of the search, he is often surprised at the burning persistence of his obsession. Michael found himself thinking about the search when he woke up and he stayed preoccupied with it while attempting to get work done at the office. He vacillated between anger and resentment at being blocked from information, and anxiousness and doubt that he would ever find his birth parents.

Becoming obsessed with the search is normal. It's all part of the process. When it happens, the adoptee might feel as though he's losing his mind or emotional control. He may find himself talking about the search all the time to anyone who will listen.

Another adoptee, Dana, at twenty-five felt the same obsession. "I was very surprised at how much my search mattered to me. I really became obsessed about finding my birth parents, and every new piece of information I received just made me more determined to someday find them."

"This Is Overwhelming"—Withdrawal

Many searchers find themselves overwhelmed with frustrations, disappointments, anxieties, and setbacks. Sometimes, for a period of time, they must withdraw from the fray. Dana experienced this stage of withdrawal.

Searching often seems like a never-ending process; there's always one more letter to write, one more phone call to make, and one more brick wall to run into. I often felt overwhelmed, and I doubted sometimes if my search was worth all the time, money, and frustration that went along with the process. When this happened, I tried to step back for a few days and clear my head. I would talk with other searchers about my progress or lack thereof, and try to get suggestions from them.

Some searchers, according to Betsie, may step back from the process for more than just a few days. Some step back for months, even years. What happens is that the search brings up feelings they were unaware of and need time to process.

"Whatever Happens Is Okay"—Acceptance

Michael, after spending months in the search mode and finding one brick wall after another, made a decision not to carry his efforts any further for a while. He was at peace with this decision. Jayne Askin calls this stage acceptance. This stage comes as the adoptee accepts *whatever* is discovered. This can mean he may decide to continue the search or not. Either way, he accepts it. It could also mean that the searcher, having found valuable information, decides to take the opportunity to open the door to the new relationship.[11]

LEARN CONTACT STRATEGIES

Contact may be the most difficult part of the search process. It's important to determine if a letter or phone call will be the first mode of contact. Many factors play in this decision. The most important thing to remember is that *contact is the first impression after many years of separation!* Strategies for making contact are outlined in detail in appendix four.

Plan Ahead for the Reunion

Adoptees spend a great deal of time and energy during the search process. Some plan well ahead, formulating plans on how, when, and where to make contact and eventually meet. Others, caught up in the intensive nature of the process, fail to make such plans. One adoptee commented, "I didn't make plans on how to meet because I guess in the back of my mind I didn't think it would happen. I was surprised and completely thrown into a whirlwind because I hadn't thought this part of the process through."

Planning ahead is crucially important. According to Mary Jo Rillera, author of *The Adoption Searchbook*, there are several specific aspects to consider:

1. *Where will the reunion take place?* Deciding if the reunion will take place in the adoptee's home or birth parent's home or in a restaurant or office is an important decision. It should be a neutral point where each person feels comfortable and has the opportunity to limit the time together should the emotional need arise.
2. *Who will participate in the reunion?* Making a decision about who will be part of the initial reunion is critical. It depends on several factors—how much prior contact through mail or on the phone there has been, how comfortable a person is in larger groups, and how intense the first contacts were. It's important to get time alone with the newfound person. If the reunion takes place in a group, taking a walk together or finding another way to be alone is important.
3. *When will the reunion take place?* Deciding on a meeting time will be dictated by the geographical location to each other and the daily schedules of all involved. A meeting should be planned where time pressure is not a factor. There should be some correspondence or phone contact prior to the physical meeting.[12]

The First Contact—What It Was Like for Others

Initiating the first contact is an emotionally tense moment. A wide range of experiences confronts adoptees at this point of the search and reunion. For some, the outcome may be positive, warm, and inviting.

On the other hand, the fallout may be rejecting, painful, and crushing. What do those who have crossed this bridge say about their experiences?

Beyond My Wildest Fantasies

Though I fantasized the reunion would be perfect, I never really believed it would be as beautiful and passionate as it was and still is. Meeting Mary (my birth mother) has brought a sense of wholeness to me. I never knew what it meant to feel complete. Now I do. In addition to finding her, I found three half-sisters, a grandmother, and a whole mess of aunts, uncles, and cousins. That has taken some getting used to (Carol, age 30)

Rough at First

Learn as much as you can before you jump in not knowing how deep the water is. I thought I was prepared, but my first contact did not go well and I was absolutely devastated. I thought I was ready for anything, and I probably was prepared as well as I could have been. I had been a member of a search/support group for three years prior to finding my birth mother and making the initial contact. I strongly urge people to join a support group before making contact. The knowledge you attain through other people's experiences is absolutely invaluable in these situations. Luckily, my birth mother had a chance to think things over and called me back six days later. Now I feel that I'm forming relationships that will be in my life forever. Everyone in my birth mother's family (including my full-blooded brother and sister) is embracing me with open arms and unconditional love. (Mary, age 35)

An Awesome Experience

It was breathtaking to look at my mirror image with whom I share many personality traits and realize this was really happening. I gained three (so far) very nice friends and/or relatives, knowing there are more I have not yet had the pleasure of meeting. (Beverly, age 42)

Unexpected Anguish

I ignored advice to be prepared for anything, including rejection. I didn't allow myself to believe rejection would be part of my own journey. I just don't understand why my birth mother has no interest in even talking with me on the phone. What is so difficult about that? When I mailed the first letter, the reply came back: "Don't try to contact me ever again. You were part of my past." I have gone through such incredible periods of depression. What is she afraid of? Maybe she never told anyone about me. (Carolyn, age 43)

I Feel Like a Different Person

The result of my search has been a reunion with my birth mother and two half-brothers. I have even met my grandfather. All have welcomed me with open arms and hearts and we continue to have an ongoing and growing relationship that keeps getting better every day. I feel like the missing piece of me has now been put back into place and I am a whole person once again. (Shelly, age 39)

WHAT LESSONS HAVE WE LEARNED? SOME GOOD ADVICE

Although I'm an advocate for feeling emotions strongly and deeply, I advise keeping expectations in perspective. Do not allow fantasies to cloud reality. I would change nothing and do nothing differently than I did. I tried to allow things just to happen. I was fortunate for our reunion could not have happened any more beautifully than it did. (Carol, age 31)

Never give up searching, but have a strong faith in God and in yourself to accept whatever you find. Then go on with life. Make sure you have a good network of support to guide you and help you make wise decisions. (Tammy, age 42)

The first thing I try to get across to those I help in searches is that unless they are comfortable with their own feelings and willing to accept the bad as well as the good, they are probably not ready to search. The one thing that tips me they are ready is their concern for not making waves in their birth parents' lives.

I also tell them, don't give up. Sometimes you need to step back and go at the search from a different angle—but just don't stop. Take a vacation. Go to the beach or mountains. Come back renewed and start again. You are healing while you seek those lost loved ones and the missing pieces of your own story. (Susan, age 47)

Finding your birth parents will not solve any of your problems; in fact, it will probably create more problems. But it will help you understand yourself better and it will give you new strength to face your problems head-on and overcome them. If you feel, as I did, the need to search is so great that it just can't be overcome, then do it. Search for yourself, and realize that no matter what the outcome, you have completed an amazing task and you should be proud of yourself. (Dana, age 32)

A Word from Betsie

Our society has supported a huge amount of denial regarding some of the realities of adoption. In my search I had to acknowledge there had indeed been a loss. Before joining a support group of adoptees and birthparents, everyone I knew had only emphasized what I gained from adoption. I felt alone in realizing there was a lot more to it than that. What a relief when I found others who were speaking honestly and openly about the realities I knew but had never dared put into words.

As my search progressed, I openly talked with my friends and family about what I was doing. Many were very supportive. However, it was only the other searching or reunited adoptees whom I felt truly understood what was driving me to search.

It was a very emotional time for me with many ups and downs. I can't imagine having gone through it without a supportive community behind me.

Since my reunion, involvement in an adoption group has remained an important part of my life for several reasons. Along with my own personal benefit, I feel committed to helping the system change to meet triad members' needs better and to being there for others so they don't have to go through this alone.

NOTES

1. Betty Jean Lifton, *Journey of the Adopted Self: A Quest for Wholeness* (New York: Basic Books, 1993), 155.

2. Barbara Wentz, personal interview, March 1994. Used with permission.

3. Joyce Maquire-Pavao, "Counseling the Adoptee: Post Search," American Adoption Congress, Chicago, Ill, 1993.

4. Michelle McColm, *Adoption Reunions: A Book for Adoptees, Birth Parents and Adoptive Families* (Ontario, Can.: Story Book Press, 1993), 162.

5. Lifton, 165.

6. Allen Ravenstine, "The Lost and Found: A Young Woman Searches for Her Source," *Cleveland Edition: The News, Arts and Entertainment Weekly*, June 7, 1990, 1.

7. Ibid.

8. Ibid.

9. Jayne Askin, *Search: A Handbook for Adoptees and Birthparents* (Phoenix, Ariz.: Oryx Press, 1992), 27.

10. Ibid.

11. Ibid.

12. Mary Jo Rillera, *The Adoption Searchbook* (Westminister, Calif.: Triadoption Publishers, 1991), 185.

CHAPTER TEN

Patchwork Siblings: Adoptees in Postreunion Relationships

LaVonne H. Stiffler

My search took three and a quarter years. I knew I was "ordained" to find my birth family after my attorney went to Boston and "happened" to be picked up at the airport by my brother, a cab driver! I had been raised in my adoptive family as an only child, so the idea of a brother surprised me. Basically, I have accepted the idea and grown to enjoy it and relish the opportunity. What I have gained is my self, and I lost a load of isolation and negative self-worth.—Barry

After a long separation by the legalities of closed adoption, the uniting of siblings is like the construction of a patchwork quilt. Diverse pieces of handed-down genetic material may be joined in a surprising design, and then must be reinforced by creating a fabric backing of newly woven experiences. It may take years to do the stitching: either carelessly, so the connections fall apart; or attentively, pleasing in detail and securely bound. The ultimate feeling of comfort depends on the depth and resiliency of the inner "stuff." The work-in-progress may be used and enjoyed daily, occasionally, or stuck in a closet for the next generation to unfold.

From recent research, we are aware that a birthmother and her found child often have an instant reconnection, because of their shared prenatal and perinatal bond, their mutual separation trauma, and a cathexis or unconscious longing for the missing part throughout their lives.[1]

Sibling reunions are more complicated. Many were never told of the other's existence.[2] They may share both or only one of their birthparents, have different ethnological features, and speak different languages.

There are likely to differ in cultural values, religion, politics, and education.

I was raised as an only child. When I found my birth mother, she had three other children. The difficulty of all this was that she never told them about me.—Regina

Brothers and sisters may be unable to comprehend that life for the adoptee has not been and never will be "the same as" knowing and growing up with one's birthfamily. Depending on their personality characteristics and proximity of residence, they may be open or closed to any sort of relationship.

Birth siblings raised by either adoptive parents or birthparents have all inherited a "ragbag" of remnants that were discussed in chapters one and three. It is normal for them to struggle with the issues of loss, rejection, guilt/shame, and identity issues, whether or not they even knew they were adopted or that they had any family history of siblings being surrendered. In any case, they receive unconscious signals from either adoptive parents or birthparents who are secretly dealing in their own ways with the issues.

LOSS, GRIEF, REJECTION, GUILT, AND CONTROL ISSUES

One may imagine the variety of normal reactions to loss, grief, rejection, guilt, and lack of control that arise in each of the following scenarios:

• An adoptee or birthparent initiates the search. Birth siblings did not know of the adoptee's existence until the reunion. They feel betrayed by not knowing, lose their presumed birth order in the family, and grieve the loss of a shared childhood.

I will never forget the evening my mother called me and asked me to come over. When I got there, she sat me down and told me about my "older" brother—a child she relinquished for adoption 33 years ago. All of a sudden, I was not the oldest in the family. After the initial shock, I thought long and hard [about] what it would have been like to have an older brother. I still grieve the fact that we didn't have the chance to grow up together.—David

• An adoptee searches and finds gravestones of her birthparents at the end of the road. Then she questions—should I search for brothers and sisters?

I waited until both my adoptive parents had died before searching. I knew I would probably find that my birth mother had also died. What I found was that my birth parents had married shortly after my adoption and had four children. They were both gone. I had no one to ask if my full-blooded siblings even knew about me.—Carolyn

- Birth siblings may reject the adoptee, thereby influencing a birthparent to pull back for fear of alienating the others.[3]

The response was beyond comprehension for me. The meeting with my birth mother and two of my half siblings ended in absolute disaster. My birth mother was okay, at first. When my sisters told me that I had never been in their life and would never be, it was like an arrow pierced my heart. I had heard that sometimes birth mothers reject reunion, but never dreamed my sisters would. After that initial meeting with them, my birth mother stopped returning my phone calls. It was devastating.—Sandy

It was not until I was 25 that I learned I had three older sisters and one brother, all raised by our mother. I was angry, jealous, and hurt that they had a happy family and didn't want me to be a part of it. They got "our" mother and I didn't. I buried away that information for three years, until I took it out and began searching. Through a court inquiry, my birthmother said she did not want contact with me. I never got to speak to her, so I never had to promise I wouldn't contact my siblings. I found and called my oldest sister first. We talked for nearly 30 minutes. She was polite, but I knew she was very uncomfortable. She did not want to hurt her mother.

She did tell me about herself, and also explained she had thought of searching for me at one point. While working for the county, she was destroying some records, and ran across my relinquishment papers. That is when she found out her mother did not fall down the stairs with the result being my death, but rather I was placed for adoption.—Melissa

- An adoptee may encounter strong objections by adoptive parents or birthparents (which may or may not change later on), but as an adult disregards their wishes and goes on to find and relate well with a sibling.

My parents were never in favor of my searching for my birth parents. During my search, I found out that my birth mother had died, but that there were three younger children born to her. My parents still did not want me to go further with the search. I tried to assure them that this was not about them or my sisters with whom I had grown up. It was about completing part of my identity. I went ahead with the search, found three wonderful younger sisters, and have enjoyed getting to know them. They grew up knowing about me.—Rich

Who Does the Patchwork?

The reunion patchwork may depend primarily on who had the fortitude to do the arduous work of searching in the first place (although it may now occur rapidly through the Internet), and who is motivated to do the work of maintaining contact. In a family of "followers," there may be no one who has the initiative or social skills to work at relationship building. Initial euphoria after an intense search may end in a let-down of energy and severe depression over what has been lost.[4]

Like a patchwork quilt, the quality of sibling communication depends on *who* is trying to do the stitching, and *why*. If a birthparent tries to force upon the siblings his or her desire for their friendship, they will, most humanly, leap to a polarity response and back away. When the adoptee longs for a relationship and sense of belonging, and the other sibling is cool and rejecting, it is difficult to be patient and work through old feelings of rejection, guilt, and shame. However, if both are open to healing, change, and new pathways, it is possible to weave a satisfying friendship.

Building Relationships—Building Rapport

The building of rapport is a useful step in forming a relationship with one's stranger/siblings and in working through the identity and intimacy. As in any human interaction, the quality of either a short-term communication or a long-term relationship is directly a result of the quality, level, and consistency of rapport achieved.

Rapport is to communication as a needle and thread are to the construction of a quilt. What is rapport? It is a feeling of *joining*, of *being like* another person, of *being understood*. For some fortunate people, it is often automatic and intuitive. Rapport skills may also be learned and consciously developed, if one wishes to inspire mutual trust and a sense of genuine caring. There are four primary strands of rapport: physical, emotional, mental, and cultural.[5] How are these experienced in sibling reunions?

Physical rapport is the noticing of similar physical *characteristics* or adjusting one's body *position* and *posture* to approximate that of the other person. Spatial distance, gestures, and intensity of eye contact are other components. What did it feel like in sibling reunions?

- I see practically a mirror image of myself.
- We are alike physically and in our demeanor.
- I notice we have similar movements.
- We are similar in appearance. Our body language is relaxed, and our eye contact is constant.
- Having someone I look like has changed my life.
- I compared our noses, fingers, eyes, hair, etc. We look and act alike.
- My sister and I have the same "hooded" eyes and the same missing teeth.
- We have some physical traits in common, but differ in height. Our body language is easily understood, and we are responsive to hugs of greeting and parting.

- I feel a sibling bond in our body language and eye contact.
- The ways we move or look at each other indicate closeness.

Emotional rapport is the noticing and matching of general emotional *intensity* (high, medium, low) and *direction* (optimistic, neutral, pessimistic) of the other person, before attempting to shift to another state. What did it feel like in sibling reunions?

- My sister and I are both caring, open, and sentimental.
- My brother and I have a similar sense of humor. We can laugh together about movies, TV, music, etc.
- Our personalities are similar. We love and trust each other.
- We have the same artistic temperament and are both professional women.
- We are similar in our feelings and need to be touched. We need approval of others and are unhappy in relationships. We were all wild and angry teens, bad-tempered and bull-headed.
- If we had grown up together, I imagine we would have fought a lot. Now we share a mutual affection.

Mental rapport is noticing how and on what the other person's *attention* is focused, and adjusting one's own attention to match it. In talking about what interests the other person, a shared direction or intention may develop. How was it experienced in sibling reunions?

- Our political beliefs are similar.
- We have many of the same likes and dislikes.
- We had/have similar activities and experiences.
- We talk most about superficial things; we both like to talk.
- We have similar ideas and hobbies.
- We have respect for each other and are very curious about what we like and do, and what we want to do in the future.
- We both enjoy sewing, cooking, our kids, and caring.
- We each have predispositions to creativity, played out differently in our lives. We mutually discuss our interests and things we enjoy.

The three categories highlighted are likely to have strong genetic components, pieces of fabric handed down from parents, grandparents, and unknown ancestors. This is confirmed by behavioral genetic studies of twins reared apart. Concerning the effect of environmental influences on behavior, researchers say that many can never properly be called "shared," even by family members living in the same household, because they are uniquely experienced by each individual.[6] A fourth category, *cultural rapport*, is greatly influenced by the nonshared environments in which each person develops. For adoptees and newly found siblings, it is in this area where most obstacles seem to lie along the road to rapport.

Cultural rapport is noticing and respectfully matching the behavioral *norms* and cultural *values* of a person, group, or locality. These may include dress, etiquette, laws, music, language, and vocabulary. How did cultural rapport work out in sibling reunions? Those who found matches and mismatches in cultural affinity described them like this.

Match

- I feel pride in my sister's character.
- We are similar in our love for art, music, and literature.
- Our lifestyles are similar.

Mismatch

- My brother was raised to think success is how much money you make; I was not.
- When I hear his voice, I feel a bizarre mix of familiarity and alienation, due to his regional accent.
- We seldom see each other. We speak different languages. I grew up in the United States, and my brothers are Korean.
- My sister and I were raised differently and have different values, socially and economically.

Culture and Environment—Further Observations

One adoptee realized, "I never knew how much *language* is wrapped up in familial relationships." With no shared history, vastly different mind-body sensory representations are conveyed by such simple words as "Christmas," "grandfather," "home," "discipline," and "birthday party." Even siblings raised together have uniquely organized and interpreted see-hear-feel-smell-taste memories. For an adoptee, these memories came from an entirely different cultural environment.

For siblings reformulating their identity at this point, there is a major difference between: (1) being born into a family, with ongoing sensory experiences and an oral genealogical history from the very beginning; and (2) an adoptee in reunion with the birthfamily, gathering bits of information from that time on. In the first instance, the weaving of a sense of identity through constant experiences involves the mental function of *retrieval*. In contrast, for an adoptee, the postreunion discovery of genetic idiosyncrasies, talents, and life patterns involves the mental process of *recognition*. ("Aha! She giggles just like me!")

Anna, a birthmother, said, "It's interesting that I have been giving my

'found' son more written family history and photographs than I have
ever given to the two children I raised. I seem compelled to do that, and
to do it quickly, as though to catch him up to speed!"

For a person whose life path was behind the walls of closed adoption,
connections to the past were distorted and denied. A time line with de-
leted parts is an unsteady base from which to form a physical and spiritual identity and to construct a future. Over the chasms lie tangled
threads of loss, rejection, shame, grief, and helplessness.

What Does the Reunion Feel Like?

In a survey of adoptees and siblings who have been in reunion from
four months to sixteen years, self-reports of the primary emotions on
finding each other indicate: initial joy, excitement, and wonder; tinged
with guilt, jealousy, and confusion; subsiding into curiosity and relief.

I had grown up always knowing that I had an older brother. Our reunion felt
like wonderment. My missing brother had been like a story character, a fantasy
hero, because I was so young when I first heard about him. (Kathy)

It felt like an incredible surprise. When searching, I was so focused on my birth
mother, I never thought about the possibility of siblings. When I learned I had
two younger sisters, it simply felt like a surprise. (Jonathan)

I felt strange, just knowing I had a sibling. I had grown up an only child in a
very adult world. It felt very strange to realize that I had a sister. Then I began
to feel very sad for missing our growing up together. (Robin)

I was filled with so much excitement and joy and also with a lot of questions.
At one point, my newly found brother wondered if I had been trained by the
FBI, because I asked so many questions! (Dan, age 47)

My reactions were very mixed. I first thought, "Wow, this is great!" Later, I felt
guilty that I relate so well with one brother, yet struggle to get along with the
other. I guess it might have turned out that same way if we had been raised
together. (Mary Ann)

My initial excitement was dashed when I met the elder of my two younger half
brothers in our mother's kitchen. He said hello to my husband and was told by
our mother to "say hello to your sister." He did, and that was it. He went to his
room. As I was preparing to leave before he came in, I simply left. I've never
seen him again. My reunion with the younger half brother was not much better.
He was friendlier and spoke to me for just a moment before going in the house.
On his way, he was nice enough to say "good-bye" and "nice to meet you."
That's it.

When I mention these two men as my brothers, I don't have any emotional feelings one way or the other. I affectionately think of them like "Darryl and Darryl" from the old Bob Newhart TV show, because they live way out in the country and have long hair and very long beards. It struck me funny when I thought of my playing the part of the sister, saying "this is my brother Darryl and this is my other brother Darryl," like they always did on that show. (Karen)

What Influences Continued Contact? What Factors Limit Contact?

Whether reunited siblings remain in any type of continued contact is based on a range of both *affection* and *obligation*. (This is true of the contacts of any adult siblings.) Fifteen adult adoptees answered a questionnaire concerning the issue of continued contact. These fifteen respondents seem representative of a larger sample. Of the fifteen:

• Eight said it is 100 percent affection that compels them to meet, call, or write.

I feel truly blessed to have such a relationship with my newly found younger sister. I was the only girl in my adoptive family and always longed for a sister. We are close and email regularly. (Kelly)

We have known each other now for four years. We grew up within an hour's driving distance and meet for lunch almost monthly. It is uncanny how much she thinks like I do, and we look so very much alike. (Christy)

• One feels 75 percent affection and 25 percent obligation.

I am very thankful to have found my brother and do enjoy being with him and his family. He wants to get together more often than I do. I think it is because he wants to catch up on all the years we missed. (Ryan)

• Two of the adults acknowledged 50 percent affection and 50 percent obligation prompts their continued contact.

I feel if I turn my sister down too often when she wants to get together, I will hurt her feelings, so I say yes. I love her, but don't feel like a sister to her—a good friend, perhaps. (Hazel)

• Three attributed their letters, phone calls, or personal visits 80 percent to obligation and only 20 percent to affection.

I know, in order for my mother to feel good about this whole thing, I need to contact my birth brother at least once a month. I do it for Mom. (Jeannie)

Affection and obligation are two factors that influence continued contact. There are also factors that limit an ongoing connection in sibling reunion. One of the primary limiting factors to an ongoing relationship commonly is residential proximity.[7]

We lived three states apart when we were first reunited. It was very hard to develop an ongoing relationship. My husband was than transferred to the city where my sister lives, and our communication and sense of connection really solidified after that. (Jackie)

Living a great distance from one's reunited sibling is a strong factor in development of connectedness. Other hindrances to a feeling of closeness are cited as age difference, occupation, different lifestyles and values, and birthmother's attitude.

It has been very difficult to see my younger sibling as a brother. He is fourteen years younger than I am, and we are at such different points in our lives. He has a very young family. Both my children are out of high school. (William)

What Do Reunited Siblings Talk About?

Brothers and sisters who say that they communicate well and want to spend the most time together seem to be those who choose to focus on their *sameness* and find *differences* interesting and not personally threatening. As both persons find a comfortable pace for moving forward, they are drawn by a measure of rapport that increases as they notice they are *alike* in some aspects, yet intriguingly *different* in others. Nonjudgmental curiosity sparks intimacy and confidence.

An initial search for *sameness* frequently leads to the discovery of *synchronicity*: meaningful, awesome, or God-directed "coincidences" that have connected them through the years of their separation. Finding they both have similar bumps on their earlobes may be just as significant as learning they have the same first name, occupation, china pattern, golf clubs, or favorite vacation spot.[8]

It is fascinating to hear from those who say they "always knew" they had siblings somewhere "out there" and have a psychic connection. They may speak the same words with the same inflection at the same instant, or be able to sense at a distance when the other is ill or in danger.

It is easy to talk about superficial, neutral subjects for most reconnected siblings. For others, art, music, and literature are comfortable topics. Some say they enjoy conversing about their likes, dislikes, sports, food, traveling, their relatives, and the search process. One happy adoptee said, "We can discuss almost anything, because my brother really seems to want to know who I am. He is a good listener and can, for the most part, be objective about anything I say."

It Is Easy to Talk About

- College, nieces, men, neutral ground; she gives good advice.
- Most anything; my sister is open like me.
- Art, music, literature, because we have common interests.
- Superficial things.

- Everyday, mundane things, because we don't have mutual interests.
- We both like to talk!
- Most anything, because he really seems to want to know who I am.
- He's a good listener and can, for the most part, be objective.
- Just about anything I say.
- Everything, from likes to dislikes, sports, food, traveling, my search, and, of course, our mother.

It is often difficult to talk about family or other relationships from the past. As a sibling said, "It seems we are afraid of being rude, hurting Mom, and ruining an already delicate relationship by sharing honest feelings." No one wants to hear criticism of the parents who raised them, and loyalties are guarded. If there is disparity in education and lifestyle, these topics are also avoided. Although they wish they could, some find it difficult to say, "I love you."

It Is Difficult to Talk About

- It seems we are afraid of being rude, hurting Mom, and ruining an already delicate relationship by sharing honest feelings.
- Mom and Dad, because of loyalty. She is often negative about them.
- Family or other relationships, because it is painful. I feel rejected and misunderstood when this brother criticizes our mother. I avoid saying any sentence that has "Mom" in it.
- Mom, because my sister didn't know her.
- Bringing up the past. It's hard for me to talk about our mother's death.
- I am angry to think Mother knew about my sister, and never told us.
- My personal feelings; I am still learning to trust.
- My success and lifestyle.
- I cannot and still do not express my feelings to anyone; it's my self-preservative. I don't share even with my children and spouse, because of the fear of rejection.
- My younger brother is the "protector" of feelings and perceptions in the family, and wants everyone to like each other. This makes it hard for me to talk to him about the angry or upset feelings that I have with others in the family.
- It's difficult for me to say, "I love you."

How Has Search and Reunion of Siblings Impacted Personal Growth and Development?

The quest for personal development in control/mastery, intimacy, and identity[9] is expressed as gaining "a sense of self, of belonging, a mirror image of myself, unconditional love, filling a void, and adding a living limb to my family tree."

The most challenging aspects of a sibling reunion vary with the circumstances. Adoptees mention trying to "fit in" after so many years, having no shared memories, maintaining contact without interfering, dealing with anger at being relinquished and genetic sexual attraction. Their siblings find difficulty in sharing a mother who is intensely focused on the found child, in forgiving parents for giving up the brother or sister in the first place, and in dealing with jealousy if the adoptee had more material advantages. For everyone, learning to understand the other's feelings is often a dilemma.

The Most Difficult Part of My Sibling Reunion Has Been

- Sharing our mother.
- Forgiving my father for giving up my sister, and my not growing up with her.
- Maintaining contact without my interfering in their lives.
- Distance—not being able to see each other often.
- How to build a close relationship without memories.
- I am angry because the other siblings got the chance to know and be loved and cared for by their/our mother.
- We grew up in different countries and speak different languages. I feel sad about their situation.
- Trying to fit in after so many years. I wanted to be accepted, but it felt very awkward. My birth mother talks about me all the time, and my half sister who is only 11 months younger was jealous of me. I felt misunderstood, and it was unfair.
- On the phone, my elder brother had said he was going to take time off work and take me places and do things with me. However, when I actually arrived, it was quite different. Instead of taking off work, our visits were limited to an hour or so during the evening. Of course, I took it personally, and my feelings were hurt greatly. I assumed he just didn't want to spend time with me.
- Guilt and frustration. A lot of my brother's and my emotion is confused with physical attraction to one another, without the benefit of childhood boundaries. He has kept a lot secret from his wife, particularly since he can't reconcile his attraction to me. At times he can't separate the infatuation from the genetic bond. My husband is having to share in my emotional ups and downs, and sometimes it affects my patience level with my children.
- My sister and I have nothing in common, other than the same birth mother. We don't look alike, have no mutual interests, don't have the same lifestyles or morals. (Our mother says she favors her birthfather!) We were both adopted by upper-middle-class families and given every benefit. However, I was adopted at four months, and my sister at ten years of age. I know this made quite a difference in how we react to circumstances, and that it was much more difficult for her. I try to take this into consideration.

Coping strategies in dealing with the emotions of reunion are like those of most human beings, either: repression, silence, avoidance, and anger; using 12-Step or spiritual disciplines; taking walks, reading, or other diversions; or honest, straightforward verbal communication— with friends, a parent, the sibling, or a therapist. Many have encountered helping professionals who are not adequately trained in the lifelong, intergenerational issues of adoption. Although there have been challenges, there have also been many gains.

What I Have Gained from My Sibling Reunion

- Nieces whom I adore; having a sister.
- Seeing practically a mirror image of myself. I am confident that with time we will become very close, as if we were never separated.
- I have gained a living limb on my family tree.
- It has provided a sense of belonging. I had always felt that almost everyone else knew something about themselves that I didn't know about myself. I feel that the reunion has filled that void.
- I have gained a sense of self, having "real" family for the first time. I know who I am; I know where I'm going; and I know who's going with me.
- Truth of my identity. I finally got to touch, look at, and get to know my own flesh and blood.
- A sense of self, with another part of family to enjoy.
- To finally connect with an actual relative who looks like me.
- At age 35, to finally feel a sense of who I am. I see pieces in me that mirror different persons in my birth family. I feel more secure and confident, because I am now "like" someone else. I have also gained a new perspective on other members of the birth family by looking at them differently, through my brother's eyes.
- Affection and unconditional love—I'm not alone anymore.
- I have gained an extended family. I was able to attend my sister's wedding. We laugh together when we go to concerts or musical events we all enjoy.
- A sense of well being. A feeling that I can let go of some things that used to be important, because now I have some truth, and that is the most important thing an adoptee can have. Upon meeting my brother, I went home, cleaned out, and threw away 27 boxes of "junk" that I had been carrying and moving around since I was 18.

ADVICE FOR SIBLINGS CONTEMPLATING SEARCH

Advice for others preparing to seek and meet siblings is clear: "Do it!" In a composite of the words of those in reunion: "Don't stop looking until you find them. Follow your instincts. Don't give up hope! Don't give up, ever. Let no one talk you out of looking. Keep searching. It will never get easier, but at least you will stop wondering. Hang in there and talk about it. Read everything you can about other reunions and searches. Join a support group and keep a journal or diary of your feelings. All kinds of different feelings are OK and natural. You are not the 'only one' out there. See a therapist specifically trained in adoption issues, to deal with the overwhelming emotions.

"Upon finding your siblings, don't be judgmental. Accept people as they are. Be prepared for people whose emotional frame of reference is quite different from yours. Be respectful of others' differences and take care of yourself, because the process of finding birth family is an emotionally heavy trip. Be grateful for any degree of contact that you have, because it is more than what you had before.

"Have patience. Even things that don't look like they are working out, sometimes will surprise you and change. People are emotionally ready for things at different times in their lives. Adoption really is a lifelong process. Searching is just a beginning. Finding and reunion are also just beginnings. Even after many years, we are all in the beginning throes of what is yet to come. Every day will redefine your relationships."

The simple eloquence of that advice may be summed up: As the separate components are stitched together over time, the resulting patchwork of a sibling relationship may not be that of one's initial dreams, but it is valued as tangibly real and full of authentic history at last.

NOTES

1. David M. Brodzinsky, and Marshall D. Schechter, eds., *The Psychology of Adoption* (New York: Oxford University Press, 1990).

2. Randolph Severson, *Sibling Reunions: A Letter to Those Who Have Been Contacted* (Dallas, Tex.: House of Tomorrow Productions, 1993).

3. Betty Jean Lifton, *Lost and Found: The Adoption Experience* (New York: Harper and Row, 1988).

4. Jayne Schooler, *Searching for a Past* (Colorado Springs: Piñon Press, 1995).

5. Mary Hale-Haniff, *Training Manual* (Miami: Brief Therapy Institute, 1994).

6. E. Mavis Hetherington, David Reiss, and Robert Plomin. *Separate Social Worlds of Siblings: The Impact of Nonshared Environment on Development* (Hillsdale, NJ: Lawrence Erlbaum, 1994).

7. J.S. Gediman, and L.P. Brown, *Birthbond: Reunions Between Birthparents and Adoptees—What Happens After* (Far Hills, N.J.: New Horizon Press, 1989).

8. LaVonne H. Stiffler, *Synchronicity and Reunion: The Genetic Connection of Adoptees and Birthparents* (Conroe, Tex.: L.H. Stiffler, 1992).

9. Betty Jean Lifton, *Journey of the Adopted Self: A Quest for Wholeness* (New York: HarperCollins, 1994).

CHAPTER ELEVEN

Synchronicity in Reunion

LaVonne H. Stiffler

The final quarter of the twentieth century witnessed the explosion of an unprecedented phenomenon: the reunion of tens of thousands of adult adoptees with their birthfamilies. Television, film, and print media captured some of their euphoria and tears. There are five to eight million adoptees in the United States.[1] As more of them hear about the possibility of finding their roots, reunions multiply. A 1984 national survey by a former Washington, DC, organization, Kinship, estimated five hundred thousand adult adoptees were then seeking or had found their birthfamilies.[2] That number has now increased greatly.

Internet resources help make quick work for some fortunate searchers in the twenty-first century. Nevertheless, reunions are usually the result of an arduous search process, particularly in the United States, where adoption records are still sealed in many states. Changes toward open adoption, guardianship arrangements, and legislative action for open records are resulting from the recent societal and psychological shifts in breaking down walls of secrecy. Policymakers are being educated, as individuals and groups articulate their experiences with the shackles of closed adoption.[3]

After reunion, families begin to build relationships and to piece together the years that have intervened since their separation. They may discover mutual physical characteristics, creative talents, personality styles, distinctive mannerisms, and idiosyncrasies. Particularly surprising are incidents of intuition and synchronicity, suggesting a continuance of the prenatal bond, genetic programming, or a psychic connection that transcends space and time. Dreaming of one's child in specific danger, naming a later baby by the unknown name of the firstborn, vacationing in the same location, making identical purchases, and beginning to search at the same time are examples of the types of anecdotes gathered from seventy reunited families for doctoral research in behavioral science.[4]

A few decades ago, stories such as these were not easily obtained, because birthmothers hid behind a self-imposed and societal secrecy, and adoptees felt the subjects of origins and reunion were taboo in their adoptive homes. In the safety of adoption support groups, which arose in the mid-1970s, they started to express their feelings and embark on the journey of search. They soon began to share stories of the unusual circumstances in timing and location that led them to each other, or their identical choices in occupation, grooming, or music.

The anecdotes that follow are all from known contributors, but their names have been changed. They are extracted from the original study, in which participants told of multiple coincidences in categories of: names, search activity, places, vacation places, dates, courtship and marriage, birth, death, crises, intuition, dreams, memory, genetic architecture, religiosity, education, and occupations. Many told of coincidences between members of the extended adoptive families and birthfamilies.

The stories invite us to feel the awe of reconnected families and to speculate *When? Where? How? and Why?* How does synchronicity function when an adoptee is separated from his or her birth family? Are reunions the result of answered prayer or unconscious longing for the missing part?

WHAT IS SYNCHRONICITY?

An operational definition of synchronicity has two consistent components: (a) a coincidence, "a notable concurrence of events or circumstances without apparent causal connection"; and (b) inherent, subjective meaning, evidenced by feelings of surprise and awe, "solemn and reverential wonder,"[5] in the persons involved. A synchronicity may arise from a choice, a chance, or a change; it may be a name, an encounter, an event, a characteristic, or a hunch that is identical, slightly similar, or simply surprising. For example, an unexpected gesture or a misspelled word seems to produce the same awesome feeling of an enduring genetic connection as would a vivid premonition of crisis or the precisely timed initiation of search activity.

When I first met my son, during our conversation, whenever he was puzzled about something, he would lean forward on his elbow and pull at his eyebrow, kind of a nervousness. This was a habit his birthfather had! When I mentioned it later, he said his adoptive mother had always commented about it. It was irritating to her, and nobody else in the family did it. (Grace.)

My mother and I are both poor spellers, and we misspell the same simple words. I remember when I got the first letter from my mother and left it on the kitchen counter. My twins came home from school and said, "Who are you writing to, Mom?" Our handwriting is identical too! (Lynne)

As we examine synchronicity, we will take a brief look at how it is evidenced in the following aspects:

Synchronicity in timing of search activity

Synchronicity in location: residence, occupation, and vacation

Connection by a Designer

Connection by names

Connection by intuition

The chapter will conclude with an examination of the significance synchronicity plays in the lives of the birth families and adoptive families who experience it, and what we may choose to learn from them.

Synchronicity in Timing of Search Activity

Like the migratory and homing behaviors of animals, which have been known, admired, expected, yet mysterious to mankind of all generations, parent-child reunions have an element of awe. After their initial contact, families begin to talk about the intricacies of the search process, and many are astonished by synchronicities in location and timing that led them to each other. In the initial study of seventy families, nine of them had intersection in location during search, and twenty-three had coincidences in the timing of their search. Two searching adoptees were drawn to timely encounters with judges who unexpectedly opened records for them; four persons were approached by strangers who offered surprising information. A mother and daughter began working at the same store within days of each other. Another mother reached her son just before his planned move to a distant country. Members of four families began to make inquiries in a search for one another at the same time.

I became obsessed with finding my son in January, but did not act on it until September. When I contacted the agency, I found out that my son had requested non-identifying information on me in January! I know I will find him eventually. I am also an adoptee who found my birthmother nine years ago. We have enjoyed a highly successful reunion—extended family included. My mother and her sister made the decision to search for me the same year that I searched for them. (Mandy)

Before searching for my son, I accepted a job 700 miles away from where I had been living, unknowingly, in the university system where he had just received a master's degree! Why at this particular time did I hunt for my son? It turned out he was shortly thereafter moving out of the country for several years! When I got to the state I called him on the phone; we had a very long conversation. He wanted to see me, so we had breakfast together the next morning. We got along great. I talked with him for 12 hours, and now I'm going to be corresponding with him. (Rachela)

I had been searching for my husband's birthmother for four years and getting nowhere, so I put an ad in the paper in the town where he was born, asking for information, giving his birth name. I waited and waited and received no reply. In the meantime I wrote to two schools and received a package from one. In the enclosed photocopies was a picture of a girl with the right name. Our search assistant did a DMV check to see if this woman's birth date was the same as the date we had for the birthmother. We had a match! So we sat down to try to figure out how to contact her. Saturday morning I wrote a sample letter for my husband. When I went to the mailbox that day, there was a letter from his birthmother! She had read my ad in the paper (placed months earlier), but had been afraid to answer until this time. (Edna)

Synchronicity in Location: Residence, Occupation, and Vacation

Thirty-nine reunited families found meaning in the way their lives had intersected at certain locations or places: twenty-six were instances of ordinary residence, work, or migration; 13 were vacation spots; nine were related to search activity; and six involved persistent thoughts of a certain place. One mother had unknowingly spent an annual Columbus Day weekend in the same motel as her daughter. Another adoptee for nine years chose to spend her vacations in a small, remote area where several generations of her birthfamily had property. The following words were used by some to describe what they believed to be an extraordinary drawing toward particular locations: pull, distinct energy, like a distant magnet, strong connection, midpoint, and our paths crossed.

Residence

We lost our baby boy to a church adoption agency in 1960, and the birthfather and I soon went in different directions. Through a path that included other spouses, children, and divorce, we made an unexpected reconnection. We married in 1990 and resolved to break through every obstacle to find our son. After a two-year search, we found him, a handsome young man named Steve by his adoptive parents, in a city of 500,000. Our reunion was a remarkable thrill in itself, but the surrounding circumstances still leave us astonished. Steve and his wife had unknowingly purchased and were living in the very house where his paternal great-grandparents had raised a large family! A great-aunt still living next door had attended the christening celebration of Steve's new son, never imagining they were related. (Mona)

The search itself was uncanny. Nearing the town where I was born, I felt a pull, a distinct energy. As we traveled the town, I began to feel "hot and cold." My companion at first was skeptical, but she soon began to trust my intuition. We camped where my family always went swimming as children. We parked in a vacant lot where my grandfather once owned a store. (Jordan)

I was flabbergasted to learn that for three years I had been living just three blocks away from my mother, during the time of my search. It was a neighborhood where my husband grew up and had lived for 18 years. My mother had been there for nine years. (Cathy)

Occupation

My daughter, who was adopted in the Midwest, recently found me after a three-year search. Our first surprising discoveries are: My daughter works in the film business, as I do; she lives in Los Angeles, as I do, and lives about five blocks from me. When she first visited me, it turned out she had looked at the apartments I live in when she was first looking for a place to live, but they were too expensive. She found another place, which happened to be an apartment that I looked at previously. We use the same bank and stores, due to our proximity. Go figure! (Ken)

My long search for my mother was getting nowhere. One day at work a co-worker asked if I was having any luck. Another employee overheard us and said, "Luck about what?" I took out my birth certificate, and the woman said, "I might know somebody who can help." She asked me for a baby picture and took it home to compare with one she had. She was shocked. She was my mother! She had been trying to find me for twenty years. It is a large city of 250,000, and I started working at this store just a few days before she did. We had worked there on different shifts for six months before our wonderful discovery. And that's not all: Another girl that we worked with was raised by my birthfather! She knew exactly where he was. So it was amazing; all in one day I found my mother and knew where my father was too. (Anita)

Vacation

Especially surprising to some reunited families is uncovering the fact that they have chosen to vacation in the same place. Are vacation spots selected in a special state of consciousness?

As a child living in California, I used to say that I wanted to go to the Florida Keys. That was where my birth family went each summer! When I was 33, they took me there too. (Barb)

In 1971 my husband and I went to a town at the other end of the state for a getaway weekend. Why we went there, I'll never know; there's really nothing there. What I didn't know was that my son and his adoptive family had moved there; they were living there at the time. (Karla)

When I met my birthfather, we talked of certain things we've done and places we have gone in our lives. There is a very small town in New Hampshire that has an annual Fourth of July mayoral-type festival. It turns into a big joke, and everybody laughs and has a good time. We both attended yearly for years without knowing, of course, that I was there and he was there! I was brought up in Massachusetts, but we had a summer place in New Hampshire only a mile away from where this took place. Until I became a teenager my adoptive parents took me, but then it was my choice. As an adult I attended for 10–15 years. My father had to come 14 miles from his home to attend. (Sonya)

Connection by a Designer

How likely is it that separated family members will find connection through a meaningful coincidence? Certainly all human beings have parallels in basic life patterns: We are born, have dwelling places, eat, play, sleep and dream, go to school, mate, work, worship, and die. There are bound to be occasional chance coincidences with people, events, and circumstances, even between unrelated lives, and most of these are never known.

What could be more mutually life affecting than the unnatural separation of a mother from her baby? So when a mother has a vivid premonition that her child is in danger, or an adoptee moves across the country for no logical reason, is there a higher force directing them? After the peak experience of reunion, families often seek answers to the mystical nature of their connection.

I feel that God led me in the right way, because there were so many things that could have prevented me from ever finding my son. (Marilyn)

Could a Designer Have Directed This Connection?

It was the fall of 1994.[6] A young woman began a journey that would eventually answer lifelong questions, yet lead to a greater mystery of how the events happened. Katherine, adopted as a one-year-old, was only eighteen when her adoptive mother died following surgery. The loss to Katherine, of course, was incredible. It would be two years following her adoptive mother's death before she began her search journey. Katherine's caseworker shared this incredible story.

I remember the fall morning when Katherine walked into our agency. She wanted to talk with someone about her birthparents and family. Following the mandated court process, I was able to open up her file to give her non-identifying information. Our court also allowed me to search for the missing person and, if found, facilitate a reunion. I was devastated by the total lack of information, except for one thing—her birthmother's (which of course, I couldn't share). I relayed to her that I saw little hope of ever finding her mother. I only had only two pieces of information to go on: her birthmother's name, Crystal Litton; and where she lived, Georgia. I encouraged Katherine to keep in touch with me.

About 10 months after this visit with Katherine, I heard that a nearby county agency was computerizing all their adoption records. I wanted to do that for our agency, so I paid a visit to that county. The computer operator said to me that the best way to learn how they did it, was to watch. She reached down into a box of nearly 1,000 files and randomly picked up one. She laid it on the desk and began to type in a birthmother's name: Crystal Litton! I stared at it and then shouted, "That's Katherine's mother!" She wasn't living in Georgia, but right next door. I contacted Crystal shortly after that, and Katherine and her mother and siblings were reunited. I am absolutely convinced that there was a "Designer" in the connection business that day. (Cheryl, caseworker)

Birthparents, adoptees, and adoptive parents have not only experienced synchronicity through timing, location, and by a Designer, but also have found amazing connections in similar names.

Connection by Names

Human beings attach great significance to words and names. We name everything from our children to pets, athletic teams, and hurricanes. Until the late Middle Ages, when hereditary last names came into English usage, only one name was given to a person. A common custom in many cultures is to name a child for relatives. It is surprising and meaningful, then, when family names appear without human foreknowledge in a person who has lived apart from the birth ancestors.

My son's adoptive parents happened to choose as his middle name the name of my grandfather, who died six weeks after he was born. (Keith)

Many birthmothers were never told they were permitted to name their babies before being separated by adoption, and frequently the original birth certificate was inscribed simply "Baby Girl Smith." The last name might have been the family name of the birthmother, the birthfather, or often a pseudonym given the mother by a maternity home. Whether or not she officially named her baby, each mother knows the name by which she will remember this precious life and carries it with her, bringing it to her conscious mind on the birthday anniversary or other occasions.

When I was carrying my baby I always called her "my little angel spirit" or "my little angel." The name given to her by her new parents is Angela. I thought of the connection right away, but always kept the story to myself. (Lenore)

Because most adoptees have no access to their original birth certificates, they do not know the names given to them by their mothers. When engaged in a search, therefore, it is a breathtaking moment when real names are discovered: Instead of a pseudonym, the adoptee now knows the mother's name; instead of a fantasy, the birthfamily has a named child for whom to search. After reunion, names are prominent in the meaning making of the renewed connection, in effect producing order out of chaos. They are usually the first, most obvious evidence of uncanny similarities.

I found an older sister with the same name as one of my daughters: Kimberly. My daughter's second name is Rochelle; my mother and all of her family came from the town of Rochelle. I have an adoptive brother named Daryl; my sister, Kimberly, married a husband named Daryl. I also have both an adoptive and a birth sister called Susie. (Frank)

After locating my daughter, it was noted that her adoptive name was Suzanne Marie. The daughter that I bore six years after her was named Suzanne Marie also; only when we said the name aloud, it didn't ring well with our last name, so my husband selected the middle name of Kay. However, had we not changed it, the name would have been exactly the same as the daughter I located after many years of search! I had given the name Victoria to my firstborn, and she has decided to use that name now, since she likes it, it was her first name, and it doesn't create confusion when we talk about "Suzanne." Her adoptive parents are deceased. (Darla)

Thirty-two of the 70 families encountered similar names, including many unusual ones. There were 22 meaningful matches between adoptive families and birthfamilies, and 10 between birth relatives. Seventeen had multiple matches. Four sets of birth siblings chose the same names for their children. Four mothers named another child by the unknown, adoptive name of the firstborn. Four adoptees in some way "knew" or made unusual use of their mothers' names, as for imaginary friends. If the siblings in the following stories had been raised together, social custom would have discouraged their choosing the same names for their children. As noticed in studies of twins reared apart, the fact that they never knew each other provided freedom for a possible genetic influence to work.

My half sister's children are named Kristy and Katy, and mine are Kris and Kathryn! (Lisa)

When I was pregnant with my second child, my first choice for a boy's name was Paul Matthew. I wrote it down and still have that scrap of paper. I had a girl. I have now found out that my sister gave birth to a boy shortly before that, and his name is Paul Matthew! (Deborah)

Finding the frequency of similarities in names is noteworthy. Some were the coincidental choice of adoptive families, and some indicated a prenatal and perinatal memory component. It is remarkable that uncanny information about names seems to be transferred to unsuspecting, separated family members. Further investigation into the significance and selection of names would be a compelling project.

An adoptee's sense of family loss occurs at the concrete operational stage, when cognitive reasoning brings realization of lack of biological connectedness; there are no names for the fantasized parents. It is interesting to speculate whether the actual learning of names after reunion is one key that permits a person whose development was frozen to resume leaps in psychological growth, filling in deficiencies from the concrete operational stage.[7]

Connection by Intuition

Reunited families, who may have assumed that their broken pieces could only be connected at the point of physical reunion, are surprised to learn that unifying communication passed between them during separation. Is it possible that the intuitive call and its response have a genetic tuning mechanism?

From twenty-three families who shared their accounts of accurate dreams or intuition, the following data emerged: Seventeen were termed hunches or intuition; eight were dreams; six were specific knowledge of crisis; and three daughters knew the time when their mothers died. Information was experienced through kinesthetic sensation, internal visual representation, or internal auditory knowledge of names or advice. The thought was characteristically perceived with certainty and marked in the mind; then it was acted upon, told to a witness, or put on paper. Seven incidents were experienced in childhood and twenty as adults.

Within days of knowing that the agency had found my mother, before I talked to her, even before I received her first letter, I knew that I wanted to paint her something, as well as write to her. I did a painting of a sunroom, kind of a sun porch: there was a wicker chair; a little coffee table with a pot of tea, some teacups, and a tray of cookies; and then a vase of Bird of Paradise flowers in the background. The painting represented what our first meeting might be, that we might sit down together. When my mother received it, she nearly flipped. It was just like her sunroom! She is British and drinks tea constantly. That teapot is out all day every day. And she had just that week received the Bird of Paradise arrangement from a good friend! (Patricia)

Five children felt they knew they had siblings. One demanded that her adoptive parents adopt a sister for her (and they did) at the same time her birthmother died, and her natural sister was placed in welfare facilities.

A hunch I always had since I was a small child of eight or nine was that I either had sisters, or I wanted some so badly that I wished I had some in my adoptive family. Instead, I had an adoptive brother four years older—just like one of my three birth sisters. (Fiona)

I have a brother who was conceived eight months after I was born. We feel close. He says he always imagined he had an older sister, but didn't know about me until he was an adult. (Dorrie)

Personal Development Involves Filling in the Missing Pieces

Beginning in 1953, I made a special effort to find and talk with other adopted people. I learned from them that they shared many of my characteristics and problems. Motivated by more than a desire to find my mother, wanting now to satisfy her desire to know me (I now assumed she had this desire), but also strengthened by the discovery of the hidden world of adoption-in-adulthood, I finally did what I could have done many years before. I found her. . . . I went into the room where my mother was, she in tears, and we embraced. Then we sat down on the sofa and began to talk together and look at each other. She wanted to tell me of my birth, my early infancy, and most of all how she had wanted to keep me. I told her where I had lived and how I had gone about finding her. Still crying but sometimes now laughing, my mother reigned supreme on this day of her glory. For the love she had never forsaken lived again in this stranger who had come into her home. She died at the age of 80 in 1967. Her inner life was seldom revealed. But once she wrote to one of my friends: "I lay at night thinking of my wonderful daughter and how thankful I am to have her back again; and thinking of her dad, too. I think my love is stronger for her than if I could have kept her. Oh dear! It is a good thing no one can read our minds. Someone said one time, 'Only God can.' I said, 'Yes.' " (Jean Paton, founder of Orphan Voyage)

MAKING MEANING OF THE CONNECTIONS

A need for cognitive meaning making follows the numinous experience of reunion, to make some sort of sense out of the missing years, and to answer the lifelong questions, *Did I do the best thing? Was it God's will? Did my parents love me?* Perhaps by discovering and claiming meaningful connections of synchronicity, families are enabled to bear the results of years of discontinuity. The darkly awful puzzle of love, abandonment, and grief now has flashes of laughter or a hint of the awesome.

Following are the types of meaning attributed by some of the persons who lived these stories. Some caught glimpses of eternity through the windows of time. Many did not attempt an explanation beyond their feelings of awe. The more reflective comments fall into two major divisions: Human Relationships and Designed by the Designer.

Human Relationships
Birthfamily Connections

This statement is made by an adoptee, a foremost clinician who works with all parties in the adoption triad and who trains others to do so:

Everyone has his own internal pace for search; it must be respected. There is fear of abandonment, rejection, loss of everything. After search, an adopted person belongs in neither place, and in both. These people have lost fantasies, lost histories. When you adopt a child, you adopt the entire birth family. Whether you like it or not, whether they are visible or not, they are really a part of that family. Dr. Joyce Maguire-Pavao (Director, Center for Family Connections)

I am very happy to have found my mother, my twin sister, two nephews, and a niece. Both my adoptive parents have passed away, and last year I lost an aunt with whom I was very close. I am very happily married, but sometimes you need a family too, you know. (Dawn)

Both my birthparents had died prior to my finding the family. But I did find siblings, aunts, uncles, cousins, and one marvelous step-grandmother on my mother's side. They filled me in with wonderful profiles of my mother and father. I was not blessed to meet them, but I feel fortunate in having what little I do have. (Shoshana)

I am an adoptee, recently rewarded with a happy ending after a two-year search. Not only did I find my birthmother but five brothers and sisters as well. It has been very exciting! A few things I found out along the way are truly uncanny. My full sister and I were in the same schools at the same time. We never knew each other but had several of the same friends. We are alike in many ways—philosophies, hobbies, etc. (Sam)

Birthfathers and Their Sons

A son whose mother intuited his name, when a paper with his new-born footprints fluttered on the wall of her room, was reached by an intermediary. He has so far refused a relationship with her. She says:

All is not negative, though. I feel much better just knowing he survived birth and is happy and healthy. I know he was married four years ago, and he graduated from college last year. I also know he grew up in the town where I live, and only moved away less than a month ago! I have pictures, from high school yearbooks at the library, and know he looks so much like me that I almost wince when I look at his face. His birthfather has been very supportive every step of the way in the search, by mail and by telephone. He and I are planning to get together for the first time in 26 years to catch up on our lives and to exchange information about ourselves and our families (neither one of us is now married). We plan to compose a letter to be sent to our son, and to include pictures of all of us, to let him know he is thought of constantly, and that we all love him. Whenever he is ready, he can contact us. (Angie)

I think my coincidences are important in that they show a child can have much more in common with the father than the mother, something most birthmothers do not even want to think about. When I first saw my son as a little child, years before I made contact, my immediate impression was that he was just like his father, and would not want to know me. That turned out to be exactly right. (Carrie)

Adoptive Family Connections

I have a poem written by my birthmother the night I was born. With each passing month I'm learning much, much more about myself and my birth family. I see I am a product of both heredity and environment, just as every adoptee is. Just how much is genetic and how much is a result of my environmental influences, I am not sure. According to my full, blood sister, I am one of the most balanced people she has ever met. I have my adoptive parents to thank for this characteristic. In fact, if I had hand-picked them myself, I couldn't have chosen better. They are the most wonderful people in my life. (Kara)

My adoptive father and my birthfather both worked on the same wharf for 35 years in different jobs. (Fiona)

Acceptance of what's left is a positive way of reframing the loss

My heart is full of love for my son, and to find that he turned out to be such a good person is very humbling indeed. We can't turn back the clock. I can't take him back, and he has had a loving and close-knit family around him. All I ask is for some room around the sides of his life, and pray that we can all enrich each other's lives as the future unfolds. (Joan)

My mother is 85 years old now and in a nursing home, and I visit her often. (Ray)

Designed by the Designer

As a child I always felt special, as though someone from above was taking care of me, as well as my wonderful parents here on earth. It seemed only natural that when I found my birthmother, she would be a kind, loving Christian. I was a new Christian at the time of our meeting. I feel our "miracle meeting" was truly blessed by God. After three years of searching, I finally prayed for help in finding her. My prayers were answered through my husband, who mentioned that I might write letters to certain people. Sure enough, that very simple idea led to our initial contact. Once I had prayed about this, I was certain I would not be turned away by my mother, but would be accepted. Our reunion has strengthened my faith. I feel much more at ease, for myself and my children. Now they know where their roots lie. (Eileen)

I found my daughter when she was 14 but waited to age 18 to contact her. I believe I was led of God and waited for his timing. Separation by adoption affected my life. I changed my career choice because of it, from nursing to social welfare. I have done research on how all Bible adoption was "open," and I promote pro-life, open adoption when absolutely necessary. (Rebecca)

My mother reached me when I was 44. In my teen years I had fantasies that one day my birthparents would find me. I learned I was born when my mother was 13. She said that during holidays and my birthday she would think about me and wonder if I had a good home and if I was okay. At our reunion, she kept saying, "I'm so thankful I found you and that you had a good home." It seemed like God worked out the search; it was so easy for her. The fact that my adoptive parents had such an unusual name made it easy. I think she has peace and contentment to know where we are. I was surprised, but not shocked, because I really feel the Lord prepared me for the reunion. It's like we've been doing things together all along. (Lynne)

WHAT LESSONS HAVE WE LEARNED?

Subjective words, visual images, and feelings are the essence of synchronicity, rather than objective data. The anecdotes confirm in a unique way the relevance of *information*: The trauma of its lack for separated family members; the therapeutic value of its acquisition through search and reunion; its storage in memory and genetic mechanisms; and its meaningful transfer in various forms of synchronicity.

We must consider what is revealed about a society that separated families and then explicitly or implicitly said to each person: You must get on with your life and pretend your other family members do not exist and are not longing for you. You must never ask questions about their names, location, activities, or welfare. There is no need for you to know such things as dates of marriage, childbirth, death, and onset of medical problems. You will survive without opportunity to express love, to marvel at your genetic idiosyncrasies, and to confirm your genealogy and your unique selfhood.

Those myths are dispelled by multitudes of reunited families. Reunion itself is an awesome experience, giving a sense of focus to a backward look at a hazy past. For those who arrive there, perhaps finding rejection or death in the end, the discovery and integration of synchronicity may be the only evidence of their enduring genetic connection.

NOTES

1. E. Van Why, *Adoption Bibliography and Multi-Ethnic Sourcebook.* (Hartford, Conn.: Open Door Society of Connecticut, 1977).

2. American Adoption Congress, "Suggested Questions and Answers About Open Adoption Records." Washington, DC., 1990.

3. A. Baran and P. Pannor, "A Time for Sweeping Change," *Decree* 7 no. 1 (1990): 5.

4. L.H. Stiffler, *Parent-Child Synchronicities During Years of Separation by Adoption: Anomalous Connecting Information in Histories of Union/Loss/Reunion* (Dayton, Tenn.: University Microfilms, 1991), no. LD-02254.

5. *Oxford Dictionary*, S.V. "synchronicity."

6. This section is an addition to Dr. Stiffler's work.

7. D.M. Brodzinsky, and M.D. Schechter, eds., *The psychology of Adoption* (New York: Oxford University Press, 1990).

PART VI

Dealing with Special Issues within the Search

CHAPTER TWELVE

When the Pieces Don't Fit: Finding Dead Ends or Death

For almost four years, I've written and called and sleuthed for shreds of information, tiny clues that would lead me a little closer to information about my birth family. Sometimes one little fact like a date or something someone thought she remembered would lead to months of searching. I ran into so many roadblocks. Some people were compassionate; a few stretched the rules to help me. Many people told me to mind my own business, not to go where I might not be wanted, not to make trouble. But still I kept trying, believing in my heart that knowing something or someone is always better than not knowing.—Katie Lee, age 47

The journey began with hope. For some the hope was to find answers to questions that had plagued them a lifetime. For others it was a hope to touch the face and hold the hand of the one person who was more intimately connected to them than any other person on the face of the earth.

Yet for these, their search did not lead to hope fulfilled; it led to hope deferred. It began with trembling anticipation. It drew to a close in the midst of confusion, frustration, disappointment, loss, and pain. It was a journey that would call for a restructuring of their hopes and dreams and a reordering of the needs of the heart. For some it has ended unexpectedly, with hope redefined.

From the ranks of thousands of adult adoptees involved in the search for birthfamily members comes a number of them who find heartbreaking disappointment. For some adopted persons, the search stretches from months into years with nothing but brick walls at every turn. For others a search effort filled with passion and anticipation crumbles at the discovery of the death of their birthparents.

How do you deal with unending, seemingly unanswerable questions? How do you encounter the reality of the death of a birthparent and move on with a sense of closure and peace? What do you do when the pieces won't fit? These dilemmas need solutions that lead to resolution and recovery. Hope deferred makes the heart sick, but hope redefined moves us toward wellness and wholeness.

FACING DEAD ENDS

There are people whose searches have continued for fifteen to twenty years. These dead ends exist for a variety of reasons, from sealed, destroyed, or altered records to self-imposed roadblocks. Listening to the experiences of adopted persons who have experienced dead ends contributes a sense of empathy to those whose pieces don't fit.

Paula's Story

As a teenager, Paula, now forty-seven, discovered a secret that altered the course of her life and sent her on a journey to find someone who could tell her the rest of the story. The many pieces that came together should have finished the puzzle, but they haven't.

1971—Paula finds out about her adoption. A senior in high school with too much time on her hands before her mom and dad get home from work, Paula figures out how to get into the family safe. One envelope with Dad's handwriting says Paula Ann's Adoption. She had never heard the term, so obviously she opens and reads the contents. It was the first time she sees her birthmother's name on her original birth certificate. What a shock! She reads further. Father: unknown . . . even more of a shock. About three months later she finally asked her parents, "What does adopted mean?" Her father said nothing. Her mother was enraged and said, "You're better off, don't ask again!" Paula struggles with a conflictive relationship with her mother. Time goes on, and Paula makes up stories in her mind about her birthmother.

1976—March 17. Paula's father dies after fighting cancer for five years. He is only fifty-six. This is devastating to her as they were always close. He was always so kind and gentle, unlike the harsh treatment Paula received from her mother. He never mentioned the adoption. Paula continues to struggle with her mother's nonacceptance.

1984—Paula is now married and has two children. She visits an aunt in Houston, her mother's sister. She freely tells Paula a few things about her adoption, her birthmother, her birthsister, and her adoptive parents. Paula learns for the first time that her birthmother and sister lived with her adoptive parents prior to her birth. It is also the first time she knows she has a sister.

1984–92—Relationship with adoptive mother has deteriorated to nonexistent.

1992—June. Paula receives a call from her aunt. "Your mother is dying, it's time for *you* to make up to her." Paula and her family go to the hospital against Paula's better judgment. She wonders, "Why should I go? She rejected us." Her mother doesn't recognize them for a long time. But then she improves and is discharged from the hospital. The next ten months Paula sees her once a week.

1993—March 5. Another call comes. Her mother probably won't live through the weekend. Paula is told she must make some decisions. Her mother improves slightly and goes home.

March 21. She worsens again but survives until April 1.

April 3. The day of the funeral, Paula's cousin, her aunt's son, gives Paula her adoption papers, but the original birth certificate is missing. Paula is the only child of her adoptive parents, but their estate is left to this cousin to do with as he pleases. Paula can't afford to fight it. She cries out, "I want my birthmother more than ever now."

Although Paula searched occasionally before, she had never felt the intensity that engulfed her following the death of her adoptive mother. "It is with great passion I have begun this search again. The passion comes from the support of some of my mother's sisters and my husband. Cousins my age and younger knew all along that I was adopted. Everyone thought I knew too! I think of my father often. How could he take this to the grave with him? Why did he? Why? Why? Why?"

When beginning her search this time, Paula did so in a more thorough way.

I had explored my adoption on and off for twenty years, but never kept records of anything. When I started again last year, after Mother died, it was from scratch trying to use my original papers and interviewing family members. I have files and files of records now just from the last eighteen months. Correspondence logs, conversation logs, charts and graphs. I have read every book out there, made literally hundreds of phone calls, written dozens and dozens of letters to everyone, but with absolutely no success.

What has been the result for Paula? Dead ends and empty hopes. "I feel I've come so close, then other times I feel like I'm so far off track. I believe it's on purpose because my adoptive mother wanted it that way. Things are so hidden, lied about, names changed, information lost. There's no end to the trail of disguise and inaccuracy."

Paula's search and the dead ends that plague her have left her with unresolved issues and unsettled feelings.

I haven't put them to rest and I probably won't until I can find the answers. I feel like I'm the victim, but why? What have I done to deserve this? If my birth family doesn't want me, okay. I'd be disappointed, but no more so than with all the dead ends. I'd like to know about them . . . my birth family. Was I really better off? Do they know about me?

My feelings are mixed with disappointment, hope, hate, love, and bitterness. I would really like to have a family . . . I'm an only child with two deceased parents, but I have two children and a husband who are loving and supportive and go through my feelings with me every day.

Paula's dead ends are a result of what appears to be intended secrecy. For another adoptee, the dead ends are a result of the barred doors of closed records and agency limitations.

Bruce's Story

Bruce, a forty-year-old adopted person, has been in and out of his search for a number of years. A writer, Bruce recorded his intense feelings about a dead-end return to the adoption agency. In the process he gives voice to the heart and soul of a searcher stepping into what feels like a dark, unknown place.

Across the street was my birth place, in a manner of speaking. It was an unusually pleasant midsummer day in New York City. I'd taken a bus from the Village to the Upper East Side, the address scribbled on a scrap of paper. Nearly shaking with fear as I stood across from the building, I took comfort in the belief that this moment was at once chosen and fated. I could approach the entrance. I might even enter and speak. If I just lingered in front, wearing an impassive mask to hide my panic, everything would be okay.

I hesitated just a moment before opening the glass outer door. Before she even spoke, the receptionist recognized me. Not personally, but as a type. She made the stock may-I-help-you-sir phrase sound heartfelt.

Some thirty years ago I was adopted from this place, my sister, too. I wanted to say more, but my tongue went thick. Mercifully, the receptionist asked an easy question. What was your name? In a flash I realized I was being treated according to a therapeutic model. It was comforting. The agency had learned that people like me might arrive on their doorstep at any time and at any age. They had decided we were fragile, needy, and anxious for support, and they were right. A lost little boy looking for my parents, I gave the nice lady my name and felt sheepish relief when she gestured to the waiting room.

A few moments later, a large handsome woman in her early forties stepped quietly to my side. She confirmed my name (who else could I be?) and motioned for me to follow her. She said she would go back upstairs and pull my file, but I knew she'd just done so, and had already had a quick look at what it contained. I sat down to wait for her return, glancing at two double doors with an emergency exit sign above them. Memories came.

The last time I'd been here was 1964. We'd come in from Westchester my father, mother, sister, and I to sign papers making my sister official. I've always recalled it as the day we got Janice, though she'd been living with us for close to a year by then. Much later I realized that, in this adopted child's mind, she did not become real until we kept that appointment. Janice was a toddler; I was four.

The trip back to the agency was an essential though unplanned step toward self-empowerment. I needed to claim their space, however fearfully, and add my voice to the chorus of agency adoptees who believe that open records are the only humane choice. We have been legally divorced from our evidence of birth. A right every other citizen takes for granted is denied by state and local authorities. It is no accident of fate, but a policy decreed by naturally parented people who cannot possibly comprehend our need to know.

When the woman returned, she asked me humanely, Where are you in your search?

I answered, As I'm sure you know from my file, I contacted the agency about eighteen months ago seeking nonidentifying information. It's taken me the year since I received a reply to process it and get this far. I happened to be in New York and have a lot of questions about what I was sent.

What kinds of questions do you have? was her ambiguous reply. We were on very shaky and highly subjective ground and I couldn't tell whether this was merely rhetorical or an invitation to ask away.

For example, about my birth father. The letter provided some data on ethnicity and employment, but nothing about his family. The woman was not forthcoming. I'm really not familiar with your case, she said. The records have been returned to storage since you wrote and the caseworker assigned is no longer with us. I'd met the management. Innocently phrased probes weren't going to get me anywhere.

A confrontational tact seemed appropriate. There are also discrepancies between what my parents remember and what the letter suggested, I stated coldly. How can I confirm, or at least reconcile that with what was provided? I want to know everything you can possibly tell me. I also want to see any relevant documents that are not legally sealed.

She asked how long I would be in New York. For adoptees outside the area, she explained, letters were the most effective means of communication. In that case, I was ready to start writing. May I have a paper and a pen, please? I'd like to leave a written request with you before I go.

For the next half-hour I composed a formal letter with detailed requests for clarification and follow-up questions. It was polite and well reasoned, but restated my desire to have any and all nonidentifying information in the agency's possession. When the woman returned I asked for a photocopy and she obliged. Then I left through the glass doors with the assurance that I would be contacted by a caseworker.

The agency sent me a brush-off letter months after my visit, attributing their inaction to a shortage of caseworkers and requesting that I later remind them of my request. Preposterous, yet instructive. My next visit to the atypical birthplace I share with my sister must be negotiated. An adoptee from this agency may arrive unannounced once or twice in his or her life, but no more.

Secrecy and agency limitations imposed by the state law are just two of the seemingly insurmountable barriers creating a dead-end search. A third is caused not by something without, but within.

Joanne's Story

When Joanne put the receiver back on the phone, she wondered to herself, *Will I get any closer this time . . . and follow through?*

Joanne had been searching for her birthmother for nearly twelve years. At least, the search organization helping her had. Every once in a while the search group would call, excited with a possible lead. Their only request was that Joanne follow through with it. However, something within her stopped. She couldn't follow through. Why does that happen?

"Some people put up self-imposed dead ends," related Kate Cleary, a past president of American Adoption Congress. "They put up their own roadblocks. They say they've been searching for years but have not done the work on their own search. They want to leave the process to others. It seems they are incapable of doing anything for themselves when it comes to taking the final steps toward finding a birth parent."

Reasons for the blockage for many searchers stifled by self-imposed roadblocks can range from fear of rejection to fear of acceptance and closeness. They may fear they can't handle what they might find, such as mental illness or poverty.

Never getting past roadblocks for some adoptees brings them to a decision-making point in the road. When does a searcher know to give up? Kate Cleary suggests two guidelines:

1. When Obsession Is the Rule Instead of the Exception. There does come a time when an adopted person has to give up. A sign that it's time, according to Cleary, is when the search has consumed the adoptee for a long period of time; when it has become such an obsession over the months, even years, that everything else in the searcher's life has been shelved.

2. When the Search Is Emotionally Self-Abusive. Finding oneself in the midst of a search places the adoptee on an emotional roller coaster. When information is found—exhilaration. When information is wrong—disappointment. When a sealed record is opened—anticipation. When information is incomplete—discouragement. When the adoptee has spent too much time living on the edge of the search, it can become emotionally abusive, Kate says. There comes a time when he must make a decision to lay the search aside. When the pain created by unending barriers drains one's ability to live fully and completely, it may be time to redefine the hope. How can that be done?

Finding dead ends is very hard. If a searcher cannot find a person, he can perhaps find places, advises Dr. Joyce Maguire-Pavao. He can go to the places and explore his heritage. He can perhaps find people who knew his birth parents. It doesn't totally take away the sense of loss in not locating birth parents, but the process itself can be revealing and helpful.[1]

Encountering dead ends in the search process requires the adoptee to step back and reorganize his hopes, his dreams. Finding a different unexpected also calls for the reordering of one's world.

DEATH OF A DREAM

Hearing the disappointing words, Your birthmother (or father) has died, evokes incredible sorrow and bitter disappointment for many adoptees who intellectually knew of the possibility but blocked it from the heart. To emotionally survive such a momentous disappointment compels one to rewrite the script. Those who have walked that path can best speak of their pain. Some are still enveloped by feelings of defeat and grief. With time and process, others have worked through the anguish to redefine their dreams, to redefine their hope.

All the Signs Told Us She Was Alive

"Although I realized my search could end at the grave, I discarded that thought as quickly as an expectant woman discards the thought of stillbirth." Patti Jo, age thirty-three, made the decision to search when she was a teenager. She postponed an active effort until her early twenties.

"I joined a search group when I was twenty-four years old," Patti Jo said. "My hopes soared when I met other people who had successful, happy, joyous reunions. It was then I decided I would devote every effort toward my own search."

Over the following months, Patti Jo, with the help of Adoption Network Cleveland support group, found encouraging signs. She obtained her mother's original birth certificate, which enabled her to trace her mother through other sources.

Everything kept coming up as current. My birthmother had a valid driver's license and other reports were up to date. We finally went back to her last known address, thinking she may have recently moved. The current landlady had no knowledge of her. Past receipts of just a few years ago also showed no evidence of her ever living there. At that point, I was really confused.

The next step Patti Jo took was to check death records. Perhaps her mother had recently died.

We went to the public library and searched back two years and found nothing. Then we asked the librarian to check back further. Just a few days later, in September 1992, the horrible call came. They had found the information. My birthmother had died at age thirty-six in 1976. She had died of mysterious causes. There was no body, she had been cremated and buried.

Patti Jo reacted to the harsh news as understandably unsettling. "Throughout the search, all the clues pointed to a live person, so discovering her death was extremely jarring. I went into a cycle of emotions—sadness, pain, grief, and anger. The anger comes, I think, from having such high expectations and hopes and not being realistically prepared for what I found."

What steps has Patti Jo taken in working with her shattered desires? After finding the death of her birthmother, Patti Jo and her husband went to the cemetery. It was the only thing she knew to do.

Going to the grave was the closest I'll ever get to my mother. On that day, my husband and I walked through rows of gravestones looking for hers. He found it. It felt very weird to walk over to it and see her name on the stone. It made me realize the finality of it all. This is as far as I'm going to get. I sat down and cried. Occasionally, even today, I have moments when I'm still angry at the loss. I had no choice. I had no chance.

My Expectations Were Too High

Erika, age thirty-three, started her search after completing a college research project on opening adoption records. She had no clue that the seemingly innocent search would impact her life so deeply.

After Erika actively began to search, she formed a picture in her mind of what her reunion would be like.

When I was about a week away from getting the information about my birthmother, I remember thinking, A week from now and she and I will be together. I thought we probably looked exactly alike, based on the non-identifying information. I expected we'd have the same likes and dislikes, the same talents and viewpoints.

I will never forget the afternoon in the late summer when the when the search consultant helping me called. 'I don't have good news for you. Your birthmother died several years ago. It was an apparent accidental death and she died of cardiac arrest. She was only forty-one.'

The emotional downhill ride Erika experienced sent her into a whirlpool of feelings.

At first I experienced terrible sadness, disbelief, and then anger. It was very painful and emotional. I cried for a whole day, driving in the car, sitting at home. I would just cry. I couldn't talk about it because I would start crying all over again. I had always thought this would be the greatest experience of my life. I thought we'd bond and be inseparable. I thought I would meet the one person on earth who truly loved me.

Now, knowing I will never, ever meet her, see her, touch her, talk to her ever in my entire life angers me. It is incomprehensible. I just wanted to talk to her, to ask her why she gave me up and if she thought about me on my birthday. I'll never be able to do that. There will always be a part of me missing. I just hope we can be together in eternity.

Although Erika never met her birthmother, she did meet her birth grandmother. Her grandmother told her of her birthmother's lifelong grief following her relinquishment decision.

My grandmother told me she believed my birthmother really died of a broken heart. She never got over giving me up. Every birthday she became extremely depressed and sad.

What else was interesting is that my grandmother gave me a video Mother had made six months before her death. It was a uniquely relevant video. She was going through her house describing those things that were important to her and her feelings attached to those things. I haven't been able to watch the video all the way through yet. It's too painful.

Although Erika continues to feel an incredible emotional gap because of the unexpected premature death of her birthmother, she took one more step toward resolution and that was to visit the grave. *"I went to her grave for the first time two years later, on the ninth anniversary of her death. I went feeling that I would handle it pretty well. Being overwhelmed with emotion and crying was not what I expected myself to do, but that's what happened. I just stood there and wept and kept saying to myself, 'Here she is and this is as close as I will EVER be.' "*

MOVING TOWARD RESOLUTION

If one's search has ended at the grave of a birthparent, how can one resolve the losses around such finality? How can an adopted person, with high hopes and high expectations walk through this valley of the shadow and emerge reconciled and at peace? Is it possible?

"When I meet with an adoptee who has found death at the end of his or her search, what I hear initially is a deep sigh, 'Oh well,' uttered with incredible sadness," says Kate Cleary. "Then they begin the long, difficult process of grieving. It's a complex process because they are grieving an abstract someone they have no memory of seeing or touching."

In her book, *Journey of the Adopted Self*, Betty Jean Lifton comments:

It is a difficult process, for this is not the recognized loss of a mother that brings sympathy and comfort from family and friends. Even those who have seen their mother only a few times are overwhelmed by the impact of their grief. This dead mother was the woman who gave you life. Your body, born from hers, feels wrenched by its disintegration. . . . I did not hear of my mother's death until four months after it occurred. It was the end of a dark fairytale in which we could not rescue each other or ourselves. She took her grief and her loss and her secrets with her, just as she took some part of that child she had held onto and who continues to hold onto her.[2]

Katie Lee Crane, undaunted by years of dead ends and roadblocks, eventually found that her birthmother had died. Her walk toward resolution began at that discovery and in many ways continues today.

The years of searching were intense. I had volunteer and paid searchers from five states working with me to find my birthmother. Twice I found the wrong person. Each time I was devastated. The second time I was so distraught I created a funeral for a fantasy. Sitting at my dining table, candles surrounding a bouquet of daffodils, I wept as I officially buried my fantasy. The person I'd come to know from conversations with searchers and neighbors, the one who was a nurse, who had brown hair and brown eyes, the one who'd lived on Olive Street, who was intelligent, strong-willed, sweet and likable that person was not my birthmother.

Only two weeks before a scheduled trip to Cleveland did I discover a clue that suggested my search might end there. Those two weeks were cloak-and-dagger weeks, with a friend literally calling me en route with new pieces of information.

On my second day in Cleveland, I went to city hall and requested the death certificate of a woman who might be my birthmother. She was. She had died of a blood clot in 1968 at the age of forty-six. I was to turn forty-six in twenty-two days.

The death certificate told me where she had lived, where she had died, and where she was buried. Before I left the city I visited all three places. When I went to her grave, I took one long-stemmed red rose and placed it there. I stayed by the marker, swimming in mud from an early spring snow, and spoke these words to her:

"My hands are raw. My tears are crusting on my cheeks. My feet and ankles and gloves are covered with mud, so is your grave. I brought you a rose. It's a symbol of the blood that killed you, the blood that gave me life, and thorns that hurt us both. You gave me life. The search gave me my self and my mother and the words: You didn't make a mistake!

"Goodbye, Lois. Hello. Rest in peace.

"Now I must surrender the fantasies, bury them all today and hold up the complex and ambiguous and painful truth: You are gone and I never knew you.

I never got to love you. But I will, from this day forward, honor your memory and praise God for the life you gave me.

Blessed be. Amen."

On the long trip home in the car, I cried as if my mother had just died. She had, for me. On that trip I decided I wanted to do something on my forty-sixth birthday to celebrate my life. I did not want to spend my forty-seventh year expecting to die just because she died in hers. I planned a naming/dedication (like a baptism) in which I took back the name Lee, which had been given me at birth. It was my way of giving birth to Lee all over again, only not alone and in shame this time, but surrounded by loving friends and in great joy the way every baby deserves to be born. It was a joyful occasion in which I gave thanks for the gifts from all four of my parents, the two I knew and the two I never knew, recognizing how each in their own way, shaped me and my life.

The search is complete, but the process is never over.[3]

A WORD ON INTERNATIONAL SEARCHES

For those adopted internationally, the hope of ever reconnecting to birthfamily members seems dim. Some begin with no hope, for some hope is ignited, for most hope is redefined. Often abandoned as infants in public places like police stations or left at orphanages due to the harsh economic, social, or political conditions within their home country, international adoptees generally grow up with the knowledge that what little information they have is all that will ever be possible to obtain. This was the case for one Korean adoptee.

Susan Soon Keum Cox, director of development for Holt International Children's Services, grew up as a Korean adoptee in the '50s and '60s. She came to the United States at the age of four from an orphanage founded by Mr. and Mrs. Harry Holt. Looking into her past was something she had not planned to do, for she assumed that there would be no possibility of ever finding anything. Also, she felt no compelling need.

"I never expected to search," Susan related. "I had not even seriously considered it. In fact, for a long time I didn't quite understand what compelled some adoptees to want to search for their birth family." However, as Susan reached out to help another Korean adopted person, that action impacted the direction her own life would take.

Susan visited Korea in 1990, attempting to locate the birthmother of an adoptee who required a bone-marrow transplant. She was successful in the search and met the young man's birthmother the following summer in Korea. That encounter ignited something within Susan.

That experience caused me to reflect on my own birthmother and wish I could somehow reassure her that I was all right. In the summer of 1992, I placed a small ad in the weekly newspaper of In Chon, which is in northwest Seoul. The ad included my Korean passport photo and my Korean name. Within a few weeks I had a reply from a woman who said she was my stepsister.

In the weeks that followed, as more and more information reached Susan, it created new and unsettling emotions for her. "My search was connected to deep feelings that evoked a wide range of responses. Each new discovery was attached to an emotion, excitement, anticipation, fear, sadness, happiness, and confusion. I think my most defining emotion was fear. I was going into the unknown. I had no control over the process or over how it would turn out."

A portion from a journal entry written in the fall of 1992 reflects Susan's strong emotions:

> Dear Mother,
> I'm coming to find you . . .
> Perhaps what I really mean is,
> I'm coming to be found . . .
> I'm so scared.
> What if I really do find you?
> After all these years
> How will that feel?
> For both of us.
> I pray this doesn't hurt either of us,
> beyond wounds that will never heal.
> I understand clearly
> this is the risk I am taking
> And I accept responsibility for that.
> That's why,
> I'm so afraid.

Eventually the news that Susan received from Korea brought incredible disappointment and pain, yet also hope. She learned her mother had died fourteen years earlier. However, she discovered she had two half brothers who didn't know of her, but would gladly welcome her as their sister.

In August 1993, Susan had the opportunity to visit her mother's grave and meet her brothers. Of that period of time, Susan wrote:

I can't believe how hard this is. . . . But I do not regret that I am standing here above this tangle of weeds that is my mother's grave. . . . As time goes by, it is a little easier. I believe it will become easier still. The feelings will continue to move and change until they melt into a comfortable pattern for all of us. It's nice to see faces that look like my own. Not because they are beautiful, but because they provide a mirror for me that reflects our mother whose face I do not remember.

Although Susan walked through intense emotional pain and confusion prior to, during, and after the search, it would be a journey she would not undo.

This experience was difficult. I don't regret having done it, but there were times in the process when I did. I could not have predicted the intense emotional roller coaster experience this would be. I was strongly supported by friends and family, but ultimately, the feelings belonged to me, and I was the one who had to live with them.

I believe the process of searching has great risks. There is so much that is out of your control, and it continues at an intense emotional level that is sometimes very difficult. I am still discovering what all this means to me. I hope adoptees who are considering searching for birth parents do so carefully, slowly, and with support from those closest to them.

This experience confirmed for me that family is shared history more than shared genetics. My (adoptive) family is my family—it's expanded a bit, and over time I'm still learning what this means to all of us.[4]

For the international searcher, running into dead ends or finding the death of birthparents are strong possibilities. Returning to the country of birth does help fill in missing pieces, as the adoptee connects in a broader sense to his heritage, culture, and ethnicity. The same experience can benefit adoptees from this country who find such disappointing realities at the end of their search.

WHAT LESSONS HAVE WE LEARNED?: OFFERING A RAY OF HOPE

Those who find death at the end of a search, by returning to places of the past, may have the opportunity to learn more about their birthparents from those left behind than they would have if they were still living. They will hear both the bad and the good. What they find will have a lot to do with who they are as an adopted person, for the search is the symbol of a search for self. The clues they find will be clues to themselves. There is really no such thing as a bad search, for the search will find out truth and truth is ultimately what one is looking for.[5]

A Word from Betsie

Those whose search ends by finding death, or dead ends, experience the lowest point on the emotional roller coaster of the search. Death or dead ends are so final.

In these situations, can a person achieve the resolution he started the search to find? We hope he can, at least in part.

- Don't avoid the grief process. Grief is normal and healthy. Others may not understand this loss you are suffering, they may not realize that, yes, you have lost a very real, very important person in your life. Turn to those who do understand.

- Don't be afraid to share your tragic story with your adoption support group. You are not the only one this has happened to, and others need to be aware of the full range of experiences.

- Do not isolate yourself, even though this may be what you feel like doing.

- Find ways to take care of yourself. Acknowledge the extent of your loss and give yourself time to interpret what this means to you. Gather all the information you can. Cry. Scream if you want to.

In the Adoption Network Cleveland, we have begun a tradition of sending flowers to members who find death at the end of their search. Our members have often told us that this was the most concrete, or sometimes the only, acknowledgment they had of their loss; this allowed them to begin the grieving process. Sadly, the flowers were usually the only expressions of sympathy they got, as others may not have grasped how real their loss was.

NOTES

1. Dr. Joyce Maguire-Pavao, personal interview at the Adoptive Families of America Conference, Minneapolis, Minn. June 25, 1994.

2. Betty Jean Lifton, *Journey of the Adopted Self: A Quest for Wholeness* (New York: Basic Books, 1993), 180.

3. Katie Lee Crane, edited excerpt from "Complete Searches," Adoption Network News, July-August 1993.

4. Susan Soon Keum Cox, personal interview, July 1994.

5. Pavao, interview.

CHAPTER THIRTEEN

Revisiting an Old Wound: Encountering Denial or Rejection

The One She Permits Me To See

One who rejects unconditional love
Having forever lost precious time
One who is unwilling to freely love
Abandoning and rejecting the most primal of bonds

One who allows the voices of society to dominate
Denying consent to life's challenges
One who lives deeply in denial
Refusing to glance into the soul

One who channels energy into painstaking avoidance
Festering secrecy, shame and foreboding
One whose detachment is the panacea to life's strains
Securing tightly Pandora's Box

One who evades acceptance of the past
Rejecting coldly the child she named Robin
One who appears loving in the eyes of family
Crushing, all the while, a daughter in turmoil

One whose priorities are scattered
Agonizing over what others may see
One who is kindhearted to the unsuspecting
Manipulating to maintain sacred anonymity

One without concept of her potential power
Showing weakness when strength was crucial
One who struggles to control the baggage and skeletons
Scarring her character and ignoring the suffering spirits

One in whose shoes I will never walk
Seeing solely the one I do not understand
One legacy I never will live up to
Nor shall I try
—Robin Weidemann (Denice Bertino)

Denial or rejection stands as perhaps the greatest fear for any adopted person who makes the decision to search for birthfamily members. Rejection is an opposing response to a shaky, uncertain extended hand. Rejection is the dashing of a hope to embrace and to be embraced, to love and to be loved by the one person who has existed only within the deep recesses of the heart.

To come full circle toward wholeness and healing of the pain of rejection by a birthmother or other birthfamily members, an adoptee must recognize and verbalize her own depth of feeling. Often, unable to reach down far enough for herself, it is helpful to listen empathically to the feelings of others. A second step in the process toward healing is to look at the "whys" behind the rejection, for surface appearances fail to tell the whole story. The adopted person must step into the shoes of someone who perhaps has pierced her heart severely and examine the reasons why the arrow flew from the bow. Finally, she must learn how to deal with the issue of rejection and to allow the process to mature her and enable her to stand tall once again.

DENIAL OR REJECTION: THE RESULT WE ALL FEAR

It can feel like death to an adoptee when the birthmother refuses a meeting, as if only she can sanction the reality of the adoptee's life.[1]—Betty Jean Lifton

"Rejection is difficult," says therapist Sharon Kaplan Roszia, "because with it comes a loss of hope. The fantasy before the reunion allows one to hope for the best. When the search ends in rejection, one feels robbed. It is a shock."[2] What does the experience look and feel like?

It Was Not What I Expected

"All of a sudden I realized that somewhere there is someone who looks like me, might sound like me, even act like me."

For thirty-four-year-old adult adoptee Teresa, dealing with adoption issues was something she had ignored. As a young child, she stuffed away thoughts and feelings about being adopted only to find herself facing them in adulthood.

Teresa's confrontation of the reality of her adoption is quite similar to many adult adoptees. Some look for answers in teen years. Still others, like Teresa, wait until a major life transition looms before them. For her, the death three years ago of her adoptive mother brought the issue to the surface.

Following this loss, the reality of another person with whom she was intimately connected by birth emerged. Finally, at age thirty-four, Teresa faces what adoption really meant in her life. She had two sets of parents. She had two mothers—one who had died, one who perhaps was still living. It became consumingly all-important for her to initiate a search to find out as much about her birthmother as possible.

With the help of her husband, Ted, and two supportive friends, Teresa set out on a journey to locate her birthparents. It took over eighteen months, and finally she found her birthmother, making her first contact by letter. Her mother's response was abrupt, stunning, and painful. It was a shocking, disturbing day when Teresa received the following letter:

Dear Teresa:

I was extremely upset that you contacted me. Do not, under any circumstances attempt to contact me again or any of my relatives. The only people in my life who knew of the baby were my parents, two friends, and my husband. My children know nothing of this and it must remain that way.

I do agree that it would be right for you to know some medical history. My father died of a heart attack at the age of fifty-eight, twenty-three years ago. My mother died just last year following a car accident. She was eighty years old and was in good health. I have no brothers or sisters. I do have a medical problem with arthritis and high blood pressure. There is a history of heart problems on my father's side. One aunt on my mother's side died of breast cancer when she was forty-nine.

There was never any consideration on my part to keep the baby. Thirty-four years ago, most women did not keep a child if they were not married. I will not send any pictures, and I have nothing to tell you about your birthfather.

I hope this letter gives you the information you sought. Do not make any more attempts to reach me. I do not want anything to do with you or your family. I have gotten on with my life. You should, too. I hope that the people who adopted the baby were good people with love. I understand wanting to know who your biological mother is, but it must end here.

Martha Joanne

The pain Teresa experienced after receiving the letter was deep, and it hounded her for months. "I have had a great problem with depression and being hypersensitive to the treatment of others. This rejection has carried over into other relationships. I find myself walking on eggs and wanting to keep the peace at all costs—even to myself." Teresa's heartbreaking experience is not unique, for others have had similar encounters.

It Came As a Shock

When I was twenty-five, my mom told me about a search and support group for adopted persons. Without her approval I may not have searched, because I loved my parents and didn't want to hurt them.

After I received my non-identifying information, it took me three years to actually go further. One day at the library I found my birth announcement. My parents had been married at the time of my birth. I contacted the court to make sure the record was correct and the court personnel took it upon themselves to contact my birthmother. She told them she didn't want contact.

At first, it was a shock. Then in a few days the shock turned to anger and disbelief that someone I had these deep feelings for would not return them. I had to deal with the rejection and understand that it was not me she rejected, but her own feelings. I have emotionally and spiritually matured and dealt with my pain. (Bonnie, age 33)

I Just Don't Understand

I am experiencing a lot of sorrow and distress when I attempt to understand why my birthmother and birthfather have no desire or interest in even meeting me. Can it really be that hard to do? Don't they understand the pain they've created in my life?

I am thirty-one years old and I still go through periods of incredible sadness and depression when I allow myself to dwell on the fact that these people, of whom I'm a part, just don't care. I have been anguishing with this for over three years. What in the world are they afraid of? Me? (Lynn, age 36)

I Have Waited So Long

I found my birthmother over five years ago. The last time we talked was about eighteen months ago when I called her on Mother's Day. She was short and abrupt with me. It's so hard, because it's obvious she doesn't want any relationship with me. Neither do my two full-blooded sisters. In my mind, I have been given up twice. I thought things were going well at the beginning, but over time she has gotten more distant. I feel so alone sometimes, because the people related to me by blood want nothing to do with me. I waited thirty-three years for them to reach out to me, but now I guess that won't happen. (Russell, age 39)

Some Days Are Extremely Rough

Because I have four precious children, I deal a lot with feelings of sadness regarding my birthmother. Some days, if I allow myself to think about her, it can get pretty rough emotionally. We talked for the first and last time over three years ago. She told me she was forced to give me up, that she held me at birth and held onto that memory. But she just can't see me. I guess she has never dealt with all of this and it's too hard for her to do so now. I had dreams of a warm, tearful reunion with my birthmother, full of excitement and anticipation, but I guess that will have to wait. Hopefully, someday. Maybe. (Janet, age 41)

I Just Wish She Would Give Me a Chance

What I would like to do is to visit my birthmother and talk things out. But I just can't show up at the door. I don't want to force myself on her. She's told me very clearly that she isn't my birthmother. However, everything I've found, including talking with other relatives, disproves her claim. I just don't know what to do—really rock the boat and go to the house or just let it go. (Charles, age 44)

I Just Want to See Her

When my search consultant contacted my birthmother, she was plainly told my mother did not have any other child. She had given birth to a boy in 1950 and he had died at the age of two. There were no other children. However, birth certificates do not lie and I know Ruthanna is my birthmother. I have no idea why she has to perpetuate the lie. All I want from her is just to see her, just once. (Sarah, age 47)

Experiencing rejection or denial from one's birthparents can not only be devastating to self-esteem and push one into depression, it can create guilt. "When I first contacted my birthmother," Kate Cleary says "and experienced initial rejection, I wanted to take it all back, to believe it didn't really happen. My first thought was that I didn't want to cause her pain and I did."

Shuffling through the many emotions generated by the rejecting experience can do one of two things for adopted individuals: leave them emotionally stuck in anger, bitterness, and depression or push them toward understanding and healing. A method to avoid becoming emotionally stuck is to step back a generation or two into the societal context of that day. Within that backward glance are the "whys" a birthmother rejects the contact from her son or daughter today.

WHY BIRTHMOTHERS REJECT

Curry Wolfe, founder of Birthparent Connection and leader of Adoption Connection of San Diego, has worked with many adoptees and birthparents as they move through the search into the reunion experience. In observing a few rejecting encounters, she believes they occur for a number of reasons.

Mothers Who Carry Shame

Many women still carry the shame and guilt of becoming pregnant out of wedlock. The pressures of family, clergy, social workers, and society created the belief that women who were pregnant out of marriage and surrendered their child were worthless. Most were told they should never share the fact of the pregnancy or surrender with anyone, not even their future husbands. Many have taken those words to heart and are not able to get past those instructions and the accompanying shame when found by their surrendered child. When the surrendered child makes contact, old feelings of shame and guilt rush to the surface.[3]

Mothers Who Fear What Releasing the Secret Will Do

Another reason some mothers reject, according to Wolfe, is that they have never told another person of their surrender experience.

A woman may be married and never have shared this personal information with her husband or children. This prospect can be extremely frightening. Many women fear their husbands will leave them, and their children no longer love them. This fear of loss can be overwhelming.

I do believe that fear is the key element in poor contacts. It is much easier to deny or ignore than to face something that may be painful to one's self or others. Many times women believe that if they deny the contact, the other person will just go away. In most cases, that is not true. Fearing to tell one's adult family is part of the blockage, but so is dealing with one's family of origin. Some women never told their parents. They were able to mask the pregnancy. The fear of having to face their parents after so many years can be so frightening that they choose to deny or reject their child before facing their parents or siblings. Some women have been able to mask the pregnancy even to themselves.[4]

Mothers Who Have Unresolved Anger

Some adoptees who have contacted their birthmothers have encountered anger. "I believe," says Wolfe, "that this anger is never for the person. It is an anger for a situation that was out of their control." This situation never really left them; it followed them well into midlife and beyond.

Kate Cleary, former president of American Adoption Congress also believes anger is not directed at the child but is directed at the whole experience of having to place the child in the first place. When the now young adult reenters the birthmother's life, feelings of being out of control resurface.

"Years ago, if a young woman had to give up a child, the message she received was 'You are not a good person,' " Cleary explains. "We tended to treat birthmothers as 'those people,' or 'that woman'—shaming them with labels most have never forgotten. Not only were they shamed, but many were forced to make a decision that altered the course of their lives—forever—and left them with incredible sadness and emptiness."

When I Relinquished My Child . . .

My son was born over thirty years ago and we didn't have many choices. Back then, having a baby and not being married was considered nearly a crime. All those years there was a big empty space; a part of me had been given away. I never let myself get really close to anyone, afraid they would be taken away too. So for twenty-five years I never told anyone that I had a son, not until he contacted me and I had to finally tell. I was angry at first, not at him, but at the fact that now I had to deal with something I had quietly put away as my secret. (Diane, age 57)

When I Relinquished My Child . . .

I was seventeen years old and a senior in high school. I was quickly sent away to an out-of-state, unwed mother's home, given a false name, and told not to contact any of my friends. My parents made the decision to place my baby. I was never consulted, just told to sign the papers. When he was born, I never saw him. I was told that was best. I was angry then, and when he contacted me, all that old anger came to the surface. I didn't want to see him, not at first. He didn't realize that my giving up a child colored every decision I have ever had to make. I've felt immeasurable loss, incredible guilt over him, my family, and myself. I've dealt with depression off and on for years. I didn't know if I had the emotional stamina to face him. (Dorothy, age 59)

"One thing the adoptee is not usually aware of is the mental and emotional process a birthmother goes through when contact is made," says Wolfe. "She will most likely begin reliving the relationship that created the pregnancy, the pregnancy itself, and the surrender. These often are raw and untouched emotions she may find devastating to feel."

She may start having angry feelings and expressing them to the adoptee, when she's really angry about what she's remembering. She may be angry with her family or her boyfriend (at the time) for not helping her when she needed it the most. She may be angry with herself for not being stronger and standing up for what she truly wanted—to keep her child. She may be angry that she was sent away from home to live in a maternity home. She may be angry about the loss of her teenage years after childbirth. And all that anger could manifest itself in anger toward the adoptee. It's important to understand this.[5]

Shame, fear, and anger are three of the major barriers that block a positive contact between some birthmothers and their relinquished children. Knowing what to do with that experience can enable the adopted person to move through the pain and avoid getting emotionally stuck in anger and depression.

WHAT TO DO IF REJECTION OCCURS

Rejection is a strong word. It does not happen often, according to Wolfe. Yet, for those to whom it does, the word sounds so permanent.

"I wish there was another word that could be used instead of rejection when talking about a contact that doesn't go well," Wolfe says. "Rejection is such a negative word and it sounds so final, when in reality, it may not be final at all."

Denying a contact with the adoptee will leave in its wake a sense of incompleteness because for so many adopted adults, total acceptance is one of the hidden needs of the reunion.

"I don't feel an adoptee will totally gain a positive sense of self if the contact fails," Wolfe states. "There will always be issues and questions that remain unclear if not answered by the birthmother. The feeling of incompleteness is one some adopted persons must learn to accept." There are, however, some practical things you can do in the wake of a rejecting experience.

1. *Follow up with a letter.* If you have not received a good reception to a phone call, Wolfe suggests following up with a short, kind letter expressing that you understand your birthmother needs time to process the contact. It's a good idea to give your name and phone number at the beginning of the conversation so that your birthparent has it for future consideration.

2. *Don't contact siblings without sharing this desire and possible action with the birthparent.* Many adoptees feel it is their right to know their birth siblings, but as pointed out by Wolfe, "not at the expense of their birthmother, her well-being, and existing family relationships."

3. *Put the search in perspective.* One thing all searchers need to realize is that they went into the search for answers to many questions, not necessarily a relationship. If you get some answers, it may be enough to help you put together the missing pieces of your life history.

4. *Don't deal with the rejection issue alone.* Find and participate in a search group. It's a good place to find people who truly understand.[6]

In considering the issue of rejection, Betty Jean Lifton writes:

I am often asked whether I think a birthmother has the right to shut out the child she brought into the world. My answer: an unequivocal no. As for whether the adoptee has the right to meet with the birthmother at least once to hear their life story: an unequivocal yes. As one birthmother said, "You can't relinquish all of the responsibilities for parenthood just by relinquishing the child."

Does the child have a right to demand a relationship with the birthmother after she gives him the information he needs? No, the child does not have the right to intrude on the life the birthmother has made for herself after relinquishing him. Does the birthmother have the right to be part of the adoptee's life? No, the birthmother does not have a right to anything the adoptee is not ready or willing to give. . . .

When adoptees, at any age, need to know their origins, those needs should supersede those of the other adults in the triad. No birthmother has the right to confidentiality from her child at the expense of her child's well-being. As Dr. Randolph Severson points out: "All people who walk the face of the earth possess the inalienable right to know their history and to meet the man and woman from whom they drew breath."

Yet, in reunion, we are faced with psychological rather than legal and moral dilemmas. Violent acts, such as having to give up a child unconditionally, can cause violent responses. The birthmother is as much a victim of the closed adoption system as is the adoptee, traumatized to such a degree that when [the child] returns, she may not be able to recognize her own.[7]

A Word from Betsie

I have seen many contacts that initially met with "rejection" turn out well. If you've experienced rejection at first, you need to give it time and show respect for your birthparents' feelings, but also keep trying. While this can be an overwhelming emotional situation, it's important to keep in mind that the "rejection" is not of you, it is of the past circumstances and the resulting emotions of the birthparent. There is still hope and often the situation turns around with careful handling.

Here's my advice:

1. *Don't do anything impulsive!* Check out your actions with others who are experienced in these situations.

2. *Wait the time necessary for your birthparent to process what has happened.* Each day may seem like a long time to you, but it's important to give your birthparent the time she or he needs to think this through and deal with personal feelings.

3. *Communicate clearly and make yourself available.* Be sure your birthfamily knows exactly how to contact you should they want to.

Remember, the goal of the first contact is simply to open the door. It may take some time from there.

NOTES

1. Betty Jean Lifton, *Journey of the Adopted Self: A Quest for Wholeness* (New York: Basic Books, 1993) 191.

2. Sharon Kaplan Rozia, personal interview, February 24, 1994.

3. Curry Wolfe, personal interview, July 1994.

4. Ibid.
5. Ibid.
6. Ibid.
7. Lifton, 190.

CHAPTER FOURTEEN

Facing a History of Abuse or Neglect

The need to search is not about looking for only happy outcomes—it is about needing to find the truth—Betsie

Kathy, age twenty-nine, has very few friends. She stays at home, seldom venturing out. She calls her husband, Jeremy, at work at least three times a day, just to make sure he is there. Jeremy has tired of the smothering he feels from Kathy and is thinking about what to do about it. The more she envelops him, the more he withdraws. The more he withdraws, the tighter she clings.

Kathy is the product of an abusive, neglectful family. Memories of being locked in a bedroom as her parents left the children for endless hours remain vivid and frightening. At the age of five, she was removed from her birth home. She lived in three foster homes before her adoption by a family at the age of eight. She was separated from three other siblings, one older and two younger.

Kathy's early childhood was devoid of feeling safe and being able to trust. These issues still haunt her in adulthood. She knows she's in trouble, and she wonders if finding her birthfamily would help her to stabilize emotionally.

Richard is what is commonly called a workaholic. At thirty-three, he owns his own business and works sixteen hours a day. He's obsessed with the need to succeed. He wants to completely eradicate memories of what it was like to have absolutely nothing to eat or anything clean to wear. Displaced from his birthfamily when seven years of age because of severe physical neglect and adopted soon after, Richard still vividly recalls bare cabinets, an empty refrigerator, and the deep gnawing of hunger. He will never forget the day his mother left him with a friend with a promise to return. She never did. He's so determined to overcome his past that he's in danger of losing something in his present—his wife and children.

As an adult, Richard is still controlled by the images of a severely dysfunctional family imprinted on his mind as a child. He suffers shame and embarrassment about his past. He refuses to talk openly about it, denying its grip on him. Lately, when alone and afraid, he considers, "Maybe a journey back to meet them would free me to live life in a better way."

Walking out on her third marriage, Lisa struggles with intense feelings of loneliness, depression, and emptiness. Her three marriages were a vain attempt to fill up the hollowness that consumed her. She always hoped her life would be different someday. Yet a fear of intimacy and an inability to express herself blocked growth and led eventually to disillusionment and abandonment.

Throughout her early childhood Lisa was a victim of physical, sexual, and emotional abuse. Taken into foster care at age six, she was eventually placed for adoption at age nine. Even at that young age she vowed never to trust or love another family.

Because of her pain at the hands of her abusive birthfather and her emotionally absent birthmother, she spends all her energy longing for those elusive words, "I love you," from the people who hurt her. "Maybe," she ponders, "if I can find them, maybe now they will love me."

Adults who entered their adoptive homes as older children usually carry with them memories of people and places. They also cart along a history of physical, emotional, or sexual abuse or neglect. Some choose to ignore the effects of such raw early life experiences. However, for most, escape is nearly impossible.

In his book, *Adult Children of Abusive Parents*, Steven Farmer comments: "The abuse suffered in childhood continues to substantially affect them. They long for a break from their cycles of repetitious, self-defeating patterns of behavior, yet they cling to familiar habits because they know no other way. Conflict and struggle dominate their lives as do persistent feelings of being victimized, exploited, and betrayed by others."[1]

Most adults who were victims of abuse carry no outward signs; there are no broken legs or arms, only wounded spirits. Many talk of moving into adulthood under the cloud of anxiety, depression, low self-esteem, and chronic loneliness. Unconsciously they continue to be controlled by the faint memories of a painful past. They are simply unaware that their present difficulties are most likely intricately tied to the trauma of a lost childhood.

Marian Parker, a veteran adoption social worker in Ohio, has encountered many struggling adult adoptees from abusive backgrounds. "Self-doubt becomes a real issue for these young adults," Parker states. "Being placed for adoption and dealing with thoughts of 'What's wrong with me, I was given up' is compounded with the feelings of knowing that one was abused or neglected as well. They think to themselves, 'It's worse than not being wanted; they hurt me besides.'"[2]

Why do many adults, adopted as older children with a background of abuse and neglect, choose to take the journey back? How does an adult, adopted as an older child, move beyond the maze of emotional pain created from his abusive past? It's a journey not easily undertaken. The first step is to find out as much factual information as possible. The second step is to become aware of silent, hidden issues created by the past that may have an impact on emotional well-being. The third step toward healing from a broken past compels the adult to examine what to expect if a reunion with the family of origin takes place. Finally, the adoptee must ask and answer a difficult question—"How do I know I'm ready for this?"

WHY SOME JOURNEY BACK

According to Kay Donley Ziegler, trainer and consultant for National Resource Center for Special Needs Adoption, almost all adults adopted as older children have thought about trying to piece together their lives. "The thoughts of searching are universal. They are normal," she said. "Some think about it. Some talk about it. Others take action, pushing on in an attempt to find some resolution to their pain."

"I believe," Ziegler continues, "that for these adults, it is an issue of closure as to why they return. They are trying to figure out what happened to them and why. They have perhaps grown up with a sense that they were at fault for the abuse—they had something to do with causing the family problem. They wonder about being defective—imperfect. Going back and finding out what happened enables many to put it into the right context."[3]

For many, facing the events of their past becomes an absolute necessity to finding emotional stability.

A Walking Time Bomb

Until now, Michael, in his early twenties, has pretended that his adoptive parents were his birthparents. He deliberately crammed away memories of his alcoholic father's violent outbursts and the sight of his mother

cowering in a corner of the room. He refuses to talk about his birthparents, even to acknowledge their existence. However, incredible anxiety
stalks him, making him feel like a time bomb ready to explode. He finally
admits that his emotional problems are perhaps related to a past he tried
to erase.

Dr. Randolph Severson, an adoption counselor in Dallas, Texas, sees
a similar scenario.

Many come to me as adults saying they feel like a time bomb ready to go off.
This happens often in those who were under the age of six when the abuse or
trauma occurred.

They have not seen their family of origin since that time and because of their
young age, they do not have any context for relating to those persons outside
the memory of the abuse.

Life is a continuum of human experience and the abusive event was so over-
powering it is their only memory from which they can develop a sense of identity
from a historical context.

As these adults move through adolescence and attempt to develop self-image
from their historical context, two issues present themselves. First, they don't have
much memory to serve them and second, what memory they do have is often
traumatic and even horrifying.[4]

Defusing the Time Bomb

Kathy, Richard, and Lisa all made a decision to address the clicking
time bomb in their lives by seeking the help of a professional capable of
addressing the memories of their painful past. The role of such a professional in preparing an adult adoptee to face the past and make future
connections is vital. How this individual helps the adoptee to walk
through these issues is pivotal to a successful recovery.

"When I can," Dr. Severson says, "I work to get into the historical
context of the person's memory. No one person abused a child twenty-
four hours a day. I try to help this person recover any memory, however
small it may be, that is positive." Another step in a therapeutic approach
moves the adoptee toward healing and resolution. Severson adds:

Using what I call "explaining therapy," that is, giving them as much information
as possible, is a successful tool. That information includes such things as factors
those contribute to the intergenerational patterns of abuse, social/economic influences, and the psychological make-up of the family of origin. Fifty to sixty
percent of my work is explaining therapy. Going back to an agency and getting
as much information as is relevant to them is essential.[5]

When Kathy returned to the child welfare agency that had been involved with her family situation, she was met by a caseworker who

understood the value of giving her as much information as possible. Dealing with the touchy subject of needing identifying information wasn't an issue for Kathy. She had known her original name and the names of most birthfamily members all her life. What she needed were the facts about what had happened.

Kathy found that the image she carried in her mind of lazy, irresponsible birthparents who sat around in a filthy house was basically incorrect. What she did discover was that her birthmother was a young woman in her early twenties of somewhat limited capabilities. Her birthfather, a product of a severely dysfunctional family, was overwhelmed with the incredible responsibilities of raising four children when he himself was not much more than a child. Abuse was the only way he knew to control their behavior. Neither parent had any concept of how to provide a nurturing, safe environment. With each day, their load grew heavier. Out of desperation, with no help or positive future in sight, Kathy's birthfather abandoned the family. Her birthmother was incapable of carrying on. The authorities stepped in.

When Kathy learned through "explaining therapy" the events and circumstances of her birthfamily, she experienced an unexpected and overwhelming sense of relief.

"One main reason I hold on so tightly to Jeremy," Kathy realized, "is that I never felt worthy of being loved. I didn't want to lose out again. I thought we must have been pretty terrible kids for someone to dump us. Now I'm beginning to understand a little of what pushed them to do what they did. I feel freer to work on the issues from my past that are controlling the present and will interrupt my future."

Kathy did not find a fairy-tale ending. She found something far more important—the truth.

"The truth is paramount for searching adoptees," Marian Parker says, "no matter what is found. Finding out answers is immensely important, because what fantasies exist for the adoptee may be far worse than the truth that may have been magnified by secrecy."

Looking into the historical context of one's circumstances is part of the healing process for adults adopted as older children. Another piece of the picture is to look at the hidden, silent issues that surface when faced with the question of reunion.

Issues That Surface as Reunion Thoughts Emerge

After Richard faced his past, hidden feelings that were directly related to his early life experiences emerged. Others adopted as older children, like Richard, speak of similar emotions and thoughts. What feelings do these adults uncover as they choose to face people and places from another time?

"Why Was I Rescued?"—Survivor's Guilt

Part of a family of five children, Lauranna carries with her the knowledge that she was "rescued" from an abusive home environment and that three of her sisters were not.

I was about three and a half, the fourth child of five, when the authorities placed all of us into foster care. My parents were given time to get their lives together, I am told. After three years, the court decided they could have three of us back— my three older sisters. My brother and I were placed together in an adoptive home. I was six when that happened.

Now as an adult, I've learned that things did not go well with my three sisters. I look back with incredible guilt. I was raised free from abuse. I had the opportunity to go to college and make something of myself. I have trouble allowing myself to feel good about my life. Right now, I feel sorrow for them and wonder, "Why was I spared?"

Ronny Diamond, an adoption expert in the field of postadoption services, works with adults who deal with abuse issues and are considering initiating a reunion with birthfamily members.

"One of the concerns I see these young adults carry is what I call 'survivor's guilt,' " Diamond offers. "There's a sense of relief that they were rescued from an injurious home environment on the one hand, but guilt for leaving on the other. They ask themselves 'If I could have stayed, could I have helped them?' They feel this especially if other siblings were left at home. Some even go so far as to think their leaving left the family in far worse shape and they should be blamed."[6]

Closely related to survivor's guilt is another issue that looms overhead. It comes from a message the adoptee received from the birthparents.

"You'll Be Back Someday"—An Obligation to Rescue

The scene remains frozen in Benjamin's mind. Although now twenty-three years old, he still remembers the day, at age seven, when he said good-bye to his mother. He recalls the blue dress she was wearing, the hole in the toe of her shoe, and her disheveled hair. Most of all he recalls what she said to him. "Someday, Benje, you'll be back. They're taking you now, but someday you'll be back and you can take care of me then. I know you will be back." That memory drives his need to find his mother.

A message often given to older children by their birthparents prior to the final separation is simply, "You must come back; I know you will."

Nancy Ward, also an adoption expert, says this farewell experience sends two profound messages to the vulnerable youngster, which he jams deep into the back pocket of his mind to retrieve at a later date.

The first message is an extreme obligation to his birthparent to reconnect. For some adoptees, it goes beyond the faint promises made by a frightened child, mushrooming into a driving, motivating force—*a vow that cannot be broken.*[7]

The second message of unrelenting obligation is the need to rescue the birthparents. "There's a perception," Ward explains, "that the birthparents need to be rescued. Some have created a fantasy of 'the poor people who lost their children.' These adults deny the reality of the abuse and neglect. This idealization of their birthparents propels them toward reunion."

"Maybe This Is Who I Really Am"—Identity and Feelings of Shame

Both Ronny Diamond and Nancy Ward, in counseling adoptees, walk with them on a rocky, thorny path as they grapple with a sense of who they really are.

"I think an adopted person's roots in his biological family are no different for a child who has been placed at birth or as an older child," Diamond asserts. "It's still a question of 'Who am I—what is my identity?' "

Diamond feels that many adoptees whose wounds are the product of physical, emotional, or sexual abuse carry a deep sense of shame. They say to themselves, *This is part of who I am.* They wonder, *How far away from being like them am I really? Can I surpass them? If I want to reconnect, do I have to become what they are and not absorb the values of my adoptive parents?*

For many, a wrestling match of the heart and soul takes place as the battle to define themselves continues. They wonder who they will become.

Mitch, now twenty-five, recalls the struggles he felt in late adolescence as he attempted to discover who he was and what he would become in relation to his birthfamily and adoptive family.

I was adopted at the age of six and I still have memories of a pretty rough home environment. When I was a teen, I wondered just how hard I should try in life. If I wanted to be like my birth family, it wouldn't require much effort. If I wanted to identify with my adoptive family, it would pull out the best I could do. I felt that reconnecting with my birthmother and birth family members would fill in an identity gap for me. It did help me to define what I had become with the help and support of my adoptive parents. I didn't particularly respect the lifestyle of my birth family and made a decision that I wanted more out of life than that. I still see them maybe once or twice a year, but the visits are short and tense.

Stacking the emotional shelves of life with such issues as survivors' guilt, obligations, and identity questions is further complicated by the feelings created by another issue, perhaps the most controlling and destructive one.

"Do I Dare Feel It?"—Acknowledging and Resolving Anger

Barbara, age thirty-eight, recollects all too well what it felt like to hear the back door swing open and hear the blustery, angry rantings of her violent, abusive father. She remembers all too well the many occasions, after his fits of rage, that all members of the family had to pretend as if nothing happened. No one could be sad. No one could be scared. And, of course, no one could be angry.

My birthfather would come home from work usually drunk. It was like a tornado hit the front room. He would just blow the place apart, leaving us in the wake, physically in pain and emotionally traumatized. I learned early in life to be afraid of anger because it was so connected to violence.

I went inside with my anger, where it rotted over time but never went away. As I grew older, that anger rose to the surface as depression and substance abuse. I finally got help and learned that I could openly express the rage I had buried for so long. I want to see my birthfather again; I was ten the last time I saw him. But I will see him as a healthier person than I used to be. I now know how to be liberated from the anger that so consumed me.

For many adults adopted as older children, anger is not only the product of the abuse that took place in the family of origin, but is further complicated by the deep pain of separation from birthfamily members. What to do with that anger is the next question. Author Dwight Wolter, who also experienced an abusive dysfunctional family, shared valuable insights as he resolved his anger.

I began to enjoy the expression of anger. Anger, sarcasm, and wit make a potent combination. The adrenaline my anger released had a druglike effect. My heart beat fast. My blood flowed quickly. My face was flushed and, best of all, I felt right! Look at the way I was raised. No one could deny me the right to be angry. Anger became the fuel that propelled me through difficult situations. Anger became the passion that let me know I was alive.

. . . Then I realized that it was not getting angry but remaining angry that had become a problem for me. If someone hurt me, I would get angry instead of feeling the pain. It was difficult to let go of my attraction to anger. . . . I want to wear my anger like a suit of armor to spare me from pain. But I can't. Now I'm losing my anger about never having had a childhood. What I'm left with is sadness. And facing sadness is not easy. All of my life I would rather have been dragged across a field of boulders by wild horses than feel the immense sadness within me. Anger was so much easier to feel.[8]

Emotional issues of guilt, obligation, shame, and anger, if left unattended, can sprout like weeds within the life of an adult with a disturbing past, choking off growth, emotional health, and quality relationships. Choosing to rip out the festering weeds with the help of support groups or counseling will enable the adoptee to manage whatever comes as a result of the reunion. Dealing with expectations of a reunion in the light of reality then becomes possible.

Dealing with Expectations

What can adoptees expect to find when making plans to reunite with birthfamily members whose abuse or neglect has left painful memories? Marian Parker suggests, "Be ready for *anything*. Be prepared for the worst possible outcome or maybe a positive encounter. There is just no way to know."

Dr. Randolph Severson makes several more observations.

First, the human mind tends to freeze a person in our minds just as we remember them. We forget that life goes on. People may change, and of course, they may not either. They have to be able to move that person on in time. Often the abusive family is made up of young parents overwhelmed financially and emotionally. As the years have passed, they have matured and gotten on top of the early problems. I caution those who are searching and making contact that the people they will meet are not going to be the same people they were twenty years ago or like they remember, if there is a memory. They may find a person who has incredible guilt over the past and feels great remorse. They may find a person living in denial of any responsibility and even refusing to discuss the past.

Ronny Diamond agrees with Dr. Severson. The memory is frozen in time—on both sides. "Often the work of the adoptee in considering expectations," Diamond interjects, "is to look at the range of possibilities. On one end of the continuum they may find the family with their act together, which causes them to ask the question, 'If you did it now, why not then?' On the other end of the continuum they may find the parents still strung out. It validates the history but keeps the door to reentering their lives closed. Either discovery creates conflicting feelings."

Another possibility adoptees may find as they return to their birthparents is a "revised history." Adoptees must be aware of the strong possibility that when they seek the "hows and whys" of what happened, their birthfamily may not come clean, according to Kay Donley Ziegler.

"A person who slips back into his abuse history may find a parent who denies that history, maybe out of pride, maybe out of shame, or maybe from a pathological refusal to face the truth," Ziegler explains. "The problem with going back is that a vast majority of the pieces may be filtered through a revisionary process and one may unearth only remnants of the truth."

Confronting the historical context of their lives, facing issues, and processing expectations prepare the adoptees to reconnect with their birth families. Yet how do they know they are emotionally, psychologically, and spiritually ready for such a meeting?

HOW TO KNOW IF YOU'RE READY

Michelle, now thirty-three, made a decision to find and reconnect with her birthfamily. She had been removed due to severe neglect. All of her adult life she had wondered why her birthparents couldn't get their lives together. How could she know if she was ready to see them again?

"One of the initial factors I look at when counseling adoptees on readiness," Ronny Diamond says, "is what their process has been up to now—what work the adoptee has done emotionally. Have they taken a few steps, stopped and processed, and begun again? Or are they impulsive and quick acting? I then urge them to slow down.

"I also ask them 'future' questions like *What are your concerns? How do you feel about those concerns and how do you think you will feel about them in six months or next year? What impact do you expect it to have on your life if you meet your family?* All these are important issues to filter through one's present life situation."

Dr. Severson also feels that readiness must be assessed before an encounter. "One of the questions I ask myself in dealing with an adult adoptee in this circumstance is, Do they have enough life experience and enough self-knowledge to forgive? If the answer is no, I am pessimistic about the reunion. If the answer is yes, I am much more optimistic."

Why are life experiences so important at this stage of the reunion process? According to Severson, "Life experiences create a judgmental system that can work for or against a positive reunion outcome. Here's one of the key life experience factors I look for: Is this person a parent? If they are, they probably know something about parental rage.

"I also look for life experiences that have prevented a 'black-and-white' judgmental perspective—How could anyone do that to a child?—and encouraged more of a gray perspective—a willingness to look at the abusive person's whole life context."

Life experiences create the ability to forgive, another important dynamic to a successful meeting, Severson feels. For many adopted persons trying to bridge the gap from the past to the present, the ability to look beyond the memory to forgiveness unlocks the door housing rage, bitterness, and resentment. Dwight Wolter knows something of that journey.

The process of forgiveness might begin by looking at our parents, but it always ends by looking at ourselves. Forgiveness is more about us than it is about them.

Many of us who were raised in dysfunctional homes use unforgiveness and resentment as a means of keeping away our true feelings. By focusing on our parents' failings, we don't have to look at our own character defects. Rage, fear, and anger lurk within an unforgiving heart. To forgive implies a willingness to admit that our old ways of dealing with our parents don't work anymore. We sense a need for change but are unsure of how to go about it. After a lifetime of focusing on our parents, it might feel terribly selfish to consider our own welfare first. We may feel we will once again open ourselves to the same abuse we were subjected to as children. . . . We stare at an image of our parents until our eyes hurt. We probe their lives more than our own because it might be much more painful to turn our eyes around and look into ourselves. We may claim it's not that we aren't willing to forgive but that they don't deserve it. Sometimes we might believe they deserve to be forgiven. Sometimes we would still rather focus on what we believe our parents might be forgiven for than on our own ability (or inability) to forgive.[9]

The Journey toward Forgiveness

Randy spent a portion of her earliest years in an abusive home and in an orphanage prior to adoption. The issues discussed in this chapter moved her to unravel an unknown past. Her story is one of pain, confusion, discovery, and forgiveness.

As I entered adolescence, damaging thoughts took root in my heart and mind. I convinced myself that since my family life was different from anyone's that I knew, I wasn't as good as the rest of my friends. Tremendous feelings of inadequacy barred me from trying new things or from branching out into friendships.

By the time I was nineteen, I was still plagued by feelings of deep resentment. I had a lot of anger toward the parents who had abused me as a two-year-old. I became more and more bitter all the time. I don't know how many times I thought to myself, Mom and Dad, you left me. You were never there for me.

I felt stuck in a downward spiral of negativism that drained me of happiness and peace. I had to put the fragmented pieces of my life together. I know that from the beginning, my search was directed by God, for it was just a matter of weeks before I located many family members.

Like many adopted kids, I manufactured fantasies about my birthparents. I hoped to see them as wealthy people who deeply regretted giving me away. As I stood on the front porch of a small house that summer day, looking at the disheveled woman who had given birth to me, all sorts of emotions welled up within me. I spent three hours with her. Our conversation was empty and strained. What I heard and saw jarred me to reality. It was obvious that alcohol still permeated this home, just as I had been told. When I walked out the door, I left my fantasies behind. The process of healing began that day as I encountered the desperate, tragic state of my birth family. Their lives were empty—ravaged by alcohol, drug abuse, and poverty. God had spared me such a life.

Compassion filled me. I did forgive those who had left me with so many missing pieces. Now I could freely go on with my life, stronger with the reality of what my life has become.[10]

For many years, adoptees—some with courage, some with timidity—have reconnected with their birthfamily members after years of separation. For some, the encounter was positive and restorative. For some, it was flat and emotionless, as if trying to resurrect something that had long ago died. For others, the heartache of seeing continuing devastation brought grief but liberating truth as well.

WHAT LESSONS HAVE WE LEARNED? MOVING BEYOND A DIFFICULT HISTORY

I Still Loved Him

I was adopted when I was ten years old. When I turned twenty-one, I wanted to go back and find my dad. When we met, it was really weird, it was like I had only been gone a short time. I didn't know what to do with what I felt—should I trust him? I did know that I still had some love left in me for him. (Shane, age 31)

I Thought They Would Care

When I turned eighteen, I remember announcing to my adoptive parents that it was time to go back and live with my birth family. I was separated from them when I was seven. My adoptive mother wisely told me to do what I needed to do, their door would always be open. I found my birthmother only an hour away. I thought she would care about seeing me. She didn't. I thought I would have deep feelings about being with her. I didn't. It was like nothing was left. After staying with her for a few weeks, I called my parents and asked to come home. I hoped they would care. They did. (Michelle, age 32)

I Felt Only Pity

From the time I was seven years old, I vowed I would return to my birth family. I just knew in my heart that by then they would be a happy family doing well and glad to see me. After finally finding them, my fantasy was shattered. My alcoholic father stumbled to the door and struggled to find a memory of me. My mother had died, also a victim of alcohol. I couldn't feel anger, just pity at the tragedy of their lives. At least now I knew the truth and it was just like I was told. (Justin, age 35)

A Word from Betsie

If you came from an abusive family of origin, it's important to keep an open mind during your search. Remember that just as you have changed over the years, your birthfamily has changed, too. Hopefully this change has been for the better. But keep in mind that you are an adult now; you have a lot more choices and control than you did years ago. Your future can be as positive as you want it to be.

NOTES

1. Steven Farmer. *Adult Children of Abusive Parents: A Healing Program for Those Who Have Been Physically, Sexually, or Emotionally Abused* (New York: Ballentine Books, 1989), 4.

2. Marian Parker, personal interview, May 19, 1994.

3. Kay Donley Ziegler, personal interview, June 10, 1994.

4. Randolph Severson, personal interview, April 1994.

5. Ibid.

6. Ronny Diamond, personal interview, May 1994.

7. Nancy Ward, personal interview, May 1994.

8. Dwight Lee Wolter, *Forgiving Our Parents: For Adult Children from Dysfunctional Families* (Center City, Minn.: Hazelden Foundation, 1989), 32.

9. Ibid., 27–28.

10. Adapted from Jayne Schooler, *The Whole Life Adoption Book* (Colorado Springs: Pinon Press, 1995), 206.

CHAPTER FIFTEEN

Searching in Midlife: What Are the Implications?

Since my reunion, I now have no doubt that my birthmother did what was right for me, and I have thanked her for placing me for adoption. My birthmother gave me two wonderful people. I call them Mom and Dad.—*Joan, age 49*

Kathleen Schultz wasn't an impulsive teenager when she began her search for her birthparents. She wasn't in her midtwenties anxiously awaiting the birth of her first child. Kathleen wasn't even in her thirties, busy with her career and raising a family. When Kathleen began her search, she was fifty-five years old, a grandmother, and looking forward to an early retirement from the teaching profession.

Kathleen is not alone as a searcher at this stage in her life, for some adult adoptees postpone their search efforts to the midlife years—forty and beyond. In looking at the unique issues for midlife searchers, several questions need examination:

- *What are the typical life issues for adults in the middle years?*
- *Why do some adults choose to wait until this point in time to search?*
- *What are the special concerns?*
- *What do they find?*

UNDERSTANDING MIDLIFE ISSUES

Someone once said, By the time I am forty I will have something to say about life. I will have lived enough of life to learn from mistakes and have the maturity to make wise decisions for the future.

Many see the forties and fifties as the prime time of life. Careers are solidly established. Children are becoming more independent. It's the high point for earning power. People at this age still have enough youth to be energetic, but already have enough life experience to be wise.[1] With the maturing years before them, adults in their forties and fifties face important emotional and psychological tasks. The impact of these challenges can be the impetus that propels many adopted adults to initiate a search for birthparents.

Dr. David Brodzinsky, in his book *Being Adopted: The Lifelong Search for Self*, states that one important psychological task during the middle adult years is generativity—a word coined by psychologist Erik Erickson, that describes the need to leave behind something of yourself, the urge to construct a legacy.

Dr. Joyce Maguire-Pavao, author, therapist, and an adopted person, says generativity is part of every adult's life. It is not only looking ahead, it is also looking back. It is a developmental stage where most adults experience a heightened interest in looking back to grandparents, to greatgrandparents, to family history.[2]

According to Dr. Brodzinsky, generativity takes multiple forms, from the passing of wisdom to children to the creating of art works to the transmitting of ideas to the next generation. The desire to pass on something is not confined within the context of the family, but involves a legacy that can be left behind by a teacher, inventor, minister, or mentor.

Brodzinsky not only cites the need to construct a legacy as a task for midlife adults, but points to four other challenges for adults in their forties and fifties as outlined by Dr. Robert Peck, a psychologist at the University of Chicago.

1. Acceptance of the inevitable decline in physical prowess and greater reliance on mental prowess for life satisfaction.

2. A redefinition of relationships with others; they become broader and more social.

3. The capacity to shift emotional investment to new people or new activities.

4. An ability to remain mentally flexible and open to new experiences or new ways of doing things.[3]

For many middle-aged adults, a reexamination of life emerges as they contemplate themselves, their family relationships, their social interactions, their careers, and their leisure activities. It becomes a period, according to Brodzinsky, for thinking about where you have come from, what choices you've made, and whether any of your past choices should be undone. Because it is midlife, not old age, there's still time to initiate new relationships, change the course of one's life, and reconstruct old decisions.

As a midlife adult reexamines the past, a very subtle change in how he views time occurs. As Brodzinsky points out, the question used to be, How long have I lived? Now it tends to be, How long do I have left? The ever growing sense of one's own mortality creates a whole new urgency to accomplish tasks left undone.

Midlife is the time in life, said Dr. Dirck Brown, family therapist and author, where the realization of one's mortality becomes evident. There comes a time for one to come to terms with his identity.[4]

The need to construct a legacy, a changing perspective on the meaning of time, and the realization of one's mortality are all issues confronting adults in midlife. With a sense of the clock ticking away, adult adoptees in midlife begin to realize that perhaps only a small window of time remains to resolve their personal issues of adoption, which may include finding their birthparents. It may be the first time the adopted person experiences an overwhelming, intense need to search. A whole new burst of emotional energy propels them to open doors that had previously been closed.

Why Do They Wait?

One might conclude that if an adoptee waits until midlife to consider or act on searching, issues related to adoption have not been a part of their thinking. However, that's not the case. Thinking about their adoptive status and subsequent search appears to be more than a fleeting, occasional thought. What are some of their questions?

Does She Want to See Me?

I reflected on my adoptive status at least once a week, sometimes more. I wondered who I looked like and what potential health problems my children and I risked in the future. By the time I began my active search, I reflected quite a bit about the probable age of my birthmother. I worried that she wanted to see me before she died. (Robert, age 42)

How Could You Give Me Up?

I thought about my adoptive status on a fairly regular basis, but it wasn't an obsession with me. When I had my first child, my being adopted had a new impact on me. For the first time in my life someone belonged to me and had features like me. It made me wonder even more, Who did I look like? What was my birthmother like? I also wondered often how she could have given away her baby. (Martha, age 49)

Does She Remember Me?

I often thought about being adopted. I don't mean that I dwelt on it, but it seemed the older I got, the more I wondered about my background. I especially thought about it on my birthday each year. I wondered if my birthmother was remembering and thinking about me, where she might be, how she felt as the years went by, and if maybe she'd like to know who I was and where I was. (Judy, age 62)

Adopted adults who wait until midlife do not do so because they never thought about their adoptive status. It was very much a part of their thinking. So why did they wait?

Waiting to begin search and reunion for adopted persons in their forties and fifties and even beyond is equally as emotional and traumatic as for searchers of a much younger age. The reasons for postponing the search until this point are as varied as the searchers themselves.

I Didn't Want to Hurt My Adoptive Parents

As I got older, I decided that I'd like to try to locate my birthmother. I really got serious about searching when I was in my late forties. I made the decision when I turned fifty, with the encouragement of a good friend, that it was the right time. I was also fortunate to have the help of a cousin when I started my search. My husband, Bob, was very supportive and understanding, and I will always be grateful to him.

I did decide, however, to tell my mother that I wanted to search and I asked for her support. She gave it to me wholeheartedly, and I promised her I would let her know as things developed. I had always been afraid of hurting my adoptive parents if I searched, but over the years I decided it was my right to know, if possible, and that I wanted to do it before it was too late. (Judy, age 62)

I always knew in my heart that someday I would look for my birthparents. I felt, however, that somehow the search couldn't begin until both of my parents had died. My father died four years ago and my mother died last spring. After the first of the year, I joined a search group and I'm now in the process of finding my birth family. I just couldn't bear the thought of hurting my adoptive parents, so I just waited it out. (Celina, age 52)

Adoption therapist Sharon Kaplan-Roszia finds that allegiance to adoptive parents is a major factor in why many adopted persons postpone their search. Some may believe it is an either-or situation, that to search would be to lose the adoptive parent relationship.

Many adoptees feel strong loyalty to adoptive parents, Roszia says. They would not do anything to hurt them. As they see their adoptive parents aging and facing death, they feel freer to consider searching. They probably have wished to do so for a long time, but have chosen to wait.[5] Some choose to wait until the passing of their adoptive parents. Others wait until time and maturity help them stabilize emotionally.

I Had to Resolve Difficult Childhood Issues

When I was a child, all my friends had parents who loved them and with whom they were very close. I wanted my family to love me and treat me as though I had worth and value.

But my adoptive parents kept me as an outsider. For many years, I had been through verbal, physical, and emotional abuse, and in view of the fact this was the only model for a parental relationship I had, finding additional parents, my birthparents, wasn't high on my agenda.

There was always something deep inside though that reminded me of a loss somewhere—a feeling of being incomplete. Driven by the possibility of a positive outcome, I decided at age thirty that I would take the first step and get a copy of my original birth certificate. When it came, I was overwhelmed.

In 1984, when I was forty-nine, nineteen years after I had gotten a copy of the birth certificate, I was working for a major company. My life was stable and my emotional strength was such that I felt as though I could handle whatever came along. I had finally recovered from my childhood experiences. Also, I had no delusions about being related to rich and famous people. My goal was simply to find a family. If I found something distasteful or detrimental, I was confident I would not get involved. I finally went to the courthouse where the adoption records were kept. From then on I have been actively searching.

I waited so long to search because to delve into circumstances that have been a mystery and a dark secret ever since childhood promotes great fear in me. Also, searching requires great emotional stamina. There must be a commitment to handle and deal with anything one finds. Previously, each time my intellect posed the question in regard to searching, my soul said, I can't.

The reality was, I didn't know how to begin the search, and I didn't have the emotional stability to deal with a frightening set of circumstances until I reached this stage in my life. Although I continue to search, I have never found my birthparents. (Robert, age 64)

Adopted into an affluent, dysfunctional family, it never occurred to me that family life could be anything other than what I had experienced.

The consequences of growing up in a dysfunctional family and facing those issues necessitated such sweeping changes in my personal life that it was four years after I entered counseling before I could find the energy or the time to begin the search. I would have started years ago. However, I couldn't begin to search while I was still trying to form a workable relationship with my adoptive parents, even after all those years. The reality is that I went into the adoptive family as an orphan. I lived with them as an orphan and I am now an adult living as an orphan. I hope any natural family I have will be closer to normal than I am. I expect to be at a disadvantage when meeting them because of my dysfunctional family experience. (John, 50)

Robert and John are not alone in waiting until midlife to face the issues of their adoption. According to Roszia, "Sometimes it's the first time in life they feel settled within themselves. They feel they have matured enough to take the risk and to attack something that feels frightening."

I Just Didn't Have Enough Time

I thought about searching for my birthparents when I was around twenty years old. However, I got married and had three children pretty quickly. I was so busy, happy, and fulfilled with the responsibilities of my family that I just didn't have the time to devote to a search. As the children grew older and their emotional demands became more intensified, I focused much of my energy in helping them. I just didn't have the emotional strength it would take to tackle such a big issue. I put it away until now. The children are grown. My husband is nearing retirement. This just seemed like the best time for me. I know that now the chances of my birthparents still being alive are pretty slim. (Rebecca, age 59)

Right after I graduated from college, I took a teaching job, married, and had three children. When they started middle school and high school, I went back to get my master's. I have been so busy with my career and family that I just didn't want to take the time especially emotionally to deal with my own adoption issues. Perhaps it was my way of denial, but someday I knew I would search. I just joined a support group and have begun the process. I think I have enough energy left to tackle anything I find. (Maryann, age 54)

I Didn't Know You Could Do It

When I was younger, I thought of my birthmother when I was in trouble. I thought she would come and save me! When I had my first child, I began to think of what she must have gone through in giving me up for adoption. I'm sure it ran through my mind a lot. But I never knew you could, in fact, find your birth family. So I tried to keep my needs put away. (Jackie, age 49)

My whole experience as an adoptee has been one of secrecy. I didn't find out I was adopted until I was eighteen. Then no one would talk about it, so I put it aside. I figured since it was all such a secret there would be no way to find out any information about my past. It wasn't until I read an article in the newspaper that I learned it was something I could do. I didn't waste any time in contacting a search group in my area for help. (Richard, age 43)

These are just a few of the reasons for waiting until past forty to search for information about one's birthfamily. Many waited for other reasons, yet finally came to a decision to act. What finally motivated them?

Death of Adoptive Parents Left Them Orphans Again

As some adoptees encounter the impending death of their adoptive parents, they realize that soon they will return to an earlier status, that of orphan. Dr. Brodzinsky says that the death of the adoptive parents may make the adopted person feel abandoned and longing for a replacement family.[6]

For some who vigorously undertake the search at age forty or fifty, it is simply that they do not want to be orphaned again, adds Roszia.

They Needed a Better Parenting Relationship

Another propelling force is a negative experience in the adoptive home. Once the parents have died, adoptees anxiously begin looking for elderly birthparents to fill in the gaps. They are fully aware that time is quickly passing and their birthparents may be gone. The search may be an effort to gain a parenting relationship they never had. It may or may not meet that need or expectation.

Their Own Children Encouraged the Search

As the child of an adopted person, some occasionally find themselves dealing with the same dilemmas as their parent, *Who I am? What is my history?* Many adopted persons are spurred on to search due to the interest of their children.

Often the decision to search is encouraged by the adult children of the adoptee, says Dr. Joyce Maguire-Pavao. They develop a strong interest in locating medical information and birthfamily history and sometimes these adult children take on the searching characteristics of an adopted person. It becomes a passion for them, too.[7] Connie, age sixty-one, found this true in her life.

As my children married and became parents, they began to question the genetic inheritance they, too, were passing on. My second daughter saw a TV program about search groups and asked if I would object if she pursued the issue. She and her older sister drove to the state capital and got my original birth certificate. It was at that point, seeing my birthmother's name, the address of the hospital, her age nineteen, that I began to wonder if she was still alive, and if she was, whether she would be willing to see me. That was in 1993 and I was fifty years old with three children and four grandchildren.

They Faced Their Own Mortality

Perhaps the strongest force in moving adoptees in midlife to search, especially for men, is coming to terms with their own mortality.

Men tend to defer these emotional issues for a long time in their lives, says Dr. Dirck Brown. Men are less likely to deal with feelings and then to act on those feelings that are so tied to the search. There comes a time when men, who once felt invincible, begin to realize that time is ticking away. What they must do is something that should be done with no further delay. Searching and finding birthparents are those issues typically tackled later in life for men. There's a strong sense that time is simply running out.[8]

Many issues keep adult adoptees from beginning their search until midlife. If an adopted adult begins the search of people and places from an unknown past, special concerns regarding the search, reunion, and midlife should be considered.

Concerns of Adults Searching in MidLife
A First Concern

The longer you wait, the greater the likelihood your birthparents have died and told no one of the child born decades ago.

Sharon was completely aware of the possibility that because she waited until she was forty-eight to search, one or both of her birthparents would be dead. What she wasn't prepared for was that they had told no one of her existence. When she first contacted her birth siblings, they reacted with anger and disbelief.

A searcher at this time in life faces what could be a unique challenge, says Sharon Kaplan-Roszia. There may no longer be people around who can validate the adoptee's story. There is no one to mediate, and it can stir up an incredible hornet's nest.

A Second Concern

Because you are in midlife, you have a lot of living to continue with during the search and reunion. You must not allow the search to take over and control everything else.

Although he dreaded doing it, Richard's boss called him into the office. He knew Richard was in the midst of a search for his birthparents and that it understandably occupied a great deal of his thinking. However, it began to occupy a great deal of his time at work with phone calls and office conversations. He had to ask Richard to put it aside from eight to five.

Adults searching at this time in their life must keep the search in balance. They must be able to find a place in their life to put the search, otherwise it can take over and control all their other responsibilities.

Phil, an adoptee in his early forties, experienced an obsession with his search once he decided to begin.

It became so consuming, so difficult for me. I was so impassioned by my need to find my birth family that everything else, including my marriage, became secondary. I spent every available free moment working on the details. If I wasn't searching through some information, I was consumed by two fears, that I wouldn't find anything out, and if I did, I couldn't handle it emotionally. Finally, after I attended a search group and heard a speaker talk about how to work through search obsession, I realized what I was doing to my wife and to myself. It helped me to settle down.

A Third Concern

If your birthparents relinquished you forty or fifty years ago, you may find a less receptive environment in which to search than the more open one that prevails today.

Diane, at age fifty-two, had searched for her birthmother for over two-and-a-half years. When she finally located her, Diane was surprised at the response. Her mother denied the faintest possibility that she was the birthmother. She asked Diane to go away and never return.

Diane was sure of the accuracy of her information. This woman who so vehemently denied she was her birthmother had to be covering up. This had to be her mother. Why wouldn't she admit it?

What Diane had encountered, without emotional preparation, was the consequences that adoption secrecy created and preserved several decades ago.

The person searching in midlife must recognize he is searching in an environment today that is totally different from that of his birthparents, advises Kate Cleary. Bearing a child out of wedlock evoked such incredible shame that denial of the whole experience became a way of survival for the birthmother. The shame and guilt, in many cases, followed these birthmothers well into their seventies or eighties.

A Fourth Concern

The search and reunion will have an impact on your immediate and extended family.

According to both Kate Cleary and Dr. Joyce Maguire-Pavao, some adopted persons overlook this significant concern.

"For some, the search becomes an obsession," says Cleary. "It is all they think and talk about. Family members who were once supportive become tired of hearing about it. If you are searching, be careful not to get narrowly focused in relationships at home. Work at informing your family members about issues of the search and reunion. Be open to their questions."

"The immediate and extended family members, in order to be supportive, must be educated about the search and reunion issues," says Dr. Maguire-Pavao.

They must be educated about how normal it is for an adopted person to want to search. They must be informed about how important it is for the adopted person to know about his medical history, his background, and the people of his past.

The family must be helped to understand that the search and reunion is a process that evokes an incredible amount of conflicting emotions. It is beneficial for the family to learn about what might happen during the search, like finding death or rejection or finding overwhelming acceptance. For some, finding the good things, like unconditional love and acceptance, makes it more difficult to reconcile issues of loss. If the family is aware of this possibility, they can be supportive.

An often-troubling concern for adoptees regarding the extended family is whether to incorporate one's adoptive parents into this process. Do seventy-year-old adoptive parents help a fifty-year-old son or daughter with the search? "Yes," says Dr. Maguire-Pavao, "I have seen it many times."

She continues, "For real healing to occur, I think it is tremendously important for the adoptive parents to be involved in the process. For years we have given adoptees the message that you can have only one set of parents. Reality is they have two sets. Integrating both sets of parents into one's life is a real step toward healing."[9]

A Fifth Concern

You may experience major changes within your emotional and psychological makeup, changes that will impact how you relate within the family and beyond.

Prior to her reunion, Connie was a real people pleaser. She felt so incredibly inadequate within herself that she thought the only way to be accepted throughout her family system and friendships was to make everyone happy at her expense. Connie grew up and carried into midlife this sense of inadequacy, due to the feelings of abandonment and rejection that lay buried within her.

In December 1991, Connie initiated a search and found her birthmother. Although initially hesitant to meet Connie, her seventy-year-old birthmother finally invited her to her home. As Connie visited with her mother, she learned the circumstances of her relinquishment. It was a picture far different from the gloomy fantasy she had cultivated for over fifty-two years.

Connie's birthmother became pregnant at the age of eighteen, just after the outbreak of World War II. Her birthfather, a soldier, left for overseas with a promise to marry upon his return. Six months after he left, she received word of his death. She had skillfully hidden the appearances of pregnancy from her family, but now it was impossible. Her parents made hasty arrangements for Connie to leave the area and place the child for adoption. All this was done against the deepest wishes of her heart. In fact, she was never permitted to see the child and was never told if it was a girl or boy. She had wanted the child all along.

As the months followed, Connie allowed the reality that she was truly a wanted child to sink deeply within her. She felt herself becoming more confident, more assertive. The changes that happened within her not only called for changes in her marriage relationship and with her children, but even with her adoptive parents. Connie wisely sought the direction of a counselor as she worked through this stage in her life.

It is not unusual to see these changes happen again and again. Some adoptees "tap-dance" as fast as they can to the tune everyone else plays. But in the months and years after the search and a good reunion experience, that person begins to like himself. He becomes surer of himself and has a clearer self-identity. The whole dynamic of his life shifts. As mentioned earlier, this is a reality of which the immediate and extended family needs to be aware. Even in a good marriage, it creates a crisis that needs to be worked through.

WHAT LESSONS HAVE WE LEARNED? A LOOK AT LIFE EXPERIENCES

Recognizing one's need to search in midlife and confronting the concerns that midlife searches create prepares one to undertake a life-changing journey. What have those who have walked this path found?

I Found Unconditional Acceptance

I found my birthmother and two sisters in December 1993, one day before my forty-first birthday. We met in January at my birthmother's home in Los Angeles. The reunion went exceptionally well. I felt at peace and so did my birthmother. She didn't stop holding me and crying for twenty minutes. I felt as if I were home from a trip, not home for the first time. The only thing I would have done differently is to start earlier. Although I'm grateful to have found my birthmother, I feel cheated out of the last twenty years when I could have known her. Since our reunion, our relationship grows stronger every day. We talk often on the phone and my birthmother is planning a trip to meet my whole family. I feel God has blessed me by giving me two wonderful mothers. I love them both. (Robert, age 49)

I've Gone On with My Life

My mother refuses contact, but I send her Christmas cards every year. It has been two years since the first contact and I haven't received a call or even a letter of acknowledgment from her. I do have an ongoing relationship with a brother and a sister. Even though it has been rejecting from her position, I would still do the whole thing again, because knowing the truth has been tremendously helpful. I've been able to put this behind me and get on with my life. It's made our adoptive family closer and I have deepened in my love and appreciation for them. (Jackie, 51)

I Feel Truly Blessed

I have found my birthmother, in fact, it took me about half a day to locate her, thanks to the group Reunite in Columbus. We had our first wonderful reunion in her home. It went very well. Her first words to me as I walked up the porch steps were, Well, my dear, a big hug, and surprisingly, no tears on either of our parts, and then just a couple of hours of conversation. She was willing to answer any of my questions. It will be 12 years this May since I found Mama Irene, as I call her. I feel as if I have been truly blessed, things just couldn't be any better. Our relationship grows continually we write every couple of weeks and call each other on special occasions.

I feel a certain peace and I just feel better. It's so wonderful to know she didn't hate me that she wanted me to search for her. It's so much fun having two brothers after being an only child for so many years. Also, my adoptive mother was very glad for me and couldn't have been more supportive. (Judy, 62)

A Word from Betsie

Adoption has changed so much in recent years that many adoptees who have thought of searching, but held back, may feel freer to take action now.

Generally, the more years since the adoption, the harder the search. So, adoptees searching in midlife may need to be especially persistent.

I personally find it sad when because of emotional baggage from the "old" system, adoptees put off searching until it is too late to find their birthparents alive. I would tell people who are considering a search to do it when they feel ready instead of repressing the need for years and then regretting it later.

Adoptees searching in midlife should seek support and invite their family or other significant people to join in their experience as much as possible.

NOTES

1. David Brodzinsky, Marshall D. Schechter, and Robin Marantz Henig, *Being Adopted: The Lifelong Search for Self* (New York: Anchor Books 1992), 149.

2. Joyce Maguire-Pavao, Personal interview on June 25, 1994, at the Adoptive Families of America Conference in Minneapolis, Minn. Used with permission.

3. Brodzinsky, 152.

4. Dirck Brown, personal interview, June 9, 1994. Used with permission.

5. Sharon Kaplan Roszia, personal interview, June 1994. Used with permission.

6. Brodzinsky, 158.

7. Maguire-Pavao interview.

8. Brown interview.

9. Maguire-Pavao interview.

CHAPTER SIXTEEN

Postreunion Relationships: Now What? New Beginnings

I've been reunited now for over fifteen years. Over time my relationship with my birthfamily, and my feelings about the role of adoption in my life have evolved. My birthfamily is now an important part of my extended family and my relationship with them, most of the time, no longer focuses on adoption. My birth and adoptive parents know and like each other. I've been in my birth brothers' weddings; my son knows my birthfamily members as grandparents, uncles, aunts, and cousins. Yet, being a member of my birthfamily to the extent that I am has not detracted at all from my place in my adoptive family.—Betsie

Much of what we hear about and see in the media about adoption search and reunion revolves around the excitement of the search process and initial contact made. Talk shows feature hugs filled with surprise and tears of joy, newspapers display stories about interesting reunions, adoption organization newsletters carry articles by excited members reporting what happened when they made contact with their found family members. But, what happens after all the initial frenzy and excitement wears off? Although reunited adoptees and birthparents will tell you that the reunion is just the beginning, we do not as often have the opportunities to hear how these relationships develop and unfold—the joys and the challenges.

The search and reunion experience changes life forever. Once an adopted person searches, no matter the outcome, he is never the same. Once a birthparent finds her relinquished child, whatever type of relationship develops, she is never the same. The reunion experience has a far broader impact than just on the two persons involved, for it reaches far beyond them. It has implications for the adoptee, the birthparents, the adoptive parents, birth siblings, adoptive siblings, spouses, children, and others.

Once the reunion begins, it impacts multiple family systems and changes the lives of many people and many relationships—forever. That's why it's crucial to understand the dynamics that are a part of the reunion and postreunion period. Reunions often go through stages, and although there is no handbook to follow, we can learn from each others' experiences.

While of course there are some reunions that do not work out, in this chapter we will take a look at those that have become ongoing relationships, and the joys and challenges involved.

UNDERSTANDING THE DYNAMICS OF THE EARLY POSTREUNION PERIOD

After contact is made and accepted, there are a whole range of feelings that come with major intensity; many call this a roller coaster of emotion. For most it begins with relief, then euphoria—feeling that things are unreal, too good to be true. That's one end of the roller coaster. There's another end of the roller coaster, letdown. So much energy has been expended in the search process, and often the searcher has become accustomed to the frantic pace of search activities. Once the adoptee or birthparent gets all the answers, and the high intensity energy is no longer needed, a letdown feeling often comes. The rush of feelings includes acknowledging and grieving losses that were never recognized before, fearing the loss of what one has just gained, confusion over roles or reactions of other family members, and sometimes deep insecurity and even depression.

Jeanne describes not knowing how deeply buried her feelings were about having placed her son for adoption in 1957. She describes her prereunion emotional state now as "detached"; she had even forgotten his date of birth. Over the years Jeanne had told the sons she raised and even some friends about her other son. However she rejected all ideas of searching—for fear her son would reject her as his father had, due to embarrassment of not remembering his date of birth, and in an attempt to "follow the rules"—after all, she'd given up all her rights.

Three years ago Jeanne was found by her son; she was sixty-two and he was forty-one years old. "I was ecstatic. I called everyone I knew, I told everyone, even people at the grocery store! I wrote to all my family members, even those who had never known about him. It was truly joyous. I even brought him to church and introduced him to the congregation."

After about a month on cloud nine, Jeanne crashed. "I didn't know what was going on. I cried, I didn't know how I could continue. I was obsessed with my son who had found me. I felt guilty for not thinking as much about my other sons—the young birthmother in me was still hungry for love—I needed to integrate 'her' into 'me' now. I felt jealous (of his adoptive parents), angry (at my lack of control in placing him), and incredible grief (over the lost years)."

Jeanne struggled intensely for a year. Her relinquished son offered her unconditional love, but worried that maybe he'd done the wrong thing in finding her—that he'd caused her so much pain.

Many adoptees, too, are unaware of the losses for them, and the reunion experience unleashes the whole grief process—from anger to sadness, and finally, acceptance. A reunion, although a positive encounter, hits many in the face with the realities of what was lost to them—biological connectedness, history, and for some, the opportunity to have been raised by their birthparents.

As an adoptee who searched and found my birthmother over ten years ago, I still recall trying to figure out just why I felt so unsettled and depressed after having such a successful reunion with both of my birthparents. I have come to realize now that this is just a part of the healing of the pain and scars many adoptees feel from being "plucked and replanted." One encouraging word: With time the low feelings go away, for they are common to all of us who deal with this unique thing called reunion. (Paul, age 33)

In the beginning there was a sense of trying to "catch up" on all that we had missed and even a sense of concern that perhaps they might disappear out of my life again. Once that stage passed we were able to settle in and get to know each other. (Donna, age 44)

ESTABLISHING ROLES: WHO WE ARE TO EACH OTHER

A New Role for Adoptees

One of the challenges for me was defining the nature of the new relationship. My whole question was—who am I to these people? I struggled with being biologically related to them while being a total stranger. I grappled with the fact that I didn't know anything about any of these people, but they are blood relatives. It felt really strange. I didn't know what to call my birthmother. I didn't know how to integrate them into my life. (David, age 28)

Defining the role and integrating the new people into one's life is one of the first challenges, and the resolution doesn't happen overnight. It often happens over a period of two or three years or more and at different levels. Growing up as an adoptee, knowing little about your own history, then suddenly having access to so much information can be overwhelming. Vicky describes:"I would listen to pieces of my family history over and over again and ask questions about other relatives. A lot of integration took place just as I experienced being with my birth family on and off over the last eight years, seeing commonalities, gestures. It just takes time, a lot of time."

THE NEW ROLE FOR BIRTHPARENTS

For birthparents, the initial issues are often about how to tell others about the adoptee and how to establish meaningful communication, especially if the adoptee lives in a different city.

For Nancy, "telling" took on a different twist. She had placed two daughters for adoption at two separate times in her life. Her family knew of the first, but not the second. Then, she was found by her second daughter seven years ago.

Sue was a secret from my family. I had not told them about her because I was embarrassed about being pregnant a second time. She contacted my parents first, so I had to be open about her birth. . . . The main "stage" I remember is worrying that Sue would change her mind about wanting to know me. I would go months without hearing from her. I did a lot of "what ifs." Thank heavens I got e-mail about that time and learned that she had just inherited my dislike of writing letters. It had nothing to do with me. She e-mails short notes all the time and so do I. I didn't want to push her or interfere. I didn't know how she was feeling. Now that I know her better, I just write or call whenever I feel like it. It is a much more comfortable relationship.

A NEW ROLE FOR ADOPTIVE PARENTS

For adoptive parents the early reunion period can be an anxious one— even for those parents who fully supported their child's right to know their birth family. Insecurities can abound, and the adoptee's parents may worry if the adoptee will turn away from them or like their new family better. For Alyce, an adoptive mother who, responding to her daughter's physical and emotional needs, herself searched for her daughter's birthmother when her daughter was seventeen years old, this was still true. Even though she had herself initiated the contact, it still was difficult.

Ann was less than a month from her eighteenth birthday when she was invited to spend Christmas with her birth family. I hated her being away for Christmas and was apprehensive. However, Ann definitely did not want us to accompany her—she wanted to deal with the reunion alone. I had spoken with her birthmother on the telephone several times and felt good about her, and Ann knew many people (our close friends) in her birthmother's city whom she could call if any problems arose. We, also, kept in close touch with her on the telephone during this period.

It is not uncommon during this "honeymoon" stage for the birthparent and adoptee to have very intense and frequent contact, as if they are making up for lost time. In many cases this sooner or later becomes overwhelming for one or both parties, and someone pulls back. Sometimes this can lead to pain and misunderstandings. In retrospect, many who have been through this stage say that if they had to do it over again, they would go much slower.

In the beginning it was so exciting and we were so intensely drawn to each other. Our lives began to revolve around each other, and I was always so nervous about the impression I was making. Looking back, this created imbalances in other parts of my life and set a stage for the relationship with my birthmother that neither of us could maintain forever. Luckily a few months into our reunion, we both began to realize at about the same time that while we wanted to be close, we had to back off a little and let our relationship develop more naturally. We talked about it. Now after four years we know each other much better and have a comfortable relationship. (Anne, age 36)

BUILDING RELATIONSHIPS: A BRAND-NEW UNCHARTED JOURNEY

While of course there is no road map to successful postreunion, we can recognize and learn from experience and examine common patterns. After the honeymoon period of elation, uncertainty, excitement and in some cases obsession wears off, what happens next?

In *Birthbond: Reunions Between Birthparents and Adoptees: What Happens After*, the authors describe a process of postreunion that parallels a child growing to adulthood and completing, as much as is possible, the unfinished business and emotional baggage that came with adoption. The authors state:

By the time a birthmother and her adopted son or daughter are able to forge a genuinely adult-to-adult relationship—the kind of relationship a "regular" mother might have with a grown-up child—they have probably completed a scope of work that includes:

• Filling up the information vacuum—that is, finding out the story (birth heritage, adoption circumstances) and what's happened since in each person's life

• Resolving the psychological issues (to the extent possible) and coming to peace with the past—for birthmothers, whatever issues are associated with relinquishing their children; for adoptees, the issues associated with being given up

- Catching up [on] present relationships—that is, informing family members and others about the past; integrating the new relationship into other existing relationships
- Growing a shared history—accumulating experience, which will enhance feelings of connectedness, warmth, and closeness; putting pages in a joint book of memories
- Negotiating and inventing a mutually acceptable relationship—that is, deciding how to relate to one another in the postreunion "ever after."[1]

Patrick, a forty-three-year old adoptee now reunited for ten years certainly found this to be true.

Over 10 years, we have been through many stages. Honeymoon, distancing, lots of contact, little contact, but I've felt we were both in this for the long haul. A part of me began growing up all over again with her, going through a 2-year old stage, kid, and teen stage, and hopefully now, an adult stage. It has taken 10 years to begin to feel integrated. Also, the first eight years of our relationship were long-distance with few visits. The last two, we've lived 90 miles apart, and it has been like starting over, with lots of hills and valleys again, but we both recognize the value of working on our relationship. The ripple effects fan out to all areas of my life.

PITFALLS AND TREASURE MAPS

Pitfalls

1. Degree of resolution of past issues. The journey of reunion is often significantly more smooth for people that have mastered some degree of resolution about difficult aspects of their past. Birthmothers and birthfathers who have found ways to feel in control of their lives and let go of anger and blame for past events are much more ready to embrace reunion in a way that will allow them to live into a positive future instead of remaining stuck in a difficult past. Adoptees who have moved past anger at having been placed for adoption, at secrets they were told, or mistakes they feel their adoptive parents made will likewise be more available to move forward into a rewarding postreunion experience. Adoptive parents who feel secure in their role as parents will be more accepting and see the rewards instead of the risks.

I went to an adoption support group for over two years before I actually started my search. Now several years into reunion I see that that's one of the most important things I could have done. When I first started going I was angry, sad and often felt needy. I was reliving a lot of issues from the past instead of living in the present. I resolved a lot, so now I'm able to enjoy my relationship with my daughter without those feelings spilling over into our relationship. I saw reunions of some in my group that happened so quickly and then seemed to have some issues or problems that could have otherwise been avoided. (Christine, age 49)

Likewise, not resolving past issues can cause pain.

My relationship with my birthmother grew for the first few years. Although she seemed open, she was always hesitant and "hands-off" and seemed scared to get too close. I can tell there is still a lot of pain for her to deal with me. Lately, we have not communicated at all. She does not seem to want to put forth any more effort toward a relationship with me or my children, therefore, I have chosen at this point in my life, to not make the extra effort to have a relationship with people who do not want to make time for me. As noble as that sounds, it still hurts that your own Mother will not make an effort to get to know her own child. (Julie, age 34)

I have not welcomed contact with my birthmother, in over a year, as I found she had a problem with being honest, and I guess I still have hurt feelings as she adopted me out and kept my sister, who is only 12 months younger than me. (Nikki, age 31)

2. Lack of open communication. When establishing the postreunion relationship, it is important to be open, and deal up front if possible, with difficult situations. The relationship that develops will be stronger for it.

The response from my birthmother initially was warm and inviting. She wanted to know all about me and my family. We talked on the phone several times before meeting. We met first at her home and then on several other occasions. A few months into our relationship, her contacts became brief. She was abrupt on the phone and refused to meet me. At first, I was terribly hurt and concerned that this was the end. Finally I asked her. Reluctantly she told me she was convinced that she would never be the type of person I would want for a mother. She had failed me once. She knew, eventually, she would do it again. After I reassured her, the burden lifted and we are now able to talk more openly and honestly. (David, age 28)

A sensitive and important issue to me was that I had to let my birthmother know I couldn't call her Mom. She gave me life, but the woman who stayed up with me when I was sick and drove me to school on rainy days is the one I call Mom. (Joan, age 25)

The only difficult issue has been convincing my birthmother that I'm not angry at her for giving me up. From time to time it pops up and I don't know how to make her feel better. (Robert, age 22)

3. Unmet expectations. One of the most common pieces of advice to those in search is to try not to have any set expectations. However, being human, most people do have expectations, or at least hopes. Sometimes the reunion does not yield what was hoped for. Soraya hoped to have

her emotional needs met and to find someone who would show he cares. Her hopes were not realized.

I have not spoken to my birthfather in three years. I have become tired of his inability to even try to meet me half way on our relationship. If I don't call him, I don't have a relationship with him. He doesn't call me. I was stationed in Korea while in the Army and tried to maintain contact with him at that time, he once sent me a letter telling me how it was my mother's fault that he did not have a relationship with my brother by my birthmother. This made me distance myself from him. One thing my birthmother never did was say negative things about my birthfather, but it wasn't hard to gather that she didn't care for him, she just simply warned to be careful, because he may still be capable of hurting me, emotionally. Where my birthmother wanted to give me a shield with which to protect myself, my birthfather wants to blame his own inequities on everybody else.

Donna found that her birthmother struggles with alcoholism and mental illness, yet she hoped for a relationship. "I met my birthmother a few years back after several years of corresponding by letter and phone. Since that initial meeting she has chosen not to keep contact with me. Initially this was very painful for me, but I am now at peace with it because I believe that some things are just not meant to be."

Carl on the other hand, based on what he had been told, expected that he was not going to have much to do with his birthfather. Upon getting to know him, he has been pleasantly surprised.

I was skeptical of my birthfather at the beginning of our relationship. My birthmother certainly didn't speak positively of him. From the fables my adoptive parents had been told, he was the one responsible for my surrender because he left my birthmother to fend for herself and her children. Over the years, I have found my birthfather to be a gentle, compassionate and personable man. He is nowhere near the image that I had of him prior to meeting him. He has never tried to control our relationship other than to try to develop a good relationship with me and my family as individuals. He never tried to become a father figure for me. He respected my adoptive father and his role as my parent, even though the two of them had never met. I can best summarize the relationship evolution as going from an emotional high to stagnation with my birthmother and going from [an] unsure to a strong friendship with my birthfather.

4. Different values—different lives. Some adoptees and birthparents find that there are big social, cultural or emotional differences between themselves and the other. Patterns that emerge in these cases include:

• accepting each other and the differences and moving forward with the relationship
• experiencing an ongoing struggle with the relationship and the differences

- eventually losing interest or making a decision that continuing the relationship is too difficult and reducing contact or terminating the relationship altogether

For Melanie there have been many positive aspects to her reunion, but she silently struggles with some of the differences.

After six years, there is still an artificial nature to some dimensions of my relationship with my birth family so I silently endure the things I dislike about them, which is difficult at times. The family in general is pretty racist and bigoted and I was not raised that way, yet I don't feel comfortable picking fights with them about it. We occasionally have a weird thing about religion because I'm Jewish and they're Catholic and never really knew any Jews. I feel sensitive that she can't just sort fold me back into Christianity (like I dislike it when she wraps presents in Christmas paper or when she sent me an Easter card—I think it's just hard for her consciousness to assimilate that not everyone is Christian).

Nikki describes many disappointments in her reunion, eventually leading to no contact. In the beginning, things went well with her birthmother. Due to the lack of acceptance of the reunions by her birthmother's other daughter and her birthfather's wife, Nikki's relationship with each of her birthparents was off and on in different stages over a twelve-year period. Although things improved for some time, the struggle got to be too much. "Not one of my birthparents have acknowledged one of my birthdays, the birth of my children, or my marriage, which I find very hurtful. My birthparents have no interest in meeting my adoptive family. My adoptive parents have looked forward to meeting them and have formed a close relationship with my adoptive brother's birth family."

Robert, a fifty-five-year-old adoptee of mixed racial background, learned that his birthmother had passed away. He found a sister and several brothers. After a terrific initial reconnection, he found that they had varying discomfort with him coming into their lives and with his life choices. Reactions ranged from a warm and enthusiastic welcome and continuing contact to resistant warnings to their "new gay/black brother." Contact from the sister diminished and he learned that his lifestyle was considered a major sin from some of his self-proclaimed "redneck" blood relatives. Both Robert and his brothers and sister continue to wade through the wide differences in their beliefs, educational backgrounds, and views of the world.

However, despite the differences, Irene focuses on the connection present. "My birth family and I have vastly different worldviews—influenced, one imagines, by the different times, opposite societies, and extremely different educational backgrounds of the homes we were raised in—but we have the same emotional reactions, and can finish each others' sentences."

5. Bad Timing. The person who initiates the search has a choice over the timing—the found person does not. Whatever else is going on in the lives of the person or family who is found can have a big impact on the reunion. The found person or family may be dealing with a death, an illness, a new or stressful work situation, or a multitude of other circumstances. Rachel's situation illustrates the type of impact this can have. Rachel, an adoptee and now the adoptive parent of two, had attempted to search for her birthparents for two years after she turned eighteen. She gathered a lot of information, but stopped short of completing her search. Rachel describes what happened about ten years later.

One day, one of the agencies we were working with (which happened to be the agency I was adopted through) called, but not with news of our status as adoptive parents. They had just received a letter from a woman looking for her daughter and when they went into the records, they discovered that the daughter was me. It was a beautiful letter and contained a photo—this was the first time I had ever seen an image of anyone biologically connected to me. Unfortunately, the timing of the letter was during a difficult and emotional time for me. I was coping with many failed invitro attempts, and a lot of my effort was going into trying to adopt a child which seemed like it would never happen. I sent word back through the social worker that I got the letter and would answer, but that it might take a while. It did take a while—maybe a few years. Then we exchanged cards, photos and a few phone calls.

I look at what we were going through at the time I was contacted by my birthmother—infertility treatments/procedures and the whole adoption process along with a new, growing business. Each of those alone were capable of taking up my energies, time, and emotions. Then the arrival of our 2 children within a couple years, and of course the children becoming my top priorities. With each child also came communications with their birthparents. I did not have the energy (or did not choose to have the energy) to develop a relationship with my birthmother in addition to relationships with my adoptive parents, my in-laws, our son's birthmother and daughter's birthparents.

Rachel finally did meet her birthmother about ten years after the first contact, and keeps in touch through cards, gifts, and e-mail, but she has never formed a close relationship. And, although she says, "It's unsettling for me that I haven't given the relationship with my birthmother the attention it probably should have," she doesn't feel the inclination to give it more focus at this point in her life.

She does however say, "I think that the difficulty I've had in establishing a relationship with my birthmother at age 30, 40 and beyond has prompted me to work even harder to help and encourage our child with the open adoption to maintain the relationship with her birthparents and to be receptive to relationships beyond birthmother and father—and, to try to help our child with the more closed adoption communicate with his birthmother and her other children."

Treasure Maps
The Journey to Meet Siblings

An added joy in many reunions is the discovery of the existence of siblings.

My relationship with my oldest brother has steadily grown over the past 17 years and I often feel like we've always been together. We have grown to know each other on a much deeper level and found that even though we were separated for 23 years we are very much alike. (Donna, age 44)

My relationship with my sister is very rewarding. I look to her for inspiration, advice, and friendship. We share a similar sense of humor and some of the same interests. I have the feeling that if we met socially we'd be good friends. (Joanne, age 29)

As Paul found however, it doesn't always go smoothly.

After I found my birthmother, she told me of three other siblings, two half-brothers and a half-sister. Up to this point, she had not told them about me. When they found out, one of my brothers and my sister were pretty angry at my birthmom for keeping such a secret. They were not ready to meet me. However, my youngest brother thought it was terrific that he had another older brother. We hit it off. I've had to come to a point where I realize that, hopefully, time will take care of my brother and sister's anger. I realize I just can't push myself into their lives. The revelation of me was a pretty difficult pill for them to swallow, I guess.

Joanne and Robin have found that incorporating the new family member takes time.

I feel strange reminiscing with my family when my birth sister is present. I feel as though I'm excluding her, even though she has her own memories of growing up. As the years go by, we find ourselves remembering "old times" from the beginning of our reunion though, which is great. (Joanne)

One might think that adults wouldn't have a problem with jealousy, but I really believe my newfound sisters became jealous, at first, of my relationship with my birthparents. My parents married a year after I was born and I have three full-blooded sisters. Since our reunion, and it has been terrific, my parents and I have spent a great deal of time together. In the early months, my sisters would not have much to say to me. Finally, I went to them and shared my feelings. That really cleared the air and now we are doing great. We meet at least once a month for lunch. I was raised an only child, so having three instant sisters has really enriched my life. (Robin)

When the circumstances around relinquishment were especially difficult, the adoptee may be viewed as the "lucky" one.

Another difficult issue is in learning the childhood experiences that my birth siblings had to endure while I was the one relinquished. To hear them tell it, I was lucky to be the one who got away from that lifestyle and was given an opportunity to have a more positive life experience than they have had. It is an odd feeling to be both abandoned yet guilty at the same time. (Carl, age 42)

Relationships with the adoptive siblings can be affected, too.

My relationship between myself and my adoptive sister (7 years my senior) was strained when I first started searching. I initially made sure my adoptive parents knew I was searching and that they were okay with it. When that news funneled down to my sister, she had a hard time understanding why I had to do this and she was very protective of our parents. As time has gone by, things are back to normal—we just don't talk about the past! (Julie, age 34)

For my adoptive siblings, my search and reunion served as a catalyst. Upon my sibling's request, I helped my younger sister and brother search for, locate and reunite with members of their birth families as well. (Carl, age 42)

I think my sister feels upset that my birthmother found me, but her's did not find her. I've offered to help her search, but she says she doesn't want to. (Vicky, age 34)

REUNIONS FROM THE PERSPECTIVE OF ADOPTIVE PARENTS

Birthparents and adopted persons are not the only ones touched by the long-term effect of reunions. With some fear, but with open hearts, adoptive parents have supported their adult children's need for a reunion contact. Some have had the opportunity to meet birthparents and even develop positive relationships with them.

What Adoptees Say about Their Parents Who Supported Them in Their Reunion

It has strengthened our relationship. My adoptive mother has been my rock as far as dealing with my extended adoptive family. She was the one who would stand up to disagreeing relatives and say "Well, if it was you, wouldn't you want to know?" (Julie, age 34)

The first holiday after meeting my birthmother was Thanksgiving. I really appreciated my adoptive parents because as the holiday was approaching, they sensed it was a dilemma for me. They told me honestly to do exactly what I needed to do. If being with my birthmother on that first Thanksgiving was important, I should do exactly that. Because they were open about it, I felt free to make that decision. Now I alternate between Thanksgiving with one and Christmas with the other. (Paul, age 33)

My adoptive mother went from not speaking to me initially about the reunion to continually asking if I've heard from "my mom" or my brothers and sisters. We have normal conversations and she has taken a vested interest in my extended family. What a phenomenal feeling it is to be able to share this with my parents. (Donna, age 44)

On Birthparents and Adoptive Parents Meeting
Adoptees Speak

My adoptive parents have met my birthmother and her husband. It was very emotional the first time, but everyone thanked everyone else for "me." They subsequently met a few more times at birthday parties, baptisms, births, etc. I think it was healing for both mothers and for me to see each other and talk about what happened 34 years ago. (Julie, age 34)

My two moms have met twice. Once three years after finding. This was mainly because I asked them to. Then I thought they needed to meet each other to dispel illusions about who each other was. Now I realize there was apart of me that was looking for permission from a-mom and wanted to show b-mom who raised me. On the surface it went well. Under the surface, there was a lot of tension.

The second time was seven years after finding. On my 42nd birthday, both moms came into town, and we all went to brunch. There was much less tension, as well as a moving moment between them when both expressed gratitude for what the other had done. (Patrick, age 43)

A Birthmother Speaks

I met my birth son's adoptive parents about 6 months into our reunion, and in fact stayed in their home for five days. We got along well and shared our stories of my relinquishment and how they came to be his parents. I like them and there was an easy openness between us. I was amazed that they would invite me to their home, they were very hospitable. I think it answered some questions for us all. It definitely has deepened their relationship with "our" son as his mother so graciously called him. (Ellen, age 55)

Adoptive Parents Speak

I was truly happy for both of my children who searched and were reunited with their birthmothers and birthfathers. [In both cases, the birthmothers had married the birthfathers following the babies' having been given up for adoption.] My wife and I were anxious to meet the birthparents as soon as possible. As the result of several visits with both sets of birthparents, we came to know them and we all felt a close bond because of what each of us was able to contribute to the child's well-being. Both sets of birthparents are our friends, and we're happy about that. (Brad, age 76)

I keep hearing about adoptive parents and birthparents that never meet, partly because of the adoptee's feelings but also for reasons I can't figure out. I could hardly wait to meet our children's birthparents. However, I have to admit we never met Ann's birthmother—she and Ann became estranged and before that she never seemed to want to meet us. Shall I also admit that we observed her once, unknown to her, by eating in a restaurant near where she works—and, from the photos and her mannerisms like Ann, we recognized her when she came in to lunch. That was a relief to me—I felt maybe we'd really hurt her by the search and the later alienation that occurred, but I could see she was a strong woman, doing well and definitely in charge of her life.

We have a good relationship with Ann's birthfather, whom she resembles physically (looks very much like his sister—could be twins)—he has visited us and we've visited him. He participated in Ann's wedding, which we hosted, and brought a tableful of friends and family with him. (Alyce, age 65)

Societal Messages Run Deep

Some adoptees would prefer to keep the two parts of their lives separate, even if their families are willing or wanting to meet each other. Carl, who has now known his birthfamilies for eleven years, would prefer that his birthparents and adoptive parents not meet. This might be due, at least in part, from early conditioning of how it "should" be.

Our parents told us as we were growing that they would assist us however they could if we decided that we wanted to find our birthparents. This was never spoken in contempt nor on a frequent basis but only at those times when we were trying to understand our adoption situations as children. For that attitude and openness, I've always respected my parents. Even with their positive attitude on search and reunion, I still felt the societal pressure that searching would hurt my parents. The subtle cues from movies, television and the print media are as subtle as a train wreck when you are aware and sensitized to the messages.

Lifelong Relatedness—Blending Families

As the postreunion period progresses and the mental and emotional adjustments are made to shift from the psychological presence to the physical presence (see chapter 2), or from one of fantasy to one of reality, many reunited family members describe a process of becoming family. In this stage, no longer is the "reunion" paramount. The "work" for the most part is done, and participants become part of each other's lives. If tough times do arise, there is a known commitment to the relationship that each securely feels—that both parties are "in it for the long haul."

New traditions are developed that encompass the expanded family, families merge and blend and attend each other's important events, and people accept each other—idiosyncrasies and all.

Our relationship has definitely grown over the past four years, and life without her is unimaginable now. Despite living 1400 miles apart, we have been fortunate in that we see each other every few months, have spent relatively long periods of time together, and have attended 3 American Adoption Congress conferences and a healing weekend together. It has been a period of increasing closeness and comfort, but there have been challenges as well. It was difficult to handle conflicts and disagreements because we both fear loss and abandonment, but it is slowly getting better. Trust just takes time and work, and has to be built one step at a time. We both still really dread saying goodbye—that is still painful for both of us. Our closeness is a double-edged sword—the closer we feel the more we realize what has been lost. I think we have recently made significant progress in dealing with this, and are more accepting of the past and more focused on the future than ever. (Eileen, birthmother, age 53)

The honeymoon period lasted for about a year after my son found me. When I realized I wouldn't lose him, I was able to start letting more of my true self out. I shared more and showed my true feelings. Now, after 5 years of knowing my son I see that he is not perfect—there are things I love about him, and other things I don't like. Before, I saw ourselves as kindred spirits, now I'm not sure that we are, and this is painful. Now I see our differences and realize that I *wanted* him to be my soul mate. In some ways I realize now how much I am still getting to know him. I let go of wanting a relationship that he was unwilling or incapable of giving me, and accepted him for who he is. (Donni, age 57)

Over the last two years our relationship has grown more normal. I am not on tenterhooks anymore afraid that he will disappear again and my heart will be broken. There's more work to be done though on maturing and normalizing this relationship. We live so far away from each other and have only seen each other twice, and that was during the first six months. Every time we talk or write I feel more and more that I need only be completely who I am. Thank goodness that time really does heal all wounds as far as is humanly possible. I do believe from what I have seen though that it can only get better, i.e. more real with the ups and downs of all human relationships. That is a gift. (Ellen, age 55)

Establishing New Traditions

We started a new tradition. I have a fall get-together. I invite my birth family, my dad's side of the family, my mom's side of the family, my husband's family, and a few special friends. Everyone feels they are truly part of an amazing experience and family. I tell them they are each a piece of the tapestry of my life. (Dianne, age 36)

Weddings

At Ann's wedding, we had to decide what role her birthfather would play. She wanted her adoptive father to walk her down the aisle and give her away, but the thought was that her birthfather might join them. I felt upset about this, especially as there would be no distinction at the altar because the Catholic Church doesn't let any father "give the bride away." Finally, it was worked out that she and her adoptive father would stop by where her birthfather was seated in the third row, he'd stand up and kiss her, and then she'd continue down the aisle with her adoptive father. Later, when the family candles were lighted, the birthfather lighted the one for Ann's birthfamily.

The misunderstanding of others was hurtful and upsetting. The DJ told me he would introduce "you and your husband" and then "Ann's father." I immediately told him that my husband was Ann's father—and that he must say "birthfather" in the second introduction. That went okay. But I definitely was aware of "feelings" about this.

The photographer really didn't understand even though we had explained. He took many more photos of Ann with her birthfather than with her adoptive father—even had our son with Ann and her birthfather. He apparently thought that her birthfather was my first husband. I was really angry and hurt for my husband (her adoptive father) when I saw all those photos. (Alyce, age 65)

At "our" son's wedding, I asked his adoptive father if he would mind posing for a few photos with me and so we did. That must have made for some interesting photographs in the wedding album. (Carole, birthmother, age 57)

Funerals

When my birth brother and I had found that our birthfather had died, we shared in the grief and also in arranging for his headstone. A part of ourselves had died and it meant a lot to be able to share that with one another. (Donna, age 44)

Perspectives Change over Time

After a while, I definitely realized I wasn't losing Beth. The turning point for me came about four months after the reunion. Beth was at college, and not calling me nearly as often as she had in the past (which was actually a good thing, because she had had separation anxiety, and had called almost daily). But I knew that she was speaking more often to her birthparents than to me, and felt bad. Then one night she called me from her boyfriend's apartment; she smelled fumes (his pilot light had gone out) and didn't know what to do. She had called me for advice, and I realized I was still her mother.

Through her reunion, Beth also became closer with my mother, who, to my surprise, was extremely threatened by Beth's searching (and especially by the fact that she found four more grandparents). Beth understood my mother's feelings, and was, and still is, exceptionally kind to her, calling her and sending cards. (Barbara, adoptive mother, age 52)

Extended Family

My children have additional grandparents, aunts, uncles and cousins with whom they've shared their childhood. I now know my biological connection into the rest of humankind. I have two genealogical histories that I can trace. (Carl, age 42)

In both cases, the search/reunion processes have only deepened the love, respect and mutual concern felt between us, the adoptive parents, and our children. I can't imagine how the processes could have come out better than they did.

The birthparents have become part of our extended family. The children have enjoyed discovering brothers, sisters, and other relatives they didn't know they had. When we can get together with the birth families, we do. Many times, however, distances are too great or getting together is inconvenient for some other reason. We love them and we know they love us. It's been a good thing for the children, and for us, to get to know their extended families. (Brad, age 76)

Beyond the Extended Family

About ten years after my reunion, my older adoptive brother decided to make contact with his birthparents, who I had helped him find right after my own search. He wasn't ready to contact them until he was turning 40 years old and realized that if he didn't do it then, he might never get the chance. Much to our surprise, he found that, just like in my birthfamily, his birthparents had married a couple years after his birth, and gone on to have three children that they raised! It's been four years and now I feel like his birth family is part of my extended family too. In fact, since his birthparents live in the same city where I live, my family often spends holidays with his family and birthfamily. (Betsie)

A New Relationship with Oneself

Because I know my first family and have felt the sense of belonging and connection unique to knowing them, I have moved into doing things that feel more natural to me. For example, I had done engineering and music previous to finding. I have over the years moved into another life-long interest, photography, both as a fine art and a profession. I've also developed my writing skills, am writing a book, and have developed a line of greeting cards for those touched by adoption. (Patrick, age 43)

Final Thoughts

Over the years I have come to strongly believe that searching for your birthfamily and being reunited can only prove to be beneficial. It may not always turn out the way you expect it to and you may not get all the questions answered, but you can find a sense of peace and closure. Each member of the adoption triad has their own issues, fears, and pain which can only be addressed by open records. Secrets harbor pain and it is only in truth that we can have closure. This closure is our God given right. (Donna, age 44)

One of the joys that has arisen through this process is the realization that my family is now complete. I didn't know what was missing, but now that the story is out, some of the gaps are filled in and I think my parents feel they can be more honest with us now. When you're keeping a big secret, you can't be very close with someone. Now that the truth is out we're all closer. (Joanne, age 29, sibling)

I am always so sad to hear adoptees tell of their feelings of divided allegiance and even guilt when they search for birthparents. And I feel sad for the birthparents who are not invited to family events or even acknowledged by threatened adoptive parents. I wish I knew some way to reassure these people that their openness to reunion only improves their relationship with their adopted young adults. That is surely our experience. (Alyce, age 65)

I am joyful to know my son and to be a witness to his life and maturing and perhaps even to be a little help to him by my constancy. Also I think I have become a better mother to my two teenagers than was possible before in my lack of awareness of some of my deepest feelings. These are indeed immense joys. (Ellen, age 55)

It was a nine month search. I now divide my life into before 'The First Phone Call,' and after. It was the most courageous, gut-wrenching, exciting, fulfilling, terrifying moment of my life. My birthmother was shocked, in fact said she had hoped and prayed this would never happen, but within ten minutes, was sharing freely and by the end of the 90 minute call, was glad I called. When we met face to face six months later, it was as if something inside me that had been tense for 34 years could finally relax. I felt natural connection for the first time and it has changed my life. (Patrick, age 43)

Finding my son and being reunited with him have completed myself as a person. Now I not only know who I am but so does everyone else. The whole concept has restored my self-esteem and I am now a very strong woman and a stronger person, which is what I could not be before. Therefore I condemn the secrecy and lies that are so prevalent in adoption and can truly say that the truth has set me free. (Carole, age 57, after 17 years of reunion)

As a family we were very lucky to have had such wonderful searches and reunions and to continue to have wonderful relationships. For me to be included in these relationships is so exciting and to see how beautifully my girls deal with all of this is most satisfying and rewarding. (Judy, age 64)

I have met a lot of wonderful people that have shared their stories/lives with me. I seem to be able to relate to their lifetime of concerns and their relationship paths. I also relish the information about myself that I have now. I don't care about the outcome and would do it all over again for the peace of mind it has given to me about myself. (Michelle, age 36, adoptee who has reunited with extended family, but whose birthmother has refused to meet her for 9 years)

Two years ago I had just found my birthmom, Marge, and we were beginning our relationship after being apart from one another for 27 years. We really thought we had all the time in the world when we "found" each other.

I met Marge two weeks after we first talked. Just seeing her filled part of that emptiness I had always felt. I was so much like her, it scared me. A year later Marge passed away after being diagnosed with a rare, aggressive form of brain cancer.

Marge was a kind, generous, loving person. In dealing with this loss, I have to believe that things happen for a reason. We were together in the beginning, then separated, and brought back to each other for a short time. How lucky I was to have her as a birthmom and get the time that I did with her.

Meeting Marge from the first day changed my life, changed me as a person. Marge lives on in me, and my adoptive mom even said that Marge is now a guardian angel for my 6-month-old daughter.

I still can't believe she is gone, but I will never forget her or the gifts she has given me—the most important being life. For our first Christmas together, I gave Marge a watch to signify all the "time" we had. Now I wear that watch to remind me how precious time really is. (Michelle, age 29)

NOTE

1. Judith S. Gediman and Linda P. Brown. *Birthbond: Reunions between Birthparents and Adoptees: What Happens After* (Far Hills, N.J.: New Horizons Press, 1989), 137.

CHAPTER SEVENTEEN

Changing Times

Adoption is transforming in many ways—often, but not always, for the better. Today the complexion of adoption is vastly different from the reality of most of the subjects of this book. There are over 120,000 children in foster care who need permanent adoptive homes (and not enough homes to take them), there are a record number of couples facing infertility and seeking to adopt (wanting mostly infants or very young children), most domestic adoptions are either fully open or provide for significant openness, and international adoptions abound.

In the area of secrecy relating to past adoptions, the institution of adoption has taken many strides forward in recent years. After years of unsuccessful attempts to "retroactively" legalize the right of adult adoptees to access their original birth certificates in state legislatures across America, several have met with success in the last few years. While some states had never closed their records (including Alaska, Kansas, and Ohio for adoptees before 1964) most states did so sometime in the 1930s–1950s. Over the last twenty years many states have passed new laws opening records to adoptees that are adopted from the date of the new law forward. The more difficult task has been convincing the state legislatures to go back and address the needs of those involved in adoptions during the era of sealed records in this country.

Thankfully, activists (who are usually themselves adoptees, birthparents and adoptive parents) are beginning to enjoy successes across the country as they fight state by state to "open" records that have been sealed. While no one is proposing opening records to the public, the "open records" activists seek to make the adoptee's original birth certificate available to him upon his request, in adulthood—a right enjoyed by every other American citizen. We have recently witnessed the records opening to adult adoptees in Oregon, Tennessee, Alabama and Delaware, and there is access to records legislation pending in many other states. The road to reform has been slow, and these successes have just begun after twenty or more years of sustained effort.

Important to note is that the American system of closed records is somewhat of an anomaly. In many countries—for instance Finland, Holland, Israel and Scotland—the original birth certificate has been available to the adult (or in some nations even teenage) adoptee for decades, if they were ever closed at all. In others, such as England and Wales (1975), New Zealand (1985) and state by state throughout Australia in the 1980s and 1990s, the laws around the closure of records were closely re-examined and, as a result, the records were retroactively opened.

In addition, openness in adoption is now accepted as good practice in most professional circles. In fact, the updated adoption standards (2000) of the Child Welfare League includes a new definition of adoption: "Adoption is the social, emotional and legal process through which children who will not be raised by their birth parents become full and permanent legal members of another family while maintaining genetic and psychological connections to their birth family." It goes on to say, "Adoption is more than just a simple legal transaction. It is a complex social and emotional experience as well, with lifetime implications for all parties to it. Those involved in adoption must acknowledge the very real genetic and psychological connections of the adopted child and birth family, which remain even after the legalization of the adoption."

The more this lifelong perspective and "consumer" focus of adoption takes hold, the greater will be the sensitivity and effectiveness of the laws and policies that govern it.

Growing Up in Open Adoption: An Essay of Life Experience

Sara VanderHaagen

Today, I want to tell some stories. Through some cosmic fiddling, I have had the opportunity to become the representative of so many children of open adoption and I'm here primarily to share my experience. But my experience being adopted isn't all I have. I have my humanity, my education, my family, and my faith (before which, thank goodness, stands a God strong enough to hold me there). Someday I even hope to have some wisdom. But for now I'm just going to try to represent all of the work, the ideals, the pain, the joy and the richness of open adoption through the offering of my story. This is done neither of my own merit nor even the merits of open adoption, but through the movement of Grace. My hope for this evening is that the quiet story of my own life— beautifully shaped but in no way governed by my being adopted—may breathe jubilation into the air and remind us all of the significance of our own stories.

Why a story? Well, three reasons: first, because it is where the statistics hit the pavement and are translated into life, by which we're all a lot more fascinated, anyhow. Second, because everyone has stories. I'm not an "adoptee"; I'm a person with a voice. And so through stories we may all transcend those inevitable labels and reach for the depth in life. That brings me to the third reason, that stories are honest and offer immeasurable richness for those who are willing to engage in them. A story of open adoption would appropriately celebrate the marvelous openness, marriage of joy and pain, and the ultimate fullness I have experienced in my life.

Frederick Buechner wrote a little book of memoirs called *The Sacred Journey*. In this book he touches both on the particularity and universality of story:

The crow of a rooster. Two carpenters talking at their work in another room. The ticktock of a clock on the wall. The rumble of your own stomach. Each sound can be thought of as meaning something, if it is meaning you want. After some years now of living with roosters, I know that their crow does not mean that the sun is coming up because they crow off and on all day long with their silly, fierce heads thrown back and the barnyard breeze in their tail feathers. Maybe it means that they are remembering the last time it came up or thinking ahead to the next time. Maybe it means only that they are roosters being roosters. The voices and hammering in the other room mean that not everybody in the world sits around mooning over the past, but that the real business of life goes on and somewhere the job is getting done; means, too, that life is a mystery. What are they talking about? What are they making? The ticking of the clock is death's patter song and means that time passes and passes and passes, whatever time it is. The rumbling stomach means hunger and lunch. But meaning in that sense is not the point, or at least not my point. My point is that all those sounds together, or others like them, are the sound of our lives.

What each of them might be thought to mean separately is less important than what they all mean together. At the very least they mean this: mean listen. Listen. Your life is happening. You are happening. You, the rooster, the clock, the work-men, your stomach, all are happening together. A journey, years long, has brought each of you through thick and thin to this moment in time as mine has also brought me. Think back on that journey. Listen back to the sounds and sweet airs of your journey that give delight and hurt not and to those too that give no delight and hurt like Hell. Be not afeard. The music of your life is subtle and elusive like no other—not a song with words but a song without words, a sing-ing, clattering music to gladden the heart or turn the heart to stone, to haunt you perhaps with echoes of a vaster, farther music of which it is part.

The question is not whether the things that happen to you are chance things or God's things because, of course, they are both at once.

Today, those sounds will clatter out life, the life of each one of us individually and of all of us together. For in one sense we each live our own dream or nightmare, but in another sense those dreams are inter-twined, even superimposed on each other. Buechner addresses this spe-cifically in his introduction, saying, "My assumption is that the story of any one of us is in some measure the story of us all." Let these words be my preface.

To begin at the beginning, the open adoption seed sprang from the darkness of the closed system, where things are secret and hidden. The operative word in the phrase is "open." Folks from some scattered agencies realized that things could only grow in the light, so they tried it and my life started in broad daylight. My parents wanted a family. After considerable thought and prayer, they collaborated with Jim Gritter on this new open adoption venture. This decision was the proclamation of their commitment to openness and also their first step into the story. Meanwhile, something had been working in the heart of a woman named Phoebe, and these people all came together to deliver me safely into life. Here they then entered into the covenant relationship of raising me. For this I could never give enough thanks—thanks to Phoebe for life and a love beyond language, thanks to my parents for entering into the endeavor and for giving me wings to fly, thanks to all those behind the scenes who arranged everything. Looking even more closely here, I need to thank them for the pain they embraced and the people they are. Because I know them as the people they are—broken, yet full of laughter—I can say that.

The cornerstone of this covenant was honesty. Being adopted is like knowing how to swim: I can't remember a time when it wasn't part of my reality. My first meeting with Phoebe when I was three illustrates this as only childhood can. As the story goes, I greeted her at the door with a smile, saying, "Hi, you must be Phoebe. I'm Sara. Did you know that I grew in your tummy?" A straight talker from the start. This interaction signaled the beginning of my relationship with Phoebe.

Openness was also woven through my family, leading right toward the birth of my little sister. I was almost two when we drove to the hospital to pick her up. Legend has it that we were debating between the names Laura and Jill. Once we got there, I decided that she needed to be a Laura; it sounded better with Sara anyway. Here was our family steered toward another crossroads by open adoption.

Still, there is a dark flipside to all of this. Lewis Smedes—a graduate of the college I attend—says it eloquently: "You and I were created for joy, and if we miss it, we miss the reason for our existence. . . . If our joy is honest joy, it must somehow be congruous with human tragedy. This is the test of joy's integrity: is it compatible with pain? . . . Only the heart that hurts has a right to joy." I've even heard Joy and Sorrow described as sisters who always walk hand in hand. I'm suspended here on the blessing side of the triad, and that very blessing whispers about the unspeakable loss sighing on the other side. It's there, but I haven't known it in the deepest sense. I am indebted to those who dove into pain on my behalf. That's real, nitty-gritty love. That's how we're meant to care for each other. The tale begins in a mixture of sacrifice and joy, and thus it is ushered into the middle of the tale; the mystery of the beginning fades into the nitty-gritty of daily life. This is how it seems to be with tragedy. With time, the tragic event itself diminishes in its immediate presence, yet it lives on in its effects and our responses to it. My adoption does not lie in the foreground of my identity, but rather shades the background colors. Every so often I must acknowledge the subtle beauty of the whole thing, and then return to my place in the foreground of my own life. Essentially, real-life open adoption is a covenant in action, like being married as opposed to the wedding itself.

In their initial cooperative agreement, my parents and Phoebe set the framework for my daily life. Here I was—and still am—shown how openness affects every one of my relationships in life, whether that relationship is part of the triad or not. When I was old enough to understand something about pain, I was also shown its role in my life as an adopted child. Finally, as I have been digging up my own identity, I can see the richness that my adoption has infused into my Self. Threads of these three things can be traced through various stories. Most of these stories are about relationships.

As I look back into the years of my relationship with Phoebe, I realize how much it has changed to reflect my stage in life. When Laura and I were young, Phoebe used to drive her tan little car from Boyne Falls to Traverse City (only when the sky wasn't threatening) and take us on outings to miniature golf places and kid-friendly restaurants like Schelde's. On special occasions like birthdays or Christmas, she would bring gifts to us both. Dolls and teddy bears were standard for the elementary school years, then porcelain dolls and finally quilts. I love those quilts and often show them off to people. When I introduced myself to the Residence Life staff in my dorm last spring, I used one of those quilts to describe who I am. They are artifacts of love that I'll hold on to even when we both are old and tattered.

The meetings with Phoebe were always quiet affairs, void of the awkwardness that may come with the social awareness of age. The ties of the triad extended beyond birthparent-child to include both families . . . in their entirety. My feelings on these experiences ranged from overwhelming to frightening. When my half brother Gary first visited our house, I hid under the dining room table. When Phoebe married a man named Art, I recall being in a sort of smiling daze from meeting several members of my birthfamily. But I think the most vivid memory was my third-grade church Christmas concert. Of course Phoebe was coming—she always supported my early performances. Not long before the concert, she and my mom conferred about bringing along other birth relations. My mom approached me with the idea and I approved for some reason or another. The night of the performance, a cloud of birthfamily witnesses descended upon our home. Half brothers and their wives, half sisters and their husbands, birthnieces and nephews, and two birth great-aunts. Childhood lends a certain exaggeration to memory, and my mom tells me that it wasn't quite as many people as I recall. Still, it was definitely a crowd to me. I was overwhelmed, especially when I was approached by my Polish Aunt Stasia. For some reason, I was frightened just to know that I was somehow related to a woman named Stasia. I had visions of step relatives in Disney movies. Thankfully, Phoebe and my mom navigated the evening, so I was off the hook. Nonetheless, a slightly traumatic experience. And, let me tell you, if that is the most traumatic component of my adoption experience, I've been blessed.

As I've stepped into the shoes of adulthood, I've had small opportunities to redeem myself from the Christmas concert incident. "Fond" and "pleasant" are rather fluffy words, and thus rare words in my vocabulary, but I believe my recent encounters with my birthfamily warrant their use. For example, my chance to meet Gary's son Ian and Phoebe's new husband Frank are certainly fond memories. Whether enlightening or frightening, these interactions are essential to the covenant of openness. You don't trade in experiences that stretch you toward richness. The beauty of the story as a whole lies in its unexpected dips and turns. In all of the relationships touched by this, those among the four in my family are by far the most affected. Our family was created through open adoption, so it makes sense that those three components—openness, depth of joy and pain, and richness—would be part of our lives. When I discuss my family, it is important to realize those components were there before the adoptions. Entering into the adoption process was simply a continuation of these values. My parents were open to begin with, but they had to intentionally open themselves to the idea of adoption. They were open when they told me about Phoebe and being adopted. They were open about themselves, their fears, their hopes, their lives. They were even open to NOT being open. Since I was surrounded with it, I wanted to be a part of it. So I shared with my parents. They knew how I felt about adoption, school, boys, republicans, the girl my mom baby-sat in kindergarten who also happened to my arch-nemesis, God, music, friends, myself, and even their perceived shortcomings. My parents have somehow become almost an extension of my own mind, yet never was I an extension of theirs. When friends would express frustrations with family problems, I would ask them questions like, "Why don't you just talk about it? Why don't you just tell them how you feel?" Such concepts were simply inconceivable in their environments, while they were implicit in mine. Betty Jean Lifton actually tells a story about me in her book *Lost and Found*: "James Gritter tells a story about his first open adoption placement, which he arranged between a birth mother and his best friends. The child, now seven, was recently watching a show on television with her father. It happened to be about an Adoptee searching. She sat quietly for some time, and then said to him in amazement:

'Daddy, that lady is adopted and she doesn't know who her birth mother is—isn't that weird!' "

My parents exposed themselves to heartache in order to foster such communication. Even though my mom and dad often told me I had the mind of a lawyer, I would sometimes run out of arguments to hurl at them. So I hurled cruelty in place of logic: "Well, you're not my real parents anyway." Even then my young eyes could see the old wound—though long since healed—of infertility. I wish I never would have said those words. But they've been swept into the current of our story, and I cannot retrieve them.

The tale continues today. Leaving my parents to go to school has profoundly changed the nature of our relationship. There is depth there as a result of the openness, the joy, the pain. There is richness in our reality as a family. Things don't often go unsaid, and arguments never last unforgiven through the night. Sometimes I feel like I want to say things more, things like "I love you." But if we said that all the time, the business of living—the reason behind and the actions involved in loving people—would be forgotten. So we trust the silence.

My sister Laura is an essential part of the reality we share. She is my other half and my oldest and dearest companion, even more than I often like to admit. Laura and Sara DO go together, and it will always be so. Being adopted doesn't mean you fight more or fight less. We bit each other, pulled each other's hair, kicked and screamed till we were blue in the face—just like any other siblings. But no matter what happened, we always ended up being open. Thanks to Phoebe's graciousness we were able to know a birthmom together. Sometimes I would get jealous and want to kick Laura out of the picture. "Remember, she's MY birthmom," I used to say. That's where the hurt comes in. In especially spiteful times I even reminded Laura of her lack of contact with her birthmother by saying, "At least my birthmom loves me." Again, I would eagerly take back these words. But they too are part of the story, and poignantly pay tribute to the pain present in my sister's situation. That situation was a wound not easily treated or healed. Mom and Dad were experiencing sorrow of their own as a result, and they had a difficult time explaining to Laura that her birthmom still loved her. They gently brought her to an understanding of her birthmother's painful situation—she was probably afraid to meet Laura because of the lingering pain. Though this continued to hurt my sister in small ways, she began to comprehend and invested her energy in the world around her. Just like I brag on my quilts, I also brag on my little sister. She has amazing artistic gifts (of which I, consequently, have few) and a deep capacity for empathy. We go to the same college now and people frequently say that we look alike. "Funny," we reply, "We're not even biologically related." Maybe it's a lot like an old married couple that grows to look alike. We huddled in the trenches and watched the sunrises together. We've grown together, so we're sisters. It's pretty simple.

There are also people outside the family and the triad who have been drawn into my adoption through association. I've run people who are ignorant and insensitive, like a classmate in sixth grade who wrote me hateful letters and, when I attempted the "kill 'em with kindness" plan, she retorted, "No wonder your mom wanted to give you away." The comment cut my 11-year-old heart deeply, but the pain dwindles over time. My 20-year-old heart remembers with a sigh and a lamentation about the human capacity for cruelty. Other people just lack knowledge and are indifferent about it. However, the vast majority of people lack knowledge and are intensely curious about how open adoption works.

Whenever I tell people I'm adopted, it's always followed by a statement of my willingness to answer questions. In our family, it was clear that adoption was not strange, it was unique. Because of this attitude, I've never been ashamed to tell someone I'm adopted. On the contrary, I'm proud of the distinction, as I might be proud if I were a twin or had received a special gift from my grandparents. It is not my identity; it simply adds a distinct flavor to who I am.

So what has open adoption left me with? As shown through these stories, I have gained a wealth of relationships based on openness, willingness to engage in the pain and joy of our lives, and producing a richness that would never have been discovered otherwise. And I know that through these things my adoption has infused true color into my life, for they are no longer a part of adoption—they are a part of me. They are also a part of each member of the triad, if that member has made the genuine effort to engage in her or his story. Too often people skim over life in motor-powered vessels of superficiality, never stopping to catch a different breeze or to anchor the boat and dive deep into the waters of experience. People are terrified of transparency and openness; I am terrified of transparency and openness. Only when we put our hearts in the hands of another and open ourselves to events beyond our control will we know genuine joy and pain. Only when we plumb the depths of genuine joy and pain can we come to know the richness of a life truly lived. Phoebe laid down her heart and her pride and her maternal hopes for me. She suffered on my behalf. My parents laid down their hearts and their pride and their hopes of biological children for me. They were willing to suffer on my behalf. They experienced this all to bring me into a safe place.

No one ever said I wouldn't have pain as a side effect of life, but I have never known any profound pain which sprang directly from my adoption. And besides, the pain I've known and will inevitably know becomes a burden shared by the people I love and those who care for me. At this focus lies the essence of open adoption and the birth of my story and the story of us all: when we engage in life, we receive it back a hundredfold. The aching beauty of a full life is undoubtedly something to celebrate.

Sara VanderHaagen is currently a senior philosophy and communications arts and sciences major at Calvin College in Grand Rapids, Michigan. She spent her childhood in northern Michigan with her family of four, including a sister who has also been a beneficiary of open adoption. She is blessed to have a consistently growing relationship with her birthmother, as well as connections with other members of her birthfamily, including her half brother. Open adoption has been a part of Sara's reality since before she knew what reality was. This essay was delivered in the form of a speech on two occasions between the fall of 2000 and the spring of 2001; it appears here by permission of the author.

Growing Up in Transracial Adoption: An Essay of Life Experience

Ai Loan Nguyen

"Putting the Pieces Together"

On April 3, 1975, President Gerald Ford launched Operation Babylift, his attempt to airlift as many orphaned children out of Vietnam as possible before the Fall of Saigon, which occurred on April 30, 1975 . . .

It was a spring day in April. People were clustered around in anticipation. There were reporters, cameramen, onlookers, eight families, and one schoolteacher; altogether two hundred people attended. The date was April 10, 1975. Nine Vietnamese orphans disembarked the DC jet plane into the long-awaited adopted parents' arms at Hopkins International Airport in Cleveland, Ohio. There were many tears in the crowd. I was one of those orphans. I was second off the plane, eight months old. As reporters went around busily asking questions about the adoptees, my adoptive parents' response was, "We saw these orphans and felt that we could fill that need with love."

When I was in elementary school, my adoptive mother was asked to give a speech at church about adoption. She stated, "We started paperwork to adopt a little girl in an orphanage in Cambodia. Her name was So Thun. While we waited, we were asked if we would like a little infant girl, Ai Loan Nguyen from Vietnam. When she arrived in April of 1975; she was beautiful." My parents never adopted So Thun. They couldn't get her out of Cambodia.

Fourteen years later, I felt the need to search for my birthmother. I remember going through bureau drawers and my parents' security box looking for anything in conjunction to my adoption. I found some documents with the name and address of my orphanage, Viet Hoa Orphanage in Cholon, Saigon. After making copies, I put back the original documents. I wasn't sure how my adoptive parents would react and didn't want them to be hurt. I never told my parents that I was searching at such a young age because I didn't feel they would understand, nor support me. I didn't have a good relationship with them. We were never close. In fact, I had all of my mail rerouted to friends' houses. My parents may have had an inkling as to what I was doing, but I don't think they knew how much research I had really done. I wrote to the orphanage hoping to hear from someone about my birthmother. For three years, I corresponded back and forth with two nuns and a priest. Unfortunately, I was unable to locate my birthmother. In fact, I was told the orphanage no longer had my paperwork because it was lost in the war.

Discouraged, I put my search on the back burner for seven years. During that time, I didn't really think too much about it. I went off to college, graduated, etc. Sometimes it would be discussed among friends, but I never actively pursued it.

In May 1999, I decided to start searching again. Honestly, I have no idea what triggered that thought, and I had no concept of what this task would actually entail. I basically thought it would be more or less an investigation and didn't realize how much emotion would play in it. When I was younger and searching, I remember the anticipation I felt when I received a new letter, not knowing what would be written, but it never got to the point where it was so overwhelming that I had to walk away from it.

In June 1999, I became involved with Adoption Network Cleveland, a nonprofit organization that facilitates reunions for adoptees and birthparents. Unfortunately, they focused more on domestic reunions rather than international. I also wrote to the INS and received all of my adoption papers including my Vietnamese birth certificates with my name, my birthmother's name, the hospital where I was born, and the orphanage where I was taken. Also enclosed were legal documents and the home study done on my adoptive parents.

Reflecting back to the contacts I had when I was fourteen years old, I wished I would have been more resourceful with them, but due to my age and ignorance, I didn't search properly. From those documents that the INS had sent me, I drew more names trying to focus on people who might be alive twenty-five years later.

Through the Internet, I located someone who has had a tremendous impact on my search. He was the lawyer who worked out the legal end of my adoption. I knew his name because it was scrawled all over the legal documents. I ran his name through the Martindale-Hubbell Web site, a directory of practicing attorneys in the United States. Sure enough, he was still practicing in Cleveland, Ohio. I checked out his statistics, he was admitted in 1974, a year prior to Operation Babylift. I had no idea what I would say to him on the phone and didn't want to shock his conscience, so I decided to write him a letter to see if he had any information or knew of anyone who could help me in my search process. About a month later, I received a phone call from him. He stated he wanted to meet with me. Many mixed emotions ran through me. It was fear of the unknown that gripped me. I even called prior to seeing him and asked if he was charging for the visit. It would give me an excellent reason to jump out of the boat. His secretary stated in the negative, so I stayed in the boat.

In September 1999, I met the lawyer at his office. He stated he was very intrigued with the letter I had sent him. When I showed him the letters he had sent to my adoptive parents with his signature, nostalgia wiped over him. He went through all of my paperwork and asked a lot of questions. It was an amazing experience for both of us. Can you imagine someone who you helped airlift out of Vietnam right before the Fall of Saigon, yet never met, walking into your office twenty-five years later? People had told him it was impossible to bring us over from Vietnam, but he did it despite being so young and inexperienced.

After perusing all my paperwork, the lawyer expressed how impressed he was with my findings. Basically, I had more information than he did. He was actually more excited about me finding my birthmother than I was. In fact, he suggested that I get on a plane and just go over to Vietnam and finish my search as soon as possible. I told him it wasn't that easy. I didn't have the language or the culture just to get on the plane and search.

People outside the adoption triad (i.e., birth parents, adoptees, and adoptive parents) don't realise how much emotion goes into something like this. My lawyer lacked the emotional attachment that I had, yet he was willing to listen and learn. He told me that his daughter was planning on going to Vietnam in January 2000 and said she might be able to do some research for me.

He asked me to keep in touch right before I left his office. I had so many mixed emotions that day. I think I had disassociated myself from really finding my birthmother due to the circumstances being international in nature, but after meeting with the lawyer who assisted in my adoption, my flame for searching was reignited. The next time I saw him, he said, "You fear the unknown, but do not fear it enough to back out. I am proud of you."

In October 1999, the lawyer took it upon himself to find someone who might be able to facilitate my search process and immerse me in my culture and language. He hooked me up with a Vietnamese family here in Cleveland. They had escaped an hour after the Fall of Saigon and spent approximately nine days in a boat without food or water. Viet and Sonny have a beautiful family, work very hard, and are proud of their children. Everyone is college educated.

For the first time in my life, I was immersed in my culture. I listened to my language, ate Vietnamese food, and tried to soak in as much information as possible. I met about ten people in the family, and they were all discussing my background in Vietnamese. By the time I left, I was truly overwhelmed. I actually couldn't wait to hear English on the radio just so I could understand it.

I came back to their house for Thanksgiving and Christmas and fell in love with the Vietnamese fruit salad and spring rolls they served. I remember for Thanksgiving they had a turkey, but I wouldn't eat it. I'd only eat the Vietnamese food.

As I was driving home after spending Christmas with them, I began to feel angry. Here I was at age twenty-five, and I knew nothing about my culture or language. My adoptive parents never encouraged it or felt it was necessary. I had just eaten Christmas dinner with this Vietnamese family, yet I still did not belong because I couldn't even understand what they were saying and lacked the cultural knowledge. I was lucky if I could catch my name or my birthplace in their conversations. At that moment, I truly felt that separation they talk about in adoption. I couldn't imagine finding my birthmother and not being able to speak to her.

Then I go home to my adoptive family, and I don't fit in there either. I'm with a bunch of Caucasian people who I feel don't understand me and certainly don't look like me. To even think about staring into another person's face and seeing my features in them just blows my mind apart. I can't imagine. I wonder where my traits and disposition came from. I wonder if my birthmother was a good writer. I wonder if my birthmother was very organized. I wonder who my birthfather was. I wonder so much.

My relationship with my adoptive parents never changed from when I was fourteen years old. I honestly don't know who they are, and they don't know who I am. We have lived in separate worlds for so long, yet they are my parents. I know they love me, but we were never close. When I started searching in May 1999, I honestly believed that if anything would bridge that gap with my parents, it would be my adoption because we both took part in it.

After taking some time off from my search process, it was already April 2000. It was time to confront what I had been afraid of for so long: language barriers, culture shock, fear of the unknown, and disappointment. I took it upon myself to learn as much as I could about my culture.

What wasn't learned when I was younger would have to be learned now. I could either become bitter or better about my situation. I chose better.

My next step was to look for people who were involved with Operation Babylift. I searched on the Internet and found an article that was dated back five years. I was discouraged and felt I wasn't getting anywhere. Then Adoption Network Cleveland sent me an e-mail about the reunion in Baltimore, Maryland, for the children of Operation Babylift.

In April 2000, I attended the reunion which was put on by Holt International. It was an event that changed my life. My passion to return to Vietnam increased. I met a lot of great people, and have memories that I will never forget. For the first time in my life, I was with people my own age that had experienced the same things I did growing up. It was amazing to be in a room full of Asian people who spoke perfect English.

Over the past year, I have been in contact with people who were part of Operation Babylift. That summer following the reunion, I met the woman who was the secretary of the nonprofit organization, Project Orphans Abroad (now AFSA) that my adoptive parents were a part of during that time period. I have also spoken and written to one of the flight attendants who helped evacuate us from the orphanage, and contacted one of the fathers who also had a child aboard my plane. I've met some wonderful people as I've searched. Many of them were more than willing to help, but others have had their own agendas or are fighting their own demons.

Fortunately or unfortunately, I've come to a standstill with my search in the United States. As exciting and scary as it sounds, I have resigned myself to the fact that I must return to Vietnam to complete it. Presently, I am in the process of planning my trip back and plan to stay at least six months. Though I'm not sure if I will work or study while I am there, I am trying to focus on learning as much as I can right now about the country, language, and culture through the media, literature, and other sources I discover daily. Despite many obstacles, my Vietnamese is making progress thanks to the patience of my tutor.

Aside from those things, I have been asked to speak on panels about my experience in a transracial adoption, as well as my journey as I search for missing pieces of my puzzle. As for my birthmother giving me up for adoption, I've never had a problem with it and believe she did it because she loved me so much. "Many adoptees think their birthparents didn't love them because they were given up for adoption. It is just as hard for parents to give up a child as it is for the child to accept it."

The lawyer always tells me how courageous I am and that I'm too close to the situation to see how far I've come in this journey. Truthfully, I just think of it as something I have to do to find closure or to be able to say to myself that I've done everything I could even if I don't find a family member. I've also realized going back to Vietnam isn't solely to complete my search, but to immerse myself in the culture and learn more about myself in doing so. I don't feel as though I can make other lifetime decisions until I do this for myself.

My search process has been compared to traveling down a road. There are lots of winding curves, some uphill travels and even some potholes in the way. It is hard work that requires me to face many issues, some which are not pleasant, and some very difficult. I do not have a set plan in seeking out my birthmother. Fortunately, I was given more paperwork than a lot of the adoptees who came over. From those documents, I'll have to think of ingenious ways to utilize them and hopefully something I've learned in law enforcement and investigations will kick in.

The "American Dream" wasn't given to me like so many who attended the reunion in Baltimore, but I do know that I did have a better life here in America than I would have had in Vietnam. My life experience and education are priceless. Perhaps, returning to Vietnam will make me appreciate America much more. At the same time, I think that I will fall in love with Vietnam while I am there.

The hand of God has been upon my life and throughout this search. There has been too much synchronicity that has occurred for it not to be. I wonder what God has planned for me once I leave, and I wonder what God has planned for me once I return.

Ai Loan Nguyen-Kropp was born in Binh Duong, Vietnam, then transferred to the Viet Hoa Orphanage in Cholon, Saigon. She was airlifted out of Vietnam, and landed in Cleveland, Ohio on April 10, 1975. Currently, she is working at a law enforcement agency and holds degrees in law enforcement and criminal justice. Her essay appears by permission of the author.

Search and Reunion Etiquette: The Guide Miss Manners Never Wrote

Monica M. Byrne

There are as many adoption search and reunion scenarios as there are people involved. Everyone who has worked in this field, who has been part of the process, or who is a member of one of the supporting families will tell you that this is a world of shifting sand and unclear rules—a minefield of potential disasters. Who in his or her right mind would embark on such a perilous journey without a map and compass? In fact, why would anyone leave the safe harbor of the known to travel to this unknown land?

The answer to this question lies deep within the heart of the "matter". The "matter" being that, at some time and in some way, the natural course of a family's shape and structure has been disrupted by the removal of some fundamental part—the parent of its child or the child of its parents, brothers and sisters of each other and grandparents of their grandchildren.

These disruptions may occur for a variety of reasons, not to be examined here, but the end result is one of an imbalance in the order of things and a need experienced by many people to regain that order. I have likened the reunion process to watching a beautiful mosaic spread out before us. Into this picture one throws a new tile—a tiny piece of marble—and every one of the hundreds of little tiles must shift and move to accommodate that new tile. The picture will change in many subtle ways. But the regaining of order does not come easily or without cost. Each one on this very personal journey will need to understand the variables. And each will need the help of a guide or a support system. This is where the rules of the game enter the equation.

First one has to divide the "search" from the "reunion." These are two separate and distinct parts of the adoption journey. If you think the search is hard . . . wait until you try the reunion! Many reunions take from five to eight years or more to "normalize" and reach a stage where the participants have built up shared memory and familiar relationships. Each reunion, therefore, must be studied and planned with a careful, almost military, precision, if the goal of the exercise is a long-term relationship with the new-found relatives.

THE SEARCH

It is important to remember that the onus of the search will fall on the searcher. It is his or her responsibility to learn as much as possible about reunions, to read as much as is available, to talk to experienced people, to listen carefully to the advice that is given and to work out a careful game plan. The "searchee" knows none of this. He or she will not be prepared. He or she may be shocked at being found and may feel like the only adoptee or birthparent in the universe who has been in this situation. Many books have been written about searching and search techniques. Often these books are just lists of state laws and information on the availability of personal information, with addresses for various offices and organizations. There may be some "typical" form letters to copy, but not much direction on what to really say! The books describing what to do with information that you now possess—the name and address of your birth relative, the location of your surrendered child's new family—are few and far between. Although each case is very different, there are some basic rules around searching that never lose their truth. Even Miss Manners might recommend the following, in no particular order:

1. *Do be very discreet.* Do not, if at all possible, discuss the adoption story with anyone except the person you are seeking. Many, many times searchers are so excited about finding a family member, that they will blurt out the whole reason why they are looking for "Millie," thereby blowing Millie's cover. The person contacted will now be in possession of information that Millie may prefer to discuss herself. Sometimes, discretion means being economical with the facts. Some sources of information, like funeral parlors, cemeteries, or churches, can be very helpful, but the discretion rule applies 100%. It is not necessary to tell the whole story to everyone!

2. *Do remember you may only have one chance to make a certain phone call.* Try to get it right the first time. Have a prepared list of the questions you wish answered to jog your memory. If you call back with more

questions, you risk raising suspicion about your right to know. Once a family's drums start to beat, there is no way to stop them. Phone calls can alert everyone right away. Phoning may be the wrong move in some situations.

3. *Don't assume that the other person will be as thrilled to be found as you are to find them.* There may be much more to the story than you have ever guessed. Every family has its own special dynamic.

4. *Don't phone everyone in the phone book with the same name, especially if it is a rare name or they live in a small community.* A searcher should exhaust other options first before resorting to this. Use search tools such as Internet sources instead of contacting everyone indiscriminately. The moment people start asking questions in some families, everyone knows. The person being sought may feel defensive.

5. *Do remember that every source of information you use may be of use to the people coming after you.* They would like that resource to remain available, so do not talk too much about how and what you are researching. Some libraries and archives are very willing to assist a "genealogist," but not an "adoption searcher." Even when people are not helpful, a searcher should remember that others will come afterwards, and your reaction to the non-helpful person may color how that person will react to the next searcher asking for "genealogical" information.

6. *Do make good search plans and keep good records. All original documents should be photocopied and the originals stored in a safe place, such as a safety deposit box.* Keep a search binder with clear plastic sleeves for the pages you are likely to look at again and again. Be sure to keep good notes of whom you call, whom you speak to, what was said and when. You do not want to repeat parts of your research because you kept poor records. When you meet your birth family member this careful system will show how very committed you were. In addition, it will serve you as a "diary" of your journey.

7. *Do be patient!* Rome wasn't built in a day, and a search can take a very long time and require painstaking application. But searches can also reach a point of "critical mass" and just take on lives of their own. When that happens there is sometimes no turning back—you must just hang on and ride to the end of the line!

8. *Do seek out the assistance and/or guidance of experienced searchers and support groups.* Sometimes days seem like years and waiting can be stressful, exhausting and frustrating. A good search buddy can keep you from making a move that could seriously disrupt the potential reunion. Also, a search and support group is often a safer and more appropriate place to share the emotions of search than casual friends or acquaintances. It's important to respect the privacy of what you learn in a search and support group, however. Sometimes we get caught up in the enthusiasm of

a search, our own or someone else's, and end up sharing information at a support group meeting that we later wish had not been shared.

9. Do try to make the call or write the letter yourself. If this is really too difficult or stressful, get the help of someone who is experienced. Practice your call with a friend and try to anticipate the obvious questions.

Note that the previous "Do" is also one of the most controversial in the search and reunion business. Some searchers, both those who charge fees and those who do not, argue that having the assistance of an experienced mediator will go a long way to making the initial reunion connection better. They note that the experience of the negotiator may help to bridge the awkward spaces and help an older birth mother to discuss this very private part of her life with some sense of safety and confidence in the mediator's skills. And indeed, a skilled intermediary may be able to say the right thing and ask the right questions at the right time by sensing the "temperature" of the event. Another school of thought says that nothing can replace the spontaneous nature of the one-to-one call between principal members of this reunion! It is harder to say "no" to one's own flesh and blood than to a third party, some believe. When making contact directly, the awkwardness of the questions or the moment is offset by the tears and the intimacy that are real. As in most things in life, nothing is carved in stone. The decision to use a third party or make contact directly will be up to you. If you choose to use a third party (or if you are required to), however, be sure you are comfortable with that person's style and approach before the initial contact takes place. There's only one "first" call.

THE REUNION

Reunions come in many styles and with many variations, but the essence is still the same. This is the "meeting"—the reconnection of two people who for all intents and purposes are closely related, but who are relative strangers. Like the development of any relationship, that of adoptee and birth relative takes time and effort. There is something profoundly mystical and magical about reunions. They require lots of work, lots of concentration and, above all, a sense of humor. Rules of etiquette which have been developed through experience may make things run more smoothly.

1. Do be honest. There have been enough lies and secrets.

2. Do share information as appropriate, both in the initial call (if there is one) and later, when you meet. Sometimes questions come as a reflex and may not need to be answered that very moment. For example, to "How did you find me?" you might respond "It was not easy. I'll tell you the whole story sometime. Right now let's enjoy this wonderful meeting." To "Who is my birthfather?" one might respond "I will tell you the whole story, but right now I need some time to reflect on what has happened. But I promise I'll tell you the truth." A related principle is that if an immediate answer to your questions is not forthcoming, try to be patient within reason with the other person.

3. *Do try to laugh.* This is a joyful situation. Don't make it into a frightening experience. There is enough inherent drama in the incredible event taking place without adding to the tension. Be prepared to go whitewater rafting and hang on tight!

4. *Do try to keep it simple.* In birthparent searches, do not try to find both parents at once (unless, of course, they are still together). The emotional upheaval that may ensue could spoil the hope of future successes.

5. *Do plan your first meeting in a place where either party can feel confident and safe.* The situation is emotional enough without adding to it the fear of not being able to "get away" if there is a problem. A cozy corner in a public place (behind the potted palms in a large hotel lounge) can be just fine. If you decide this is working well, you can move to somewhere more private.

6. *Do keep the first meeting shorter rather than longer, if possible.* This gives everyone time to take a breather, re-assess the situation and consider the future relationship. It is always easier meeting for the second time. (If you have to travel some distance to meet, the "second time" may be the day after your initial meeting.)

7. *Do try to avoid a huge family picnic as the way to introduce your new-found relative to the clan.* It can be very overwhelming to meet 50 relatives at once.

8. *Do keep an open mind.* The birthfamily may be very different from the adoptive family. Try not to judge one against the other until you get to know them better.

9. *Do have realistic expectations.* The moment of reunion is not the time to decide you really only wanted "medical information" or that you are not ready to pursue a relationship. It is cruel to set the other party up to expect more than you are prepared to give. Be honest with yourself and try to look at your reasons for searching and the limits of what you can accept. Talk with your support system ahead of time about the limits; if you're in an uncomfortable situation, try to resolve it directly and privately.

10. *Do have a frank discussion of how the adoptee will address the birthparent and other birth relatives, and vice versa, following the reunion.* Some birthmothers want their surrendered children to call them "Mom," but adoptees already have one "Mom" in their life and may not be comfortable using that title for anyone but their adoptive mother. Likewise, some adoptees are eager to call their birthmother "Mom," but the birthmother may not be comfortable being called "Mom" by a child she did not raise. Good manners would also direct that any discussion of how

the adoptee will refer to his or her birth relatives not take place in the presence of a roomful of relatives. One needs to be very flexible. If this issue becomes one of contention, a re-examination of expectations may be in order.

11. Don't try to compete with established family holiday procedures unless everyone agrees. Like the name issue, this is not worth the anguish it can cause. Keep it simple. Many reunited relatives get bogged down in the minutiae of names and festivals instead of being thrilled that they have found each other.

12. Do try to respect the other person's wishes about sharing the reunion with other members of the family. For some birthparents, a reluctance to share can go on too long. Try to set limits to your impatience and wait it out. At some point adoptees in this situation may need to re-assess their expectations and make decisions about the future path of the relationship. Advice from an experienced searcher or support group is recommended.

13. Do be stoic if the other party feels a need to pull back for a while. It is very wise to agree without a huge fuss, great grief, or gnashing of teeth. Such need to pull away is often seen in the reunion process. It allows the person to take stock or re-assess the reunion and its effect on his or her life. Although very painful to the other person, it is best treated with patience and lots of reading. Support groups are great for dealing with the sadness. No one can fix anyone else. They can only fix themselves.

14. Don't blame yourself for problems in the other person's life. Birthmothers often feel great guilt if the child they relinquished did not grow up as advantaged as they might have hoped, or if religion is not as important in their child's life as it is to them (or vice versa). Adoptees can sometimes feel guilty if the relinquishment experience had a negative impact on the birthmother's life. We cannot turn the clock back no matter how much we might want to. Your relationship starts from the day you meet again. Keep it positive.

15. Don't plan on moving in with your new relatives. They may be delighted to meet you but they are not looking for a permanent houseguest.

16. Do enjoy the reunion. It's a gift from God.

So . . . is the Search and Reunion a good thing? You bet! Should it be carefully thought through? Absolutely! Will it be 100% successful? If we knew the answer to that, we'd be setting up shop in Las Vegas!

Monica M. Byrne has been associated with family reunions since 1987. She is the Co-Chair of the Adoption Council of Ontario, Canadian Co-Liaison to the AAC, and Registrar of Parent Finders, National Capital Region. A member of many adoption reform groups, she is a reunited birthmother and has a positive and ongoing relationship with her daughter. She was also the proud recipient of the Governor General of Canada's "Caring Canadian" award, in 1999, for her many years of volunteer work in adoption.

NOTE

This appendix reprinted with permission from the American Adoption Congress, *The Decree*, Winter/Spring 2001 issue.

Making Contact After the Search

Curry Wolfe

When the time to make contact finally arrives, everyone is eager to move forward. Contact should be made when you are ready. Don't let others force or influence when you make contact! There are some basic things to remember about reaching out to someone that doesn't know that they have been the main focus of your life for some time.

Contact may be the most difficult part of the search process. It becomes important to determine if the letter or the phone call is going to be your mode of contact. Many factors play in this decision. The most important thing to remember is—CONTACT IS THE FIRST IMPRESSION MADE AFTER MANY YEARS OF SEPARATION! It is time to put your best foot forward.

How to choose between letter or phone?—Selecting the phone call or the letter depends on the information you have been able to gain during your search. You may have a full address and phone number. Or you may have only one. It is not always necessary to obtain all information, if you are certain that the information you do have is accurate for contact. Many searchers want to have all information about the family member before contact. That is not necessary. Learning about your family member can come after your contact has been made. Over investigation may be viewed by the receiver as an invasion of privacy.

Once you are sure that you have the correct information, it is important to determine your contact method. You can be thinking about this during the search process. This all depends on YOU! It is time to look deep inside yourself and ask how you would like to be contacted if the shoe was on the other foot.

Ask yourself if you would like to be contacted by a simple letter. Or would you prefer to receive a phone call. You know if you are a letter person. You know if you are a phone person. There is a good chance that your family member may have similar feelings as you.

There are many different views on the phone call vs. the letter contact. There are not any right or wrong answers to this question. As stated above, it is important for you to determine what is the best form for you to follow.

The Phone Call—The phone call is the direct way of reaching the person and having an instant answer to your important questions. It allows you to hear the receiver's voice. You get a true sense of how they feel about being contacted. When making a phone call you are able to make sure you are speaking to the right person and no one else can intercept the call.

Simple suggestions to prepare for the call:

1. Make your call at a reasonable time. Don't call early in the morning or late at night. Always be aware of time zone differences. It is not considered proper to call before 9:00 A.M. or after 9:00 P.M. It is not the best idea to call anyone at work. It may be against company policy to receive personal calls or it could disrupt their work day.

2. It is not advised to call during the dinner hour. We know that the dinner hour is not the same in all homes. If you know there are children within the home, it is likely that there will be dinner preparation and family time going on anywhere between 5:00 through 8:00 P.M.

3. It is not appropriate to call on a holiday. Many searching want to attach the contact with a birthday or a holiday. This is not always appropriate. Making the holiday an important part of your contact may set you up for hurt feelings and disappointment.

4. Have someone with you when you make the call if you are very nervous. Many times callers have actually lost the ability to speak due to total excitement. It is a good idea to have someone there to step in, if necessary. It is nice to have someone with you after you get off the phone for sharing.

5. Record the call if you can. Many answering machines have two-way calling which should allow you to record the call. Have several tapes handy in case your call is lengthy! The excitement level is so high when making the call, many don't remember much of the call until days later.

6. Make sure that you have time for a lengthy call. You don't want to feel rushed. Make sure that children are cared for in another room or away from your home. This is not the time for that kind of interruption!

7. If you can use the *70 feature of blocking any incoming calls, it is best to do that before dialing. You don't want to be interrupted by other calls at this

time. If you don't know about *70, call your local phone company and inquire if this feature is available to you. If you are not able to block call waiting, DON'T ANSWER CALLS COMING IN. IF IT IS IMPORTANT THEY WILL CALL BACK. This is not the time to be interrupted by a busy phone!

8. Be prepared when making the phone call. Have some questions written down ahead of time so that you will be able to gain the specific information you seek. Write your questions on lined paper and leave blanks for taking notes. These may be very important to you at a later time. You may wish to rehearse your call with someone, so that you know what you will be saying in the beginning of the call.

9. Don't leave a contact message on an answering machine. This contact is far too important to leave on a machine! If you have tried to reach the person several times, and there is never an answer, try calling at a different time. They may work unusual hours. If you are calling during a holiday or vacation time, keep in mind they may be away.

10. When you have reached the correct person, speak clearly and slowly, but not unnaturally. Ask if they have time to talk privately, because you have something you would like to discuss with them of a personal nature. They will most likely ask who you are at this point. Give them your name and ask that they write it down with your phone number, in case you get disconnected for any reason.

Then it will be time to start into why you are calling. It can be very simple by stating the birth date involved with your search and the location of the birth. If this doesn't get an instant response, then you will have to mention adoption. From this point on, the conversation will take on a life of its own. If you become overly excited, take a deep breath. This will calm you down and allow the receiver to respond.

Keep in mind that this is a shock to the other person, even if they are thrilled that you have made contact. Their mind may be working a mile a minute trying to determine how they are going to deal with this in their life. There may be many pauses in their conversation. You, as the caller, will have to allow them time to process and keep the conversation going. Be prepared!

If the receiver denies the relationship, have some prepared points of fact available in your notes to ask them. But don't hit them with a barrage of questions. This may frighten them and put an end to the conversation. If the receiver becomes upset and doesn't wish to continue the call, understand that they may need some time to think things over. Offer to contact them at another time. Or offer that they call you back. It is not good to push the issue if the receiver is not able to continue with this call. Kindness and understanding is the word of the day!

Never make promises that you cannot keep. If the receiver is upset and doesn't want you to contact again, don't make that promise. Sometimes the caller makes promises that they know in their heart will not be kept. Just be understanding and end the conversation.

Of course, you wish that your contact will be well received. You should be prepared for the possibility of a negative reaction. This doesn't mean that there will not be a relationship. It may only mean that the receiver needs time to share this with family or someone close to them. You have had the time to process your feelings during the search. Plus you have been able to understand the reason for the search and contact. Now, you may have to give some needed time to the found person. It is hard to be patient, when you are so excited and are wishing for an immediate and open acceptance. *Patience is the key!*

In all cases, it is appropriate to follow up the phone call with a letter and pictures. Do this very soon. If you have received a less than positive response, sending a kind and tender letter of reassurance with pictures may make all of the difference in the world.

Using an Intermediary—Many searchers and organizations encourage the use of an intermediary person for contact. Don't feel pressured into using this form of contact, if you are not comfortable with it. There is always the chance that a well-intended person could jeopardize your contact. You will never know for sure if the contact goes poorly. If you wish to use an intermediary, make sure they have experience in making contact. They should be totally familiar with your search. And if at all possible, you should be there when the call is made. All of the suggestions about the phone call apply to the intermediary call. Many states now have Intermediary systems or Confidential Intermediary (CI) systems in place for the search and contact. In those states, you will need to follow the rules that apply, unless you do your search on your own.

The Letter—The letter is a very nice way of reaching out after many years of separation. It allows the receiver to read the letter over and over. It becomes a keepsake forever. The letter does take time for a reply. It is not as instant as the phone call. But it may be the best way of reaching out if v⌐ ⌐ are not a phone person. It may be the only method available if you have not been able to obtain an accurate phone number. (More and more people are requesting nonpublished phone numbers, this makes the letter your only option.)

Many are concerned that the letter may fall into the wrong hands. In most cases this *doesn't* happen. Make sure you address the letter correctly. It is not advisable to send the letter by registered or certified mail. This only brings attention to the letter and may cause problems within the household. It seems that many times anyone can sign for a registered letter, so there is not really a guarantee the person it was addressed to got it!

Go greeting card shopping. There are many lovely blank cards available that would be very appropriate for a first contact. You may even find a card that does state your feelings exactly. Take some time and you will find something that is right for you. If your contact is in a card, it will probably not draw any undo attention within the household.

Writing the Letter—Even if you end up making a phone call, it is a good exercise to write a letter to clarify your thoughts and get ready for the contact. Writing the letter doesn't need to be an overwhelming task. The letter should be short and simple. Always keep in mind that this is your first contact in many years. It is not the time to express sorrows and great needs. It is a simple contact asking for communication. The letter doesn't need to be lengthy. It may be as short as 5 paragraphs! The following is a simple listing of the paragraphs and the kind of information you may wish to express in your first contact.[1]

1. Introduce yourself in the first paragraph. State your name and the connection date of birth. Offer the city and state. Then state your triad position in relationship to them.

2. The second paragraph is a good place to say why you have written. Keep this simple! It is not the time to express deep pain, hurt or unfortunate circumstances pertaining to your adoption experience or life. Simply state that you wish to share or gain medical and heritage information. You may wish to state that you have always wanted to learn more about the other person.

3. In this paragraph you can state some data about yourself. It is not necessary to tell your life story. That will come after you have received a reply. You may wish to share your education, family structure, and interests.

4. This is the paragraph where you state what you want. You may wish to receive a letter or phone reply. You may want to state that this letter may be shared with the adoptive or birth families. If pictures are very important to you, state that here. You may want to ask for letters, phone conversations, or a possible meeting. Keep in mind not to ask for too much in the beginning. Your contact may be overwhelming, be understanding that asking too many questions may offend or confuse the receiver. (For adoptees—this is not the place to ask about the birthfather!)

5. The closing paragraph should state how they can reach you. If a collect call is acceptable, state that. Make sure you offer the best times to reach you. This is very important for those that have odd work hours. Or if you are not comfortable with the phone at this time, ask that they write you back. Always ask for a note of acknowledgement. This will inform the receiver that you are waiting for a reply.

6. Selection of a closing word or phrase is difficult for many. Select a word that you feel comfortable writing: Always, Fondly, Love, Sincerely, Yours, etc. You will need to find the word that fits you best.

You may wish to include a picture or two in your letter. A picture is worth a thousand words. Of course, only send pictures that are flattering! It is not possible to sit down once and write the perfect letter. Plan on writing several drafts before formulating your final letter. Take out some lined paper. (Lines help keep your thoughts in order.) Write a letter. Then put it away. Then, write another letter. Write as many as you need. Then take out all of your letters and mark the parts you like the best. With those marked portions, write a new letter. This way you will be able to express yourself well. Once you have come up with the letter you feel shares your feelings and wishes, have someone else read your letter—a friend, spouse, your searcher or group leader. Accept their remarks and suggestions if you agree with them. If you are not a great speller or your grammar is not the best, make sure you have someone review your letter for spelling and grammar. You would hate to find that the person you are writing to is an English teacher!

Then make a final draft of your letter. Reread your letter and decide if it expresses your feelings and needs for this first contact. Write your letter in the card you have purchased or write it on separate paper to be inserted in the card. If your handwriting is not readable, it is appropriate to type your letter. But state this is why it is typed. Otherwise, *always* hand-write your letter. It is more personal. Address the envelope and get it ready to mail. If you are not ready to send the letter, put it out where you can see it daily. Ask yourself when you see it, if this is the day to mail it? You will know in your heart the right day! Most like to take the letter to the post office and drop it into the slot to guarantee that it is mailed.

Now, you will have to wait for the letter to be delivered and processed by the receiver. This does take time. You may become concerned that you didn't hear back the day the letter should have been received. Don't let this get you down. Remember how long it took you to write the letter. It may take the receiver that much and more time to process and reply. Or, they may just pick up the phone.

Waiting for a Reply—What to do if you have not heard back in a couple weeks? Wait at least two more weeks! The letter is a slower way of receiving a response. But it does offer the receiver time to process and reply. The receiver is not aware that you are sitting on the edge of your seat and that you have developed a close relationship with your postal carrier as you wait at the mailbox daily! All they know is that they need to reply, but the sense of urgency may not be there. If you have not received a reply in 4–6 weeks, you may wish to place a phone call. Or simply write a new note stating that their reply is of great importance to you. You should not have to totally rewrite the letter.

Other Suggestions—Knocking on the door is NOT acceptable. It has been done with great success, but confronting someone without warning may start the reunion off on the wrong footing. This action may take years to recapture. Many times a drive-by may be possible. If you are able to do this, don't stop and stare. Don't bring attention to yourself.

The last thing you want is to have a neighbor calling the police because they have an active Neighborhood Watch program in effect! Always keep in mind that you are looking into the lives of others that are not aware of your search. Be respectful on all accounts. It will pay off.

If you are registered with International Soundex Reunion Registry and you have had a reunion, please write them to get your information out of their database. ISRR, Box 2312, Carson City, NV 89702.

NOTE

1. If you think the person you are writing to does not live alone and you do not want to risk other household members seeing your letter, you might choose to be more discrete. In this case you may consider sending a "thinking of you" type card and simply writing that you knew the person long ago, and in fact think that you last saw the person on [adoptee's birth date]. That you have been thinking a lot about them and are hoping to re-establish contact. That your name is now [your name], your phone number and address, and would they please call or write to you—you will be very much looking forward to hearing from them.

Resources and Recommended Readings

ORGANIZATIONS

Adoption Network Cleveland
1667 East 40th Street
Cleveland, Ohio 44103-2304
(216) 261–1511
www.AdoptionNetwork.org

Also Known As, Inc.
PO Box 6037, FDR Station
New York, NY 10150
(212) 386–9201
www.AlsoKnownAs.org

American Adoption Congress
PO Box 42730
Washington, DC 20015
(202) 483–3399
www.AmericanAdoptionCongress.org

Center for Family Connections
350 Cambridge Street
Cambidge; MA 02141
(617) 547–0909
www.kinnect.org

Concerned United Birthparents
14820 Figueras Road

LaMirada, CA 90638
(800) 822–2777
www.CUBirthparents.org

International Soundex Reunion Registry
PO Box 2312
Carson City, NV 89702
(775) 882–7755
www.isrr.net

National Adoption Information Clearinghouse
330 C Street, SW
Washington, DC 20447
(888) 251–0075
www.calib.com/naic

North American Council on Adoptable Children
970 Raymond Avenue, Suite 106
St. Paul, MN 55114
(651) 644–3036
www.nacac.org

RECOMMENDED READINGS

Open Adoption

Lifegivers: Framing the Birthparent Experience in Open Adoption. James L. Gritter. 1999. 234pp. CWLA Press.
Open Adoption Experience, The: A Complete Guide for Adoptive and Birth Families From Making the Decision through the Child's Growing Years. Lois Melina and Sharon Kaplan Roszia. 1993. 416pp. HarperCollins Publishers.
Spirit of Open Adoption, The: James L. Gritter. 1997. 315pp. CWLA Press.
Story of David, The: How We Created a Family through Open Adoption. Dion Howells and Karen Pritchard. 1997. 309pp. Doubleday.

Transracial Adoption

Birthmarks: Transracial Adoption in Contemporary America. Sandra Patton. 2000. 220pp. New York University Press.
In Their Own Voices: Transracial Adoptees Tell Their Stories. Rita James Simon and Rhonda Roorda. 2000. 480pp. Columbia University Press.
Inside Transracial Adoption. Gail Steinberg and Beth Hall. 2000. 405pp. Perspectives Press.

International Adoption

Dim Sum, Bagels, and Grits: A Sourcebook for Multicultural Families. Myra Alperson. 2001. 304pp. Farrar Straus and Giroux.

I Wish for You a Beautiful Life: Letters from the Korean Birth Mothers of Ae Ran Won to Their Children. Sara Dorow, editor. 1999. 135pp. Yeong and Yeong.

Seeds from a Silent Tree: An Anthology by Korean Adoptees. Tonya Bishoff and Jo Rankin, editors. 1997. 180pp. Pandal Press.

West Meets East. Richard C. Tessler, Gail Gamache and Liming Liu. 1999. 208pp. Praeger.

WuHu Diary: On Taking My Adopted Daughter Back to Her Hometown in China. Emily Prager. 2001. 256pp. Random House.

Adoptees

Beneath a Tall Tree: A Story about Us. Jean Strauss. 2001. 290pp. Arete Publishing.

Journey of the Adopted Self: A Quest for Wholeness. Betty Jean Lifton. 1994. 224pp. Basic Books.

Primal Wound, The: Understanding the Adopted Child. Nancy Verrier. 1993. 252pp. Nancy Verrier.

Adoptive Parenting

Adoption and the Schools: Resources for Parents and Teachers. Families Adopting in Response—FAIR. 2001. 256pp. Families Adopting in Response—FAIR.

Launching a Baby's Adoption. Patricia Irwin Johnston. 1998. 256pp. Perspectives Press.

Telling the Truth to Your Adopted or Foster Child: Making Sense of the Past. Betsy E. Keefer and Jayne Schooler. 2000. 256pp. Bergin and Garvey.

The Whole Life Adoption Book, The. Jayne Schooler. 1993. 224pp. Pinon Press.

Toddler Adoption: The Weaver's Craft. Mary Hopkins-Best. 1998. 272pp. Perspectives Press.

Birthparents

And Sin No More: Social Policy and Unwed Mothers in Cleveland, 1855–1990. Marion J. Morton. 1993. 183pp. Ohio State University Press.

Other Mother, The: A Woman's Love for the Child She Gave Up for Adoption. Carol Schaefer. 1991. 1241pp. SoHo Press.

Out of the Shadows: Birth Fathers' Stories. Mary M. Mason. 1995. 270pp. OJ Howard Publishing.

Shattered Dreams—Lonely Choices: Birth Parents of Babies with Disabilities Talk about Adoption. Joanne Finnegan. 1993. 208pp. Bergin and Garvey.

Search & Reunion

Adoption Reunion Survival Guide, The: Preparing Yourself for the Search, Reunion, and Beyond. Julie Jarrell Bailey, N. Lynn Giddens and Annette Baran. 2001. 176pp. New Harbinger Publications.

Birthbond: Reunions Between Birthparents and Adoptees: What Happens After. Judith
    S. Gediman and Linda P. Brown. 1989. 285pp. New Horizon Press.
Ithaka: A Daughter's Memoir of Being Found. Sarah Saffian. 1998. 320pp. Basic
    Books.
Synchronicity and Reunion: The Genetic Connection of Adoptees and Birth Parents.
    LaVonne Stiffler. 1992. 189pp. L.H. Stiffler.

Triad and General Issues

Adoption Nation: How the Adoption Revolution Is Transforming America. Adam Pert-
    man. 2000. 272pp. Basic Books.
Child's Journey through Placement, A. Dr. Vera Falhberg. 1992. 420pp. Perspectives
    Press.
*Adoption Reader, The: Birth Mothers, Adoptive Mothers and Adopted Daughters Tell
    Their Stories.* Susan Wadia-Ellis, editor. 1995. 304pp. Seal Press Feminist
    Publications.
*Adoption Triangle, The: Sealed or Opened Records: How They Affect Adoptees, Birth
    Parents, and Adoptive Parents.* A.D. Sorosky, A. Baran, R. Pannor. 1989.
    Second Edition. 236pp. Corona Publishing.
*Clinical and Practice Issues in Adoption: Bridging the Gap between Adoptees Placed As
    Infants and As Older Children.* Victor Groza and Karen F. Rosenberg. 2001.
    215pp. Praeger Publishers.
Ethics in American Adoption. L. Anne Babb. 1999. 264pp. Bergin and Garvey.
The Family of Adoption. Joyce Maguire Pavao. 1999. 160pp. Beacon Press.
Imagining Adoption: Essays on Literature and Culture. Marianne Novy, editor 2000.
    328pp. University of Michigan Press.
May the Circle Be Unbroken: An Intimate Journey into the Heart of Adoption. Lynn
    C. Franklin and Elizabeth Ferber. 1998. 288pp. Harmony Books.

Selected Bibliography

American Adoption Congress. "Suggested Questions and Answers About Open Adoption Records." Washington, DC: 1990.

Anderson, Robert. *Second Choices: Growing Up Adopted*. Chesterfield, Mo.: Badger Press, 1993.

———. "The Nature of the Search: Adventure, Cure, or Growth?" *Child Welfare* 67, (November–December, 1988): 625.

Askin, Jayne. *Search: A Handbook for Adoptees and Birthparents*. Phoenix, Ariz.: Oryx Press, 1992.

Baran, A., and R. Pannor, "A Time for Sweeping Change." *Decree* 7, no. 1 (1990).

Blair, Jonelle, "Illegitimate Business." (Unpublished) novel based on real-life experience of birthmothers in a midwestern maternity home.

Boss, P. "A Clarification of the Concept of Psychological Father Presence in Families Experiencing Ambiguity of Boundary." *Journal of Marriage and the Family*, 39 (1977): 141–151.

———. *Family Stress Management*. Newbury Park, Calif.: Sage, 1988.

Brodzinsky, A.B. "Surrendering an Infant for Adoption: The Birthmother Experience." In D.M. Brodzinsky and M.D. Schechter (eds.), *The Psychology of Adoption*. New York: Oxford University Press, 1990: 295–315.

Brodzinsky, David, Marshall D. Schechter, and Robin Marantz Henig. *Being Adopted: The Lifelong Search for Self*. New York: Anchor Books, 1992.

Brown, Dirck. Personal interview, June 13, 1994.

Cox, Susan Soon Keum. Personal interview, July 1994.

Curran, Dolores. *Traits of a Healthy Family*. New York: Ballentine Books, 1998.

Daly, K. "Toward a Formal Theory of Interactive Resocialization: The Case of Adoptive Parenthood." *Qualitative Sociology* 15, (1992): 395–417.

Damico, David. *The Faces of Rage*. Colorado Springs: NavPress, 1992.

Demuth, Carol. *Courageous Blessing: Adoptive Parents and the Search.* Garland, Tex.: Aries Center, 1993.

Demuth, Carol. Personal interview. February 1994.

Ferree-Dean, L. "Through the Looking Glass: Birthmothers Break the Silence Surrounding the Relinquishment of Children through Past Adoption Practices." MA dissertation, Prescott College, 1998.

Fishel, Elizabeth. *Family Mirrors: What Our Children's Lives Reveal about Ourselves.* Boston: Houghton Mifflin, 1991.

Fossum, Merle, as quoted by Lewis B. Smedes. *Shame and Grace: Healing the Shame We Don't Deserve.* San Francisco: Harper and Row, 1993.

Fravel, D.L. "Boundary Ambiguity Perceptions of Adoptive Parents Experiencing Various Levels Openness in Adoption." Ph.D. diss., University of Minnesota, 1995. Abstract in *Dissertation Abstracts International* 56 (1995): 4160.

Fravel, D.L., R.G. McRoy, and H.D. Grotevant. "Birthmother Perceptions of the Psychologically Present Adopted Child." *Family Relations* 49 (2000): 425–434.

Fravel, D.L., et al., "Adoption Openness and the Psychological Presence of Birthmothers in Adoptive Families." Forthcoming.

Fravel, D.L., R.G. McRoy, and H.D. Grotevant. "Boundary Ambiguity and Adoption Openness: Birthmother Adjustment Eleven to Twenty Years After Adoption: A Longitudinal Study." Forthcoming.

Gediman, Judith S., and Linda P. Brown. *Birthbond: Reunions between Birthparents and Adoptees: What Happens After.* Far Hills, N.J.: New Horizon Press, 1989.

Gritter, James. *The Spirit of Open Adoption.* Washington, DC: CWLA Press, 1998.

Grotevant, Harold, et al. "Adoptive Identity: How Contexts Within and Beyond the Family Shape Development Pathways." *Family Relations* 49 (2000): 379–387.

Grotevant, H., and R. McRoy. *Openness in Adoption: Exploring Family Connections.* Thousand Oaks, Calif.: Sage Publishers, 1998.

Hale-Haniff, Mary. *Training Manual.* Miami: Brief Therapy Institute, 1994.

Hetherington, E. Mavis, David Reiss, and Robert Plomin. *Separate Social Worlds of Siblings: The Impact of Nonshared Environment on Development.* Hillsdale; N.J.: Lawrence Erlbaum, 1994.

Howe, D., P. Sawbridge, and D. Hinings. *Half a Million Women: Mothers Who Lose Their Children by Adoption.* London: Penguin Books, 1992.

Imber-Black, E. *Secrets in Families and Family Therapy.* New York: W. and W. Norton and Company, 1993.

Jones, M. *Birthmothers: Women Who Relinquish Babies for Adoption Tell Their Stories.* Chicago: Chicago Review Press, 1993.

Kaplan Roszia, Sharon. Personal interview. February 24, 1994.

Kaplan Roszia, Sharon, and Deborah Silverstein. "The Seven Core Issues of Adoption." www.adopting.org.

Keefer, Betsy, and Jayne Schooler. *Telling the Truth to Your Adopted or Foster Child: Making Sense of the Past.* Westport, Conn.: Bergin and Garvey, 2000.

LaRossa, R., and D.C. Reitzes. "Symbolic Interactinism and Family Studies." In P.G. Boss, *et al.* (Eds.), *Sourcebook of Family Theories and Methods.* 325–355. New York: Plenum Press, 1993.

Lewis, Jerry. *How's Your Family?* New York: Brunner/Mazel Publisher, 1989.

Lifton, Betty Jean. *Lost and Found: The Adoption Experience.* New York: Harper and Row, 1988.

———. *Journey of the Adopted Self: A Quest for Wholeness.* (New York: Basic Books, 1993.

Maguire-Pavao, Joyce. "Counseling the Adoptee: Post Search." Chicago: American Adoption Congress, 1993.

———. Personal interview, June 1994.

Mask, Michael, *et al. Family Secrets.* Nashville: Thomas Nelson, 1995.

McColm, Michelle. *Adoption Reunions: A Book for Adoptees, Birth Parents and Adoptive Families.* Ontario, Can.: Story Book Press, 1993.

McRoy, R.G., H.D. Grotevant, and L.A. Zucher. *Openness in Adoption: New Practices, New Issues.* New York: Praeger, 1998.

Millen, L., and S. Roll. "Solomon's Mothers: a Special Case of Pathological Bereavement." *American Journal of Orthopsychiatry* 55 no. 3 (July 1995): 411–418.

Millen, L., S. Roll, and B. Backlund. "Solomon's Mothers: Mourning in Mothers Who Relinquish Their Children for Adoption." In T.A. Rand (ed.), *Parental Loss of a Child.* 257–268. Champaign, Ill.: Research Press, 1986.

Phillips, Jodi. "Powerful Forces Lead Children on a Search for Their Birth Parents," *Houston Chronicle,* June 27, 1993, sec. A, 9.

Pitino, Rick. "Lead to Success." *Reader's Digest,* May 2001, 73.

Ravenstine, Allen. "The Lost and Found: A Young Woman Searches for Her Source." *Cleveland Edition.* June 7, 1990.

Reitz, M., and K. Watson. *Adoption and the Family System.* New York: Guilford, 1992.

Rillera, Mary Jo. *The Adoption Searchbook.* Westminister, Calif.: Triadoption Publishers, 1991.

Sachdev, P. "Birthmothers and Their Experience with Reunion." Unpublished study.

Schooler, Jayne. *The Whole Life Adoption Book.* Colorado Springs: Pinon Press, 1993.

———. *Searching for a Past.* Colorado Springs: Pinon Press, 1995.

Severson, Randolph. *Adoption: Charms and Rituals for Healing.* Dallas: House of Tomorrow Productions, 1991.

———. "Transformations." Paper presented at the American Adoption Congress, Cleveland, Ohio, 1993.

———. *Adoption and Spirituality.* Dallas: Aries Center, 1994.

———. Personal interview used with permission, April 1994.

———. *A Letter to Adoptive Parents on Open Adoption.* Dallas, Heart Words Center, n.d.

Sharma, Anu. Personal interview used with permission. March 21, 1994.

Stiffler, L.H. *Parent-Child Synchronicities During Years of Separation by Adoption: Anomalous Connecting Information in Histories of Union/Loss/Reunion.* Dayton, Tenn.: University Microfilms, 1991.

———. *Synchronicity in Reunion: The Genetic Connection of Adoptees and Birthparents.* Conroe, Tex.: L.H. Stiffler, 1992.

Van Why, E. *Adoption Bibliography and Multi-Ethnic Sourcebook.* Hartford, Conn.: Open Door Society of Connecticut, 1977.

Wallenfenfelsz, Carole. "Missing Pieces." *Birthparents Today Newsletter*. Cincinnati, Ohio; (summer 1993): 4.

Webster, Harriet. *Family Secrets: How Telling and Not Telling Affects Our Children, Our Relationships and Our Lives*. Reading, Mass.: Addison-Wesley Publishing, 1991.

Weinrob, M. and V. Konstam. "Birthmothers: Silent Relationships." *Affilia* 10, no 3 (fall 1995): 317.

Weinrob, M., and B.C. Murphy. "The Birth Mother: A Feminist Perspective for the Helping Professional." *Woman and Therapy*. 1988.

Wentz, Barbara. Personal interview. March 1994.

Winker, R., and M. van Keppel. *Relinquishing Mothers in Adoption: Their Long-Term Adjustment*. Melbourne, Austral: Institute of Family Studies, 1984.

Wolfe, Curry. Personal interview. July 1994.

Wolter, Dwight Lee. *Forgiving Our Parents: For Adult Children from Dysfunctional Families*. Center City, Minn.: Hazelden Foundation, 1989.

Yellin, Linda. Personal interview, January 1994.

Index

About the Authors and Contributors

JAYNE E. SCHOOLER is an affiliate trainer with the Institute for Human Services in Columbus, Ohio, where she played a major role in the development of adoption training curriculum for professionals and families used nationwide. She is also a frequent speaker at training events and conferences across the country. Jayne has over twenty years of experience in child welfare, first as a foster parent, then as an adoptive parent, adoption professional, and educator. She is the author of *The Whole Life Adoption Book* (1993), *Searching for a Past* (1995), and coauthor of an award-winning book, *Telling the Truth to Your Adopted or Foster Child* (2000).

BETSIE L. NORRIS is an adoptee who searched for and reunited with her birthparents in 1986. A registered nurse working in child psychiatry at the time, Betsie felt her search and reunion was the most profound experience of her life and developed a commitment that others should not have to face these issues without support and assistance. She therefore founded Adoption Network Cleveland in 1988, leading the nonprofit organization as a volunteer until 1995, and in the role of executive director since.

Betsie is a frequent spokesperson in the media, has assisted in over 1,400 adoptee-birthparent reunions, has worked extensively on changing Ohio's adoption laws, and has led Adoption Network Cleveland to its recognition as a successful and dynamic organization with a wide array of programs and services for the full triad. She holds a certificate of nonprofit management from Case Western Reserve University and is a former board member of the American Adoption Congress. Betsie lives in Cleveland, Ohio, with her four-year-old son, Elliot.

DEBORAH L. FRAVEL is a professor of human development and family studies in the Department of Applied Health Science at Indiana University, Bloomington. Dr. Fravel is also a Certified Family Life Educator. She teaches a course, "Dynamics of Birth and Adoptive Family Systems," each year. Her research on boundary ambiguity and adoption has occurred in conjunction with the Minnesota/Texas Adoption Research Project. She may be reached at dfravel@indiana.edu.

LAVONNE H. STIFFLER is a National Certified Counselor, currently working with grief groups and interfaith relations. Her doctoral research was published as *Synchronicity and Reunion: The Genetic Connection of Adoptees and Birthparents.* A reunited birthmother, she has studied sibling communication, conducted search-related seminars, and published journal articles and training material for adoption professionals. Dr. Stiffler lives in Conroe, Texas. E-mail may be sent to txlavonne@cs.com.